ECHOES
on the HARDWOOD

ECHOES
on the HARDWOOD

100 SEASONS OF
NOTRE DAME MEN'S BASKETBALL

MICHAEL COFFEY

Go Irish!

TAYLOR TRADE PUBLISHING
Lanham • New York • Dallas • Boulder • Toronto • Oxford

This Taylor Trade Publishing hardcover edition of *Echoes on the Hardwood* is an original publication. It is published by arrangement with the author.

Published by Taylor Trade Publishing
An imprint of The Rowman & Littlefield Publishing Group, Inc.
4501 Forbes Boulevard, Suite 200
Lanham, Maryland 20706

Distributed by National Book Network

Library of Congress Cataloging-in-Publication Data

Coffey, Michael, 1969–
  Echoes on the hardwood : 100 seasons of Notre Dame men's basketball /
Michael Coffey.—1st Taylor Trade Pub. ed.
    p. cm.
  ISBN 1-58979-124-X (hardcover : alk. paper)
  1. University of Notre Dame—Basketball—History. I. Title.
GV885.43.U55C64 2004
796.32'363'0977289—dc22   2004002965

To Nana

Contents

The George Keogan Years
(1936–1946)

The Moose Krause Years
(1947–1951)

The John Jordan Years
(1952–1964)

The Johnny Dee Years
(1965–1971)

The Digger Phelps Years:
Part I—The First 10
(1972–1981)

The Digger Phelps Years:
Part II–The Second 10
(1982–1991)

The John MacLeod Years
(1992–1999)

The Matt Doherty Year
(2000)

The Mike Brey Years
(2001–)

Foreword

"Why do you want to go to that football school to play basketball?" That's what 99 percent of the recruiters asked me when they knew Notre Dame was No. 1 on my list. The only coach who didn't ask me that question was Dean Smith of North Carolina, a very classy coach and person.

But when I visited campus, I lived the Notre Dame experience and knew I wanted to be a part of it. I spent that weekend with Bob Whitmore, who was someone I had looked up to and who was the best defensive big man I ever played against. It was a wonderful weekend, and if you don't know what a football weekend at Notre Dame is like, you owe it to yourself to have that experience once.

My freshman class was Tom Sinnott, Jackie Meehan, Jim Hinga, John Pleick, Collis Jones, Sid Catlett, and I, and it's still one of the best the school has had. When we arrived on campus, we knew basketball at Notre Dame had a strong history—maybe not like UCLA's but with its memorable moments and heroes like Moose Krause, Kevin O'Shea, Joe Bertrand, Dick Rosenthal, Fr. John Smyth, Tom Hawkins, and Larry Sheffield, to name a few. We respected that legacy and wanted to build on it.

The Notre Dame family was an important part of my experience at the school. It was great to go to different cities and know we would have strong fan support. At home, the student body supported us just like they were at a football game, and opposing teams always hated having to face our home crowd. We couldn't wait to play games in front of our fellow students.

Our coaching staff was solid with head coach John Dee and assistant coach Gene Sullivan. They put together some great game plans, especially against UCLA. Even though we didn't fulfill our dream of getting to the Final Four, we had a great run. It feels good to know that soon after we set the pace, Digger Phelps and his teams took that next step.

I still stay close to the program, and it looks like Coach Brey has it headed in the right direction. And you can believe that when they get to the Final Four, I will be there to support them.

Go Irish!

Austin Carr, 1971
Leading Scorer in Notre Dame basketball history
Record-holder for points scored in a NCAA Tournament game
Current holder of 27 individual Notre Dame scoring records

Preface
Basketball School

I f I was asked once, I was asked a hundred times by interviewees, friends, fellow alumni, and even complete strangers on an airplane: why would someone write a book about Notre Dame men's basketball?

My usual flippant response was this: the fact they would ask the question showed how much the book was needed. Notre Dame has enjoyed great success on the hardwood, but because of the high profile of the football program, it's not as apparent to alumni and fans.

References to Notre Dame as a "basketball school" are seen on the Internet occasionally, usually as a derogatory comment when the football team is doing poorly. But the people who use the phrase in that context are unaware the description is apt. Notre Dame is ranked in the top 20 in Division I in total wins and winning percentage, the only school in the nation that can say that about both football and men's basketball. Its 27 NCAA Tournament appearances are ninth on the all-time list, and it is the only school to have three players designated as Consensus All-Americans by the NCAA three times, with 10 of its players gaining that distinction at least once.

Just as it's difficult to see a flashlight in a brightly lit room, so too is it difficult to appreciate Notre Dame's basketball accomplishments given the amount of football success the school has enjoyed, and the recent history of the program doesn't help matters. Many Irish basketball fans disconnected from the program during the down years of the 1990s and are only now returning to the fold as the team returns to postseason play and success under coach Mike Brey. Those fans were looking for reference materials to reinforce memories of basketball success and since I was raised to be part of the solution to problems, I decided to provide one for them.

But what really prompted me to write this book was 35 years of interest in Fighting Irish basketball inspired by another Notre Dame graduate. In my elementary school days, my father would take my siblings and me on annual overnight trips to see a Notre Dame basketball game. We'd pile into the car for the two-hour trip to South Bend, grab dinner at Rocco's and then head over to the Athletic and Convocation (now Joyce) Center (A.C.C.) for a couple of hours of rooting on John Paxson, Tim Andree, Kenny Barlow, Tim Kempton, and their teammates. An overnight at the Morris Inn would be followed by breakfast, the obligatory trip to the campus bookstore, and walks around the snow-covered campus. Thus did we develop an affinity for the school that resulted in three of us becoming Notre Dame graduates, and thus did I develop an affinity for the school's basketball program.

Puberty creates a different sense of what's cool in adolescents, so the trips became more infrequent as we got older. But the interest in the program they had planted in me grew. After receiving my acceptance letter to Notre Dame in late 1986, I sat in the A.C.C. and watched David Rivers score 14 points in the second half and placards sail out of the stands to celebrate a 60-58 win over top-ranked North Carolina. "This," I thought, watching the mob scene on the court, "is what I have to look forward to."

Alas, it was not to be. My four years at Notre Dame saw the end of the Digger Phelps era, and like all die-hard hoops fans, I suffered through the 1990s as the program struggled to find itself.

As the program regained its legs in John MacLeod's waning years and through the season under Matt Doherty, I was presented with the opportunity to help manage a Notre Dame basketball-related website, NDHoops.com (now NDNation). I jumped at the chance to merge my passion for Irish basketball with my love of writing, and immediately took to the task of learning as much as I could about Notre Dame basketball history.

That research is the basis of the book you hold in your hands—the oral history of Irish basketball, told from the perspective of the people who created it: players, coaches, administrators, media, and other friends of the program. Each chapter has been put together based on interviews with those people and reflects their memories and opinions of what went on during their days at Notre Dame. Each season is covered to a varying degree of detail, concentrating on the major events and situations that were important either to the program at the time or in making the program what it is today. Some seasons will, by nature, require more attention than others, but I have done my best to keep things balanced.

It's difficult to write a book about Notre Dame basketball without including Digger Phelps. He coached the Irish for more years and to more victories than any of the other men who have held the job, and some of the biggest moments for the Irish on the hardwood took place on his watch. But it's a challenge I will have to accept, as he declined my request to interview him for this work. I hope that the perspective of the coaching staff during his tenure can be sufficiently expressed through his many assistant coaches who shared their stories with me.

Before we begin, one nomenclature clarification. A basketball season spans the change of the calendar year. In order to reduce confusion and eliminate the need to reference two years every time a season is mentioned, I refer to seasons by the year that ends them. For example, the season in which Notre Dame went to the Final Four is the 1978 season for the purposes of this book, even though games were played in 1977 and 1978.

Acknowledgments

One of my favorite books is *Huckleberry Finn*, and many times during the three years it took me to put this work together, I was reminded of Huck's admission at the end that if he'd known what trouble it was to write a book he "wouldn't 'a' tackled it." That I not only tackled it but also completed it is thanks to the help of a number of people.

First I would like to thank my interviewees—the Notre Dame basketball players, coaches, administrators, and others who trusted an unknown commodity with their stories, opinions, and memories, counting on him to express them correctly. I had enough material to write three books, and editing it down to the following pages was a difficult task. While I was not able to share things from everyone I interviewed, I considered every interview invaluable to the end result. That which was not quoted was still used in support of what was. The only hope I have for this book is that my interviewees come away thinking I've done their stories justice. Anything beyond that is gravy.

It takes a degree of faith to trust a first-time writer with any kind of book project. Jill Langford, Terry Fischer, Tracy Mirade, and the other folks at Taylor Trade Publishing exhibited that faith in me and helped make my dream of writing a book a reality, and for that I will always be grateful.

My involvement with NDNation.com first put me on the road to writing this book. My thanks go to Scott Engler, John Vannie, and Mike Cash for providing me with a forum to hone my writing skills and an avenue to be involved with the Notre Dame basketball program; to Tim Kelley for his sage advice throughout the process; and to his brother, Patrick, for his assistance contacting interviewees and endorsers.

This book would have been impossible to write without the cooperation and assistance of a lot of people at Notre Dame: associate athletic director John Heisler, who green-lighted the project and had my back a number of times while I was arranging interviews; sports information director Bernie Cafarelli and her staff, particularly Carol Copley, who were very patient answering my (sometimes inane) questions and providing unfettered access to and assistance with sorely needed reference materials; Karen Putt with the Notre Dame Alumni Association, who helped me track down hard-to-find former players; the late Denny Moore, who arranged interviews with Notre Dame administrators past and present; and Stephanie Reed in the men's basketball office, who passed along a seemingly infinite number of messages on my behalf to potential interviewees and helped arrange access to both the current team and the recent basketball alumni reunion. They made my life a lot easier over the past couple of years, and for that, I thank them.

Going from interviews to manuscript was a laborious process replete with speed bumps. Helping me negotiate those hazards were Edith Lindsey and Shawn Espinosa, who provided assistance with tape transcription; Christine Wainright, who gave me direction on content and structure; and Dan McGrath, whose help in editing the work from its original verbose form was invaluable.

The process of becoming a published author began way back in my childhood in the books of John R. Tunis and the newspaper articles by Mike Royko I read. My mother, Mary, gave me that love of reading coupled with a desire to express myself through writing. My father, Mike, instilled in me the interest in Notre Dame basketball that got this started. I couldn't have done this without their support and influence.

Last, and most important, I thank my wonderful wife, Trish, and our children, Katie and Michael. No one sacrificed more than they did to see this book completed, and no one supported me more when exhaustion or frustration threatened to swamp the project. I love them dearly, and hope the final product justifies their faith.

Non sunt simplices historiae

Introduction
If You Can't Beat 'Em . . .

N otre Dame fans all over the world recognize Knute Rockne as the architect of Irish football greatness. What they might not realize is he is also partly responsible for Fighting Irish basketball being what it is today.

Make no mistake, Notre Dame had a basketball program long before Rockne became football coach in 1918. In 1897, Frank Hering organized a Varsity team using the best players from the campus interhall league. That team played six games over the next two years against local civic teams before Hering's departure and a fire in the campus fieldhouse eliminated the nascent program. Then in 1908, the program was revitalized under the leadership of Bert Maris. Playing a schedule almost equal parts collegiate and YMCA, Maris led the Irish to a 78-20 record over his five years as coach.

But in Rockne's early days, the program had fallen on hard times. Jesse Harper had tried to put together teams over the years with limited success. Irish football legend Gus Dorais and Walter Halas, brother of Chicago Bears founder George, tried their hands at coaching, but fared no better.

Although Knute Rockne the football coach had little use for basketball in general, Knute Rockne the athletic director realized if Notre Dame was going to have a program, logic dictated the school should put the best possible effort into supporting it. So when Halas resigned in 1923, Rockne remembered a hard-nosed coach whose Valparaiso University football team had given his 1920 squad all they could handle. The man had also coached basketball for many years, and was definitely interested in the job. This was an opportunity for Rockne to give basketball the leadership it needed and free him from having to think about it. So in 1923, George Keogan was hired as head basketball coach at the University of Notre Dame.

Keogan's efforts quickly bore fruit. After going 26-19 his first two seasons, the Irish moved into a brand new addition on the school's old Fieldhouse and responded with back-to-back 19-1 campaigns and a Helms Foundation national championship in 1927 with players like Clem Crowe, Vince McNally, and John Nyikos.

Over the years that followed, Keogan's teams continued to play strong basketball, although another championship was not in the offing. Tenacious defense and discipline were Keogan's watchwords, and his teams from 1928 through 1935 averaged 16 wins a year, including an 18-2 finish by the 1932 squad that featured a center more known for his football exploits, Edward "Moose" Krause. It is in the seasons that follow the era of Moose that our stories begin.

The
George Keogan
Years

(1936–1946)

The Fab Five
(1936–1938)

George Keogan had been building for the 1936 season. It had been eight years since the Irish had won the Helms Foundation national championship, and while the intervening seasons had been successful, he had not been able to return Notre Dame to the mountaintop.

But for 1936, he had the pieces he needed, starting with strong senior leadership in guards Frank Wade and George Ireland and forward John Ford, who had pretty much fallen in his lap two years before.

John Ford: "I was recruited by Knute Rockne. He had sent his assistant coach, Jack Chevigny, to one of our football banquets and he had instructions from Rockne to recruit me to Notre Dame. There was nothing in writing. I was to contact Coach Chevigny when I arrived at Notre Dame that fall, and he would take care of the details from then on.

"In the meanwhile, Rockne died that March, and Chevigny left and ended up at Texas. So that left me with no contact when I arrived in South Bend. When I went in to see [new head coach] Hunk Anderson, he evidently had never heard of me. He had no idea who I was, but he did agree to provide me with a partial scholarship, which meant you waited

3

tables in the mess hall and did other jobs to help pay for your tuition. That didn't sound very good to me, because I had received offers for full rides to other schools.

"As I was leaving Anderson's office, by chance I ran into George Keogan. He heard my sad story and offered me a full ride in basketball."

Aiding Keogan in his quest for talent was Notre Dame's stature among the Catholic high schools in the country, especially in the Midwestern Catholic dioceses. The strong programs in those areas were natural feeder schools, sending Notre Dame players like Ireland, Don Allen, and Marty Peters, and meant that Irish players often came to Notre Dame already familiar with the playing habits of their teammates.

Don Allen: "My high school in Chicago, St. Mel, was one of the top two basketball teams in the country in 1932. The other team was St. Patrick's, which was in our section in the city and was led by Ray Meyer. They only had three losses that season, and all were when they played us. So we knew each other pretty well.

"Back in those days, Loyola University in Chicago had a national Catholic high school tournament, and all the top teams would come to it. In 1932, the tournament had my St. Mel's team, Ray Meyer and St. Pat's, Marty Peters's team from Peoria, Illinois, Campion High with George Ireland from Madison, Wisconsin, and Johnny Ford's Cathedral High team from Indianapolis. Marty Peters, Johnny Ford, and I all made the All-Tournament team. We beat Johnny Ford's team, but lost to Ray Meyer and St. Pat's for the Catholic national championship in the final seconds. We'd won three games against them, but lost the one for the championship."

Thanks to recruiting acumen and the Catholic connections, Keogan had assembled a talented group of five sophomores that rank among the more prominent classes in Irish hoops history. John Moir, Paul Nowak, Tom Wukovits, Ray Meyer, and Tom Jordan would finish 62-8-1 over their three years on the varsity and win George Keogan's second Helms national championship in 1936.

John Ford: "Moir was kind of a phenomenon. He was a shooting machine. He could shoot from any position if you got him the ball, and he made a lot of them.

"Nowak had been out of high school a year or so before he attended Notre Dame, and he played semi-pro ball in South Bend for Bendix. He was their big star, and one of the first great big men to play the game. Meyer stayed out as well before coming to ND. So they all had a lot of experience and were great players to begin with. Next to Krause, Novak was probably one of the greatest centers ND had ever had in basketball."

Don Allen: "Ray Meyer and I were in the same class in high school, but while I went right to Notre Dame, he spent two years in the minor seminary. In those days, you spent six years in the minor seminary and six in the major, and a lot of guys did that in those days. He left the seminary after a short time—he just didn't have a vocation, which was fine. But he played some ball during that time in the leagues on the west side of Chicago, which had some pretty good teams back then."

The 1936 team was a "point-a-minute" squad, with an average of 41 points per game. Although Austin Carr would later average almost this many points per game on his own, this was an extraordinary total in the days when there was still a center jump after every made basket.

Ray Meyer: "We had a lot of talent, and we could substitute for anybody. Moir had a broken toe. We put a substitute in, and it didn't make any difference. Paul Nowak had an appendectomy operation, we'd throw another guy in—didn't matter. I dislocated my elbow and they put a guy in for me—didn't miss me. They didn't miss anybody."

Coupled with their offensive power was an attention to defense. The Irish were scoring 15 more points per game than their opponents—again, an unusual spread in a slow-paced era. Frank Quinn, who would star for Keogan in the early 1940s, remembers the coach's switching man-to-man defense that came as close to being a zone defense as you could get without it actually being one.

Frank Quinn: "A lot of coaches didn't like the switching man-to-man defense Keogan ran because it stopped some pretty good teams. It prevented some of the top scorers from scoring. There were a lot of pick-and-rolls in those days, and we would switch off the picks and pick up the players who were being set up for baskets."

Beyond the Helms championship, the 1936 season would be known for one other event: the only tie in the history of Notre Dame basketball. On New Year's Eve, the Irish were playing their traditional game at Northwestern and the players went to the locker room thinking they'd come out on the wrong end of things.

John Ford: "I can remember how sad we were. We went to the dressing room thinking we had lost by one point. It wasn't until they started going over the scorebook that they realized one of [Ray Meyer's] foul shots hadn't been counted."

Ray Meyer: "Wilfred Smith from the Chicago Tribune walked in after we'd already showered, walks up to Keogan and asked him, 'When are you guys going to come out to play the overtime?' But it was too late; everybody was dressed.

"Northwestern had thought they'd won, and we'd thought we'd won. The newspapermen decided the game, and said they had the score 20-20."

At the end of that 22-2-1 season, Moir and Nowak were named Consensus All-Americans, following Moose Krause from two seasons before. The Helms Foundation awarded Notre Dame its national championship, giving the players what they thought would be a ticket to the Olympics as the United States' representative.

John Ford: "In those days, they were taking the champion college teams. We were really hoping to go, because that was a really big deal. Well, the school authorities nixed it because it was in Germany and it was going to be too much time away for studies and all. They ended up having an AAU tournament and selecting players from there. But none of the Notre Dame boys were included, which we felt bad about."

Don Allen: "It was a disappointment, but you have to remember that it wasn't necessarily what we were playing for. Our goal was to win. We were winning for the sake of winning, not the stuff that would come afterwards."

Keogan had more to worry about in 1937 than the team's abrogated travel plans, as three members of his starting lineup had graduated. Moir and Nowak were now juniors and would have to shoulder more of the load than they had the previous season. The fiery Keogan hated to lose under any circumstances, and having achieved so much in 1936, he was determined to get as much out of that year as he could.

One of the wins in that 20-3 that season was a 47-40 victory over the Purdue Boilermakers and their coach, Ward "Piggy" Lambert. That would prove to be the last Irish/Boilermaker game for five years. A feud between Keogan and Lambert finally boiled over and led to the suspension of the series.

Ray Meyer: "It was a personality clash. Ward had excellent talent at Purdue, and that was always a great game for Notre Dame. I know we had a lot of problems with them."

John Ford: "My senior year, we played at West Lafayette. At that time, Purdue played their games in the Lafayette High School gym, and during halftime, our dressing room was at the other end of the gym from theirs. But Lambert held his halftime pep talk just outside our dressing room in the small stairway there. He gave a fire-and-brimstone speech, and he had them all fired up. But we could hear the whole thing, and the trouble is we believed him. We went out there, and were practically cheering for Purdue rather than Notre Dame. We couldn't do a thing the second half, and they ended up beating us by something like 14 points for our first loss of the season."

The 1938 season would be the Fab Five's last playing in South Bend, and they would get a chance to show off their athleticism with a rule change handed down by the NCAA. Instead of having a center jump following each basket, the ball would be taken out of bounds by the opposing team. Mark Ertel, newly arrived on the team as a sophomore, remembers the effects it had on the game.

Mark Ertel: "With a center jump, you got a little bit of relief. Without it, the game speeded up. As a result, we got into what I'd call a platoon system. It started my senior year when Keogan finally realized something had to be done. It turned out to be a very successful move."

Ray Meyer: "It took the emphasis off the center jump, which was slowing the game down. At that time, the big men couldn't really move. The only reason they had them in there was to get the center jump. When they eliminated that, then they eliminated the big man who couldn't move.

"It wasn't a good spectator game at that time. But after they took it out, crowds really started swelling all over the nation. It was an excellent rule to get out of there."

Although Keogan was a proponent of the center jump and campaigned for it the rest of his career, Nowak's mobility at center meant the rule change didn't affect the Irish game plan much. The Irish finished the season 20-3 again, but didn't enjoy the national recognition they could have because the Stanford University teams of the time, led by Hank Luisetti, were commanding quite a few headlines.

John Ford: "We were still using the two-handed set shot. Very few people were using the one-handed shot, other than Hank Luisetti out on the coast at Stanford, and we all thought he was a freak."

Ray Meyer: "We always wanted to play Stanford. That was one of our things. We had a great ballclub; we were talented and deep. They'd have had a tough time with us."

Unfortunately, the one chance they might have had to play Stanford couldn't be worked out. A new postseason tournament had been started in New York City called the National Invitation Tournament, or NIT, that would pit the best three schools from across the nation against the best three from the New York area. The tournament hosts wanted the Irish and Stanford to participate, but Stanford declined citing travel costs. The Irish were unavailable because of a university policy prohibiting postseason play enacted after the football team's appearance in the 1925 Rose Bowl.

Mark Ertel: "I still don't understand why they did that. We were very disappointed. If you have a good season, you'd like to be able to compete further up against teams outside your regular schedule."

Ray Meyer: "We weren't very happy with it, but as long as the school had a rule. . . . At that time, the NIT was just beginning. I don't think they had much recognition at that time, so it wasn't a big deal."

Moir and Nowak were named Consensus All-Americans for the third season in a row, joining Moose Krause in the Notre Dame record books for the achievement. They, along with Tom Wukovits, became the first Notre Dame alumni to play in the National Basketball League. And George Keogan was left to carry on without his Fab Five, trying to put together another run at another title for the Fighting Irish.

2

The Doctor Is Out
(1939–1943)

Dealing with the departure of two three-time Consensus All-Americans would be a difficult hurdle for the 1939 Fighting Irish. Fortunately, they had a sophomore joining the team who would do his best to fill the gap—6-foot forward Eddie Riska.

Mark Ertel: "Eddie Riska was a playmaker. He was very fast, and very active. I remember mostly setting up picks for him and feeding him the ball, and he'd out-run the guy going to the basket."

Frank Quinn: "Of all the players I played with at Notre Dame, I'd have to say Riska was the best. He was very aggressive—a strong player, good dribbler, and great shooter. He could drive to the basket. If I could get him the ball, he could take care of the rest of it.

"He was a fierce competitor. A lot of people thought he should have played football at Notre Dame, because he was that type of guy. He'd run over people."

Riska's first season saw the Irish compile a 15-6 record—not as good as the preceding seasons, but along the lines of what fans would expect from a Keogan-coached squad. That record included a big 42-37 win against Kentucky and their famous coach, Adolph Rupp. Games against Rupp were always big ones for Keogan, who won seven of the eight games he coached against the "Baron of the Bluegrass."

Charlie Butler: "I don't recall Keogan and Lambert disliking each other. But I do know Rupp was the one he was the most competitive with."

Frank Quinn: "Adolph Rupp couldn't stand George Keogan because Keogan had his number. He never beat him badly, but he always managed to beat him, which was probably the highlight of Keogan's coaching career. He had Rupp figured out, and we always had good scouting reports on him."

Although the season had been a success, the Irish were without an All-American for the first time in eight years. The same held true in 1940, as the Irish finished 15-6 again. But as the 1941 season dawned, George Keogan had more to worry about than a win-loss record. Doctors had discovered a heart problem and suggested the coach scale back his activities—advice the workaholic Keogan was not likely to take.

Bob Rensberger: "We liked the man so much, and we all realized he was sick. The doctors told him he shouldn't coach. I couldn't understand why he kept coaching. It was obvious it was going to kill him if he kept coaching, and the doctors all told him that. But he couldn't give it up."

Keogan did, however, acquiesce to hiring an assistant coach, the first in the program's history.

Charlie Butler: "Word had gotten out that Keogan was going to have an assistant. So at every one of our games, you would see a former player or two. They would come down in the locker room, and they were talking to George. We didn't realize what it was at the time, but they were all applying for the position."

The man chosen was Ray Meyer, who had dabbled in coaching even in his days as a player. Frustrated by the team's performance in the first half against Wisconsin in 1938, Keogan watched the second half from the stands as Meyer rallied the Irish to a 33-31 win. So when it came time to hire an assistant, the choice, to Keogan, was clear.

The Irish won four of their first five as the 1941 season got under way. But after an overtime loss to Illinois, Keogan suffered a heart attack that forced him to curtail his coaching activities even further. After a win against North Dakota, Keogan checked into the Mayo Clinic and was put on bed rest for the remainder of the season, leaving Meyer in charge.

Charlie Butler: "I don't think any of us realized how bad his health was. We knew he got an assistant, which was to relieve him. But George was still coach."

Compounding the stress, Eddie Riska broke his foot against Syracuse and missed a month. But sophomore Charlie Butler ably filled his role, and the Irish didn't miss a beat.

Ray Meyer: "We were losing in New York. I come in at halftime, and Riska's gotten one of the kids to get his shoe off and he's going to try to play with a broken foot. I told him 'Whoa, you're not playing with that.'

"We had a jump ball in the center circle, and we had a kid by the name of Charlie Butler. Boy, he could jump. We had a timeout, and I knew Butler would get the tip. So he goes up, tipped it to Art Pope, and Pope laid it in the basket as the gun went off. Next day, the papers all said, 'Pope Gets Win for Notre Dame.'"

Charlie Butler: "The next game was Michigan State. George came to see us before the game, and he said, 'We'll miss Riska. But never in the history of Notre Dame has a player gone down that someone else wasn't to take his place and do the job just as well. And tonight, it's you.'

"I just about jumped two feet in the air. George could give a good pep talk. I went out and I scored 17 points, which they told me was a record for a sophomore. That was my first game starting."

With Butler shouldering Riska's scoring load, the Irish went a perfect 5-0 without him and completed a 17-5 season. But Keogan's return was in serious doubt. Having been forced off his feet for the balance of the 1941 season, questions arose about whether he could coach again. Elmer Layden had just resigned as football coach and athletic director, and the hot rumor was Frank Leahy, the new football coach, would not assume the athletic director's chair, leaving it to George Keogan, who would, in turn, turn the team over to Ray Meyer.

But it proved to be nothing more than a rumor. In 1942, Keogan retained his coaching position for home games but didn't travel with the team. He and Meyer would have to figure out how to replace Riska's scoring on a young team, and they found a solution in Cy Singer.

Charlie Butler: "Cy Singer, when he was a freshman, was older than we were. Where George got him from, I don't know. But instead of shooting like normal people with two hands, Cy swung it around from his hip. And the first time he did it and it went through the hoop, the crowd at Madison Square Garden shouted. They never saw anybody shoot like that before."

The team's offensive skill was evenly balanced with a number of players capable of providing points on a given night. The Irish ended up 16-6 and seemed ready to take a big step in 1943.

But if they were to take that step, they'd be doing it without Ray Meyer. The Irish assistant was offered the coaching job at DePaul University in his native Chicago, and decided to accept.

Ray Meyer: "Jim Enright and Arthur Morse came down. Enright refereed the game that night. It was the last game of the year. After the game, they caught me in the room and Morse offered me the job at DePaul. So I went in to talk to George Keogan before I did anything, and he said, 'Well, you're going up there as head coach. You can always come back to Notre Dame, but you should explore this and try to find out if you really want to coach or not.' So I went to DePaul."

Some may have questioned why Notre Dame would allow this move given Keogan's precarious health situation, but to the players it was a no-brainer.

Charlie Butler: "I don't think he had complete assurance in his own mind that Keogan was ever going to retire. Ray felt this DePaul job was it."

Frank Quinn: "Meyer was really just an interim coach. They brought him in to help out because George was having trouble with his heart. I think they just paid him by the week or by the month or something. He didn't really have a contract the way assistant coaches have them now. When this opportunity came up at DePaul, he felt like he should take it because he wasn't aware of the fact that Keogan was in that bad of health."

George Keogan, though, didn't seem to be doing too badly. The rest was helping him physically and mentally, and his doctors had green-lighted his return to the bench full time. His 1943 team was loaded with talent, with Bob Rensberger and Bob Faught receiving All-America mention at season's end, and won 12 of its first 13 games. As he sat in his easy chair after practice on February 17, 1943, Keogan remarked to his wife, Ruby, that he had never felt better in his life.

Moments later, he was gone.

Frank Gilhooley: "We used to go down to the basement chapel for early mass in the morning. I remember being with Jimmy O'Halloran, and we went down there for a 6:15 mass. Brother Patrick Kane, who was our rector in Brownson Hall, came up to us and told us that Coach Keogan had died the previous night."

Bob Rensberger: "It was on the radio immediately after it happened. He was reading the paper. Ruby heard the dog barking, and she went in to find he had passed away."

In the midst of their storybook season, the Irish bid farewell to their coach. On February 20, the players served as pallbearers for Keogan's funeral in the afternoon. That night, they traveled to the Chicago Stadium to take on Great Lakes Naval Station. They gave an emotional effort before falling by four points in overtime, although they were able to avenge the loss at Great Lakes later in the season.

Bob Rensberger: "The Chicago Tribune had a picture of us all sitting on the bench. Bob Faught was the last one, and then they had a spotlight shining on where George would have been sitting."

Charlie Butler: "At Chicago Stadium, they turned out all the lights and put a spotlight on an empty seat at the end of our bench. If you are in the Monogram Room, a picture of that picture is in there. When we played Great Lakes the second time up at their place, Riska claimed George was sitting on their rim knocking the ball away, and that's why we won."

Moose Krause, who had replaced Meyer as assistant coach, coached the team for the rest of the season, and the Irish went undefeated after that

Great Lakes loss. An 18-2 record would have been enough for a postseason tournament for most teams, but this Notre Dame team was still bound by the university's ban on postseason play. Given what the players had gone through, it was probably a better choice.

Charlie Butler: "It was a shock. He was our coach, and you just thought you'd never be without him. He was an unbelievably strong character—one you would never forget if you were associated with him.

Mark Ertel: "I admired George Keogan, I really did. You never saw him get perturbed about anything, and that was instrumental in instructing us about the right way to do things. I was very comfortable with him."

Bob Rensberger: "I've always been very happy that I had George Keogan as my coach during my playing days. He taught us a lot about life in general, and he was a really good man. He took a shine to me because I was from a small town, and he helped me out a lot with talks and things like that. My father had died when I was very young, and he became a father figure to me. I really loved the guy. Most of the players he had did. If my sons were playing ball, I'd love for them to play for a man like him."

Keogan finished his Notre Dame career having won 77 percent of his games. He would be named to the Basketball Hall of Fame in 1961. But it was the little things his players would miss most.

Bob Rensberger: "George always had the team over at the end of the season. After we'd eat, Keogan would get out his magic tricks. He got the greatest kick out of taking us up one at a time and having us try to do a trick that we couldn't do. He would take it and do it, and he would just roar. We'd look forward to it every year."

Charlie Butler: "Keogan every year had a spaghetti dinner after some game. Of course, we didn't have it there that year. But Mrs. Rockne had it in her house. I didn't know her. But we did go to her house. She played records of Rockne's pep talks."

Pep talks would certainly come in handy for the Irish the next couple of seasons. Their coach was gone, and there was a war on that would wreak its own brand of havoc on their seasons and their lives.

What Is It Good For?
(1944–1946)

As would be expected, World War II made things very difficult for the athletic programs of the nation's colleges and universities, not to mention the young men who participated in them. Players and coaches were being called into military service, so rosters would change wildly from season to season. Wartime rationing meant restrictions on travel, affecting the size of crowds at games and a teams' ability to create a viable schedule. And for those players who weren't on active duty, there was sometimes a guilty feeling regarding their status.

Bob Rensberger: "The seniors would enlist because the military would allow them to graduate and not call them up until then. But a lot of people had a rough time with it. Here we were in college, and some people thought we should be over there fighting. We had enlisted, and we had every intention of getting into it. But you could see why people would say that. We were out playing a game of basketball when there were more important things going on. There were some insults thrown at us at times, and some of us felt a little ashamed."

Faced with these obstacles, many schools like Georgetown and Xavier chose to suspend their programs during the war. Notre Dame, with the Navy's V-12 program operating on campus, was able to keep its program going, but had to scramble at times to keep things running smoothly.

Many of the toughest games in those years were played against military teams. Military bases and training centers like Great Lakes and Iowa Pre-Flight put together "all-star" teams consisting of athletes-in-arms stationed there, and those teams filled the scheduling voids created by the suspended programs.

Bob Rensberger: "They had so many good ballplayers that collectively it was tough. You had to come out strong. But we were one of the few teams that ever beat those guys. The All-Star concept hurt them. Most of them kept trying to prove they were the stars of the game."

The 1944 season exemplified the chaos. Moose Krause was now the permanent coach, but virtually his entire roster from the previous season was lost to graduation or military commitments. Only two returning players suited up for the Irish that season: Bernie Rutledge, the team's only senior, and junior Leo "Crystal" Klier, the younger brother of Gene Klier, who had played in Keogan's final years.

Frank Gilhooley: "Leo Klier was a great player, one of the best I've ever seen. He was a tough guy who could really go. He was a competitor right from the opening tip, and he never let up."

Richard Kluck: "He was absolutely fierce. He wasn't going to be guarded by anybody. He'd run you down if he had to get to the basket. He had a quick first step and he was a hard driver, but he also could set you up very well for you to drive with the ball."

The team finished 10-9 and Klier became a wartime bright spot for the Irish. He led the team with 15.4 points per game, and set a Notre Dame record for points in a season. His 18 points helped the Irish to a 54-51 win over a Great Lakes team that had won 21 games in a row, including a 36-point pasting of Notre Dame just 10 days earlier. And when the season ended, he was named Notre Dame's fourth Consensus All-American.

Leo Klier: "There weren't that many people from my hometown who were All-Americans, and I really felt it was an accomplishment. I remember one of the coaches in my hometown told me he didn't think I would ever make it. It wasn't my purpose to show him, but I just felt good about it."

That feeling was short-lived. Klier was called to active duty, as was coach Moose Krause. Faced once again with having to replace almost the entire roster, along with a coach, the Irish turned to an alumnus who was cooling his heels because of Xavier's decision to suspend its program, Clem Crowe.

George Ratterman: "Clem was a very fine person. I went to high school in Cincinnati, and Clem was coaching at Xavier University there. So we knew each other going in."

Frank Gilhooley: "Clem Crowe was a wonderful man. He certainly didn't die of an ulcer. He was an easy-going guy. Give him his pot of coffee and pack of cigarettes and he was home free."

With rosters decimated by the war, the NCAA relaxed transfer policies, which allowed the programs that could stay afloat to field teams. Refugees such as Johnny Dee and Billy Hassett joined Frank Gilhooley, a returnee who had played sparingly in 1944, and football player George Ratterman in the starting lineup for the Irish.

Hassett would have a wonderful season, following in Klier's footsteps as a Consensus All-American, and Ratterman would average more than 10 points per game. But the attention-getter on that team would be a freshman from East Chicago, Ind., Vince Boryla.

Vince Boryla: "My mom and dad came from Poland, so they were very poor people. There were steel mills up and down the shore of Lake Michigan, and we probably lived about a half a mile from them. The furthest thing from my mind was being given the opportunity of going to college.

"I was what amounted to an all-Northern Indiana Conference player. The No. 1 team in Indiana was in the same conference as we were, and we happened to upset them in the opening round of the playoffs. So I had a chance to go to Northwestern and Indiana and maybe Indiana State. But then Notre Dame was interested in me, and I came from a very strong Catholic family. So that's how I ended up at Notre Dame."

A hard-working, reticent young man, Boryla made a big impact on his teammates fairly quickly.

Frank Gilhooley: "People think of Vince as a center, which he was and a very good one. But with the exception of Billy Hassett, he was also the best outside shooter on the club. Boy, he could hit from all over."

Hitting from all over allowed Boryla to eclipse the scoring records Klier had set the previous season and helped the Irish to 10 wins in their first 13 games, including a one-point overtime win over Kentucky in Louisville.

Frank Gilhooley: "Vince threw in a couple of hook shots, and Johnny Dee did too in the overtime. Jack Tingle had two free throws coming in regulation that would have beaten us, and he only made one. His second missed the front rim by a good six inches, and Adolph Rupp let go with a blast of profanity. He could really rant and rave."

The 15-5 finish was certainly more than Irish fans expected that year, and with hostilities winding down and the return of players like Leo Klier to the already-loaded team, expectations were high going into the 1946 season. But again there were replacements required, with Clem Crowe deciding to take the head coaching position at the University of Iowa. To replace Crowe, the university brought in another coach idled by a closed program at Georgetown, Elmer Ripley.

Vince Boryla: "Elmer Ripley was the complete opposite of Clem Crowe. Clem Crowe was strong, hard, a tough disciplinarian. Elmer was a lot looser. He had come from the East, and he had coached at other places. So he had more of a basketball background and he ran a looser ship."

George Ratterman: "He had a different system. You might say it was Eastern-style basketball, rather than Clem's style, which was midwestern basketball where you just ran like crazy all the time. He came from the East, where they played more ball control."

In addition to adjusting to Ripley's new style, the team had an enviable problem—integrating the scoring punch of the returning Klier with that of Boryla, now a sophomore. As the players remember, it didn't turn out to be a problem at all.

Frank Gilhooley: "It was a very unselfish ballclub. Elmer Ripley instilled that in us. He was an old pro player, and talked about how it was a five-man game and you should always look to find the open man closer to the basket with the better percentage shot."

Leo Klier: "That was kind of a unique situation. I had set the scoring record the year before Vince came to Notre Dame, then he broke my record. The two of us were slugging it out my senior year . . . it was all in good fun. I thought we had good chemistry and didn't feel any vibes one way or the other. I was just playing basketball as hard as I could play it."

Vince Boryla: "I never thought of it, to be honest. The scoring races and the importance of scoring of today and so on—that never played any importance with me. We were just there to win ballgames."

With the chemistry issues settled, the Irish got down to the business of winning, which they did in their first 13 games. They contributed to a 33-game unbeaten streak at home that remains the Notre Dame record. The Associated Press, toying at the time with an unofficial poll, ranked the Irish No. 1 for six weeks.

Halfway through that opening streak, the Irish hosted DePaul and their giant, George Mikan. Mikan had originally wanted to attend Notre Dame, but George Keogan had sent him home with a jump rope, telling him to work on his footwork prior to the next year and return then for another evaluation. Ray Meyer's first act as DePaul coach was to call Mikan and tell him there was a spot for him on the Blue Demons' roster.

Frank Gilhooley: "Mikan was just too big for Boryla. George was kind of a freak back in those days—there wasn't anybody who was that big.

"At halftime we were behind by 13 or 14 points, and Billy Hassett, who was very close to Elmer, said, 'Why not let Vince get out from under the basket and move out to the corner and shoot?' Elmer asked us what we thought, and we all agreed, figuring we should get George away from the basket if we could.

"Vince went out there and hit four in a row from the corner. I can remember seeing Ray Meyer getting up finally and saying, 'Well, how long are you going to stay under there, George? Better get out and get after him.'"

Billy Hassett's last-second shot—his only made shot in 12 attempts that game—gave the Irish the 43-42 win and continued the streak, which came to an end about a month later against Northwestern.

Frank Gilhooley: "The bubble broke when we went to the Chicago Stadium and Northwestern beat us. They had a guy who was also an All-American football player by the name of Max Morris, and he had a big night. Everything he tossed up went in. He could have drop-kicked the ball and it would have found its way in. And they took it to us and won it."

Leo Klier: "That loss triggered something that caused us to slide. We lost four games against 17 wins that year, but we were better than that. We should have won 19 or more. We lost to NYU, and we shouldn't have lost to those guys. Marquette gave us a trimming as well, and DePaul beat us at the Stadium after we beat them at Notre Dame. Maybe we had a letdown. It wasn't evident. In my mind I never thought it was, and I don't think anyone else did."

Notre Dame still had a no-postseason policy, which wouldn't be tested in 1946 because of the season-ending slide. But people had taken notice of the Irish players. Leo Klier repeated as a Consensus All-American, and Hassett (first-team) and Boryla (second-team) joined him on the *True Magazine* lists. With the war over, Krause returned to campus, ready to take the reins of a loaded team that would no doubt rule the next couple of seasons.

The
Moose Krause
Years

(1947–1951)

4

The Lithuanian
and the Irishman
(1947–1949)

Edward "Moose" Krause arrived on the Notre Dame campus in the fall of 1930 from a small Lithuanian enclave in Chicago's Back of the Yards neighborhood with the dream of playing football for Knute Rockne. Not only did he fulfill that dream, by the time of his death in 1992, Krause had become such an integral part of Notre Dame football he had earned the moniker "Mr. Notre Dame."

Krause was such a good athlete that he couldn't be limited to one sport. While lettering in football all three of his eligible years, he also set a new standard for pivot players under George Keogan and was Notre Dame's first three-time Consensus All-American in basketball.

John Ford: "Moose was the greatest player Notre Dame has ever had in basketball. He had the full equipment—he could score and he could guard. Everything in those days revolved around the pivot man, and he was a master of the pivot. If you got the ball in to him, he was able to feed off or fake or take his famous hook shot, which he seldom missed. If he had one weakness, it was that he wasn't too great of a foul shooter. But he really worked hard at it and he practiced daily."

Don Allen: "Moose was so dominant, he forced them to change the rules. The three-second rule they have for the big men being in the lane? That was because of Moose. He'd get the ball down low, and he could either flip it right back to you for a score or put it up himself. I guess the other teams got tired of it."

The gregarious personality that would serve Krause so well in his later role as athletic director made him a favorite of almost everyone on the team. As a result, he developed a strong rapport with his coach—which was unusual for the intensely private Keogan—allowing him to do things an "ordinary" player might not have.

John Ford: "I remember a game we played at Marquette up in Milwaukee in 1934. There was a guy in the stands who kept heckling Keogan the whole game. He was really riding him hard, calling him all kinds of names. Finally, Keogan got fed up with it, and during a timeout, jumped up out of his seat—he was quite volatile on the bench anyway—and started up into the stands after this fellow. Well, Moose grabbed Keogan, picked him up bodily, put him back on the bench, and told him 'Just sit there, George, and don't say anything else.' Keogan didn't open his mouth the rest of the game."

After his graduation in 1934, Krause declined an offer to play for the Chicago Bears in favor of a position as athletic director at St. Mary's College in Winona, Minn. But he continued to play basketball, forming an all-star team that played exhibition games throughout the Midwest. He also brought his St. Mary's basketball team into the Fieldhouse to face his old coach, falling by 23 points.

Krause had moved to Holy Cross as football and basketball coach in 1941, when he received a phone call from Frank Leahy offering him a position as an assistant football coach, an offer he immediately accepted. Ray Meyer's departure for DePaul the next season created an opening on the basketball staff, and Krause moved into that position as well. But George Keogan's untimely death left the Irish in need of a head man, and rather than search the country for a replacement, the Notre Dame administration decided to keep the hiring in-house, naming Krause as Keogan's permanent replacement.

Leroy Leslie: "Moose was very adamant on sound fundamentals. We never played a zone defense because he was a pure man-to-man coach. He was definitely a single-pivot man—you had your center, and everything worked around your center—because that's where his indoctrination came. He was a huge man in his center position. There were also a couple of things you couldn't do. You could never leave your feet on defense, and you could never throw the ball cross-court."

Leo Klier: "I played a lot in the pivot when I was a sophomore and junior, and of course he had been a pivot man. So he gave me some good points to follow in playing the pivot, positioning myself and things like that."

Returning from a brief coaching interruption to serve in World War II, Krause was enthusiastic about his 1947 team. The nucleus of talent would be returning, and there would be talented underclassmen returning from war service to add to it.

But things didn't quite work out that way. With schools restarting their basketball programs, players like Ray Corley, Tom O'Keefe, and Johnny Dee transferred back to their original schools. Leo Klier, feeling it was "time to move on," decided to graduate with his academic class, even though he had another year of eligibility remaining. And Vince Boryla enlisted in the army and never returned to Notre Dame, choosing to finish his eligibility at the University of Denver.

Vince Boryla: "I really liked Notre Dame, but I wasn't a fanatic. I really enjoyed going to Notre Dame. It was great for me, and I have fond memories. But that's kind of where it stops. And I like Denver. I can't tell you how taken I was with the city when I came out here. Everything always kind of fit somehow with the good Lord's guiding. And to this day I have not regretted the move."

With George Ratterman the team's only returning letterman for 1947, Krause would have to rely on his underclassmen. The team was sophomore-dominated, with players such as Leo Barnhorst, Paul Gordon, and Jim O'Halloran playing a lot of minutes. But as the season progressed, a freshman from San Francisco named Kevin O'Shea emerged as a player to watch.

Leroy Leslie: "I was kind of awed by Kevin when I first came to Notre Dame. I never saw a guy who had hands that big. He just had humongous hands. He handled the ball real well, and had probably one of the first one-hand set shots in the country."

Neal Fichtel: "Kevin O'Shea was a great person. Needless to say, he was also a great basketball player. He was very down-to-earth. He didn't look down on anybody."

Eligible for varsity play his freshman year because of temporary eligibility rule relaxations, O'Shea contributed 9.5 points per game, third on the team behind John Brennan and captain Frannie Curran. The young Irish players finished the season 20-4 and received their first bid to the NCAA Tournament since 1943—which, of course, they declined as the school's ban on postseason play continued.

But O'Shea was getting national attention. Named to a number of second- and third-team All-America lists after 1947, he was ready to step into the spotlight in 1948 and became Notre Dame's latest Consensus All-American.

The 17-7 record for 1948 was a disappointment considering the results of the previous season, and there were a number of close losses. However, the Irish did manage a 64-55 win over Adolph Rupp's Kentucky squad that won the NCAA Tournament and featured Ralph Beard, Alex Groza, and Wallace Jones.

Richard Kluck: "They devised a method of isolating Kevin O'Shea on Ralph Beard and keeping the big man out of the center. What they did was put Kevin O'Shea in the middle and he played the center slot. As a result, they had Groza and Jones out on the wing chasing the center in the rebounding area. I think O'Shea went on to get like 28 points that night.

"Rupp brought Beard out of the ballgame with about a minute and a half left to play. Beard had already gotten 26 points. And Rupp said to him, 'Sonny, some nights you just don't have it.' We kind of got a kick out of that, because 26 points was a lot back then. But O'Shea put it to him."

With the noise of the partisan crowd and the placement of the band behind the visitors' bench, Rupp swore that once the current contract was fulfilled, he would never play in the Notre Dame Fieldhouse again. Other coaches adopted the same attitude, seeing little benefit in playing the Irish in their snake-pit home arena. Slowly but surely the Irish would become road warriors, playing most of their games away from the Fieldhouse.

The 1949 schedule would prove to be a harbinger. Wanting to keep a high athletic profile in alumni-heavy areas, the administration sent the basketball team on trips to those areas. Kevin O'Shea's reputation meant many teams wanted to face the Irish, and Krause ended up putting together a schedule that had but nine home games.

In 1949, the major basketball team excursion would find the Irish playing in Dallas and San Francisco over the holiday break—a trip that turned out to be a little more than they'd bargained for.

Richard Kluck: "We played Purdue and Indiana in Indianapolis, then got an all-night train ride down to Dallas. The alumni greeted us and treated us like royalty. We played SMU that year and beat them. After the ballgame, we went to some alumni's homes and they treated us very nicely.

"The next day, we got up and took a plane to San Francisco. That was New Year's Eve. We were expecting great things for New Year's Eve in San Francisco, and it was flat-out nothing. We didn't know what to do. We didn't know where to go or anything else. We ended up going to our hotel room and wishing each other a Happy New Year. It rained all the time we were there."

Neal Fichtel: "The coach flew back to South Bend, and he left the trainer, Hughie Burns, and the student manager in charge. We got on the train and had just gotten out of San Francisco and into the Rockies when a snowstorm hit."

Richard Kluck: "We were on that train from early Tuesday morning until we pulled into Chicago on Saturday night. We couldn't wash. You could brush your teeth and you could drink the water, but we couldn't shave or do anything like that. All we could see would be snow all around us. Jimmy O'Halloran and Hughie Burns played Gin all the way back. And the money at one point got to where one guy owed the other guy $1,000. Either Jimmy or Hughie handed the other $5 at the end of the trip [to square it]."

Neal Fichtel: "There was something like 13 trains ahead of us, and it got to be a long period of time stretched out. So they kept moving us up.

Somewhere along the way in one of the towns they stopped us in, we got off and went to the high school gym and shot around for a little bit.

"It was almost a week before we got back, and we got back just in time for semester exams. There was only one instructor who made any kind of accommodation for me. But we didn't miss any games—we were in the light part of the schedule that accommodated semester exams."

Richard Kluck: "We got into Chicago Saturday night, and Krause greeted us on campus Sunday morning, 'Well, boys, how did you do?' We played DePaul that Monday night and they kicked our fannies."

The Donner Party-esque foray through the Rockies was probably the most memorable moment from that 1949 season, which ended just like 1948 had at 17-7. Two weeks after the season ended, Krause was named athletic director in a reorganization of the university athletic department—a move that would set the clock ticking on his tenure as basketball coach.

Changing of the Guard
(1950–1951)

Moose Krause was many things at Notre Dame—head basketball coach, assistant football coach, goodwill ambassador. In 1949 he added a new title: athletic director. In an effort to centralize control within the athletic department (and perhaps to smooth over relationships with other schools that had been made tense by the bristly Frank Leahy), the university ended the practice of the football coach also holding the athletic directorship. The new president, Fr. Theodore Hesburgh, appointed Krause to the position he would hold for 32 years under the new executive vice-president, Fr. Ned Joyce.

But this created more demands on Krause's time. Though the players didn't complain, it became clear something would have to give.

Leroy Leslie: "He had other responsibilities as athletic director, and the kids understood that. But he never missed a practice. He was always there. He never missed a game. Strict disciplinarian. If you goofed up, he'd let you know it. He was interested in the kids. He wanted to know how you were doing in your studies and how everything was in your campus life. If he could help you out, he would."

Norb Lewinski: "We accepted that kind of stuff because the money wasn't there for specialization. Now you've got to have an athletic director who does nothing but direct, and then you've got to have a coach, and then you have an assistant. At that time, the guys were like coaches in grade school and high school now—they'd have three different jobs and were happy to do it. Moose was that kind of guy. He felt he was helping the school by maybe saving them a salary or two."

Still trying to wear many hats, Krause began the 1950 season hoping Kevin O'Shea could regain his sophomore year form. The All-American had been hampered by a knee injury at the beginning of his junior year and never quite recovered. It was thought a fresh season would get him back on the right track.

He certainly had a more successful senior campaign from a personal perspective. His scoring average rose to 15 points per game and he became Notre Dame's first 1,000-point career scorer. He returned to the first-team All-America lists after dropping to third team in 1949. But he was surrounded by youth, and the team managed only a 15-9 finish.

That youth would serve the Irish well in future years, however. Among the sophomores getting their first taste of varsity action were Leroy Leslie, a 6-foot 2-inch forward from Pennsylvania who was the team's No. 2 scorer with just over 12 points per game, and Don Strasser, a 6-foot guard who was the latest import from the talent-rich Catholic League in Chicago.

Neal Fichtel: "Our guards usually ended up defending against forwards, so I ended up guarding Leroy in practice a lot of the time. He was the most competitive person I ever played with."

Jim Gibbons: "Leroy was a terrific, gifted athlete. He could run and jump and score. He was very fluid, very competitive. He had that floating ability."

Norb Lewinski: "Leroy was a cocky, good player. He knew he was good, and he showed it. Out on the floor, he always impressed me. And Strasser was one of the best passers I ever played with."

Dick Rosenthal: "When I was a freshman we used to scrimmage against the Varsity. [Strasser and Leslie] would never let an opponent split between the two of them. They would always try to shut you off."

As the underclassmen gained confidence, they turned around a 1-4 start to win 10 of their next 12, including Notre Dame's last win over Adolph Rupp at home. Trying to negate the tremendous home-court Irish advantage, Rupp said the only time fifth-ranked Kentucky was available to travel to South Bend that season was during the week in which Notre Dame had scheduled first-semester final exams. But his effort was unsuccessful. The Irish ignored Kentucky center Bill Spivey and concentrated on stopping his teammates, which they did to the tune of a 64-51 upset win.

Leroy Leslie: "All the Notre Dame fans were behind the Kentucky bench and the band was back there. Rupp accused Moose of putting the band back there [on purpose]. And he would never play in the Fieldhouse again."

Neal Fichtel: "I remember Coach Rupp being livid because in the short confines of the Fieldhouse, he felt the band was too unruly, too close. He said in the paper afterwards he'd never come back to Notre Dame—he'd either play them on his court or a neutral court."

But the workload was taking its toll on Krause, and it soon became apparent that a change was needed.

Fr. Hesburgh: "Moose was a good coach for us, and we had a number of good years under him. But it became apparent the athletic thing under Fr. Ned Joyce was growing—we were going to have this big development that would include the Joyce Center—and although everything was moving very well, it was obvious we were going to have more problems. That made it difficult to be both coach and athletic director. It was kind of like being your own boss.

"So I had the nasty job of calling him in and saying, 'Moose, you're going to have to be one or the other. I know you love basketball, but being athletic director is more important to the whole university.' So he gave it up. He hated to, but he did."

Just before the 1951 season, Krause announced to the team that he would be stepping down at season's end. No doubt the team wanted to send him out a winner and get him over 100 victories for his Notre Dame coaching career. But a four-game losing streak to end the season meant a 13-11 record, leaving Krause two victories shy of the century mark. Had the announcement affected the team psychologically?

Leroy Leslie: "Subconsciously, it affects you because you don't know what to expect of the new coach coming in. It's always in the back of your mind that a new broom sweeps cleaner. But it didn't affect me, because once that ball was up, everything was go. You are on a scholarship and you've got a responsibility to the university."

Don Strasser: "I don't think we at that time had any knowledge as to what was going on—who was available or who was here and whatnot. We were in a little world of our own. Whoever came in came in, and that was it."

The Irish had a good record in the Fieldhouse, but played poorly away from home, which made wins tougher to come by with a more road-oriented schedule.

Leroy Leslie: "When you were at home, you had an outstanding student body. They gave you a little bit more spirit. And if you look at that time, Notre Dame was a national team. We traveled probably a lot more than our opponents. Teams like DePaul usually played around their own area."

Jim Gibbons: "We lost to Indiana with Branch McCracken. We lost to St. Louis with Eddie Hickey. We lost to Kentucky with Adolph Rupp. We lost to Michigan State with Fordy Anderson. We lost to Butler—Tony Hinkle always murdered us in their fieldhouse. We lost to DePaul with Ray Meyer—it was a war every game we ever played with them. We lost to Canisius, because that's a tough place to play in Buffalo. We lost to NYU at Madison Square Garden. We lost to some pretty good basketball teams. And all of those teams we lost to on the road we played at Notre Dame and beat them."

That schedule also had to be played without Don Strasser, who broke his ankle against Wisconsin in the third game of the season.

Don Strasser: "I was going in for a lay-up, and as I went up I got bumped. I came down on the side of my foot. I just thought it was a severe sprain, but it was broken. I had been playing basketball since I was in the sixth grade, and starting all the way through. Sitting there and watching it was very disheartening."

Neal Fichtel: "He was a very competitive leader, and the people who came in for him were not of the same temperament. Although those guys were good basketball players, [Strasser] had leadership qualities they didn't."

Leroy Leslie: "I knew what Strasser was going to do every minute because I played with him from the time I was a freshman until I was a senior. He knew me and I knew him. If he hit me and I hit the center, he knew which way I was cutting. When you don't have that guard in there, you don't have that continuity. It's like a quarterback getting to know his receivers."

Strasser's injury opened the playing-time door for a fellow Chicagoan and future Irish assistant coach, sophomore Jim Gibbons.

Jim Gibbons: "I felt sorry for him, even though that gave me a chance to play. The kid was a terrific athlete and a terrific competitor. We knew each other from Chicago when he was at Leo and I was at Mt. Carmel, so we had a kind of a good relationship."

The team's propensity to foul kept key players on the bench at key times, which didn't help in close losses.

Neal Fichtel: "Coach Krause liked contact basketball. I always said I had limited talent in shooting and Moose told me not to shoot and just get the ball to the people who were better shooters. But he liked that I would go out there and compete, run into people and maybe foul them.

"He was still coaching football at the time, so maybe the football coach mentality was coming over to our team. But he liked that type of basketball, and with that comes fouls. So we had some rough games."

With Krause leaving as coach, attention turned to his successor. Conventional wisdom pointed to Ray Meyer, but the former Irish star had found a niche at DePaul and wasn't inclined to leave.

Ray Meyer: "Notre Dame has been very good to me all of my life. I think I was offered the job every time they changed coaches. Once they had Arch Ward from the Tribune come to me and we had lunch together. He was trying to persuade me to go back to Notre Dame. Another time, Moose Krause flew up to my basketball camp in Wisconsin and offered me the job.

"There were a lot of times I regretted never going back. Notre Dame has a fantastic name. I remember I was in a hotel in Detroit [as a Notre Dame assistant coach], and Hunk Anderson came by to see me. I was in a really little room. He picked up the phone, called the front desk and said, 'What the hell do you mean giving a coach from Notre Dame a room like this?' They immediately switched me into a big suite with flowers and everything.

"But the reason I never went back was I started at DePaul, and they were very good to me in the sense that they gave me a chance to coach and put me out on my own. I liked the kind of a boy I was getting there—never a great ballplayer, but always someone from the area."

With Meyer out of the picture, the Irish would have to look elsewhere. But there were still plenty of Irish alumni in the coaching ranks, so Krause only needed to look a couple of miles further up the Lake Michigan shoreline from DePaul to find his man.

The
John Jordan
Years

(1952–1964)

6

Up on the Boards,
Back on the Defense
(1952)

John Jordan first made his name on the hardwood in South Bend in uniform. As a teammate of Moose Krause under George Keogan, Jordan finished 49-13 in three seasons as a player. His teams won 22 games in a row along the way, and Jordan was team captain as a senior.

But even in his days as a player, there was a coach trying to get out. During Jordan's senior year, George Keogan was taken ill before the team's trip to Ohio State. As captain, Jordan tried to assert some control over the game plan in Keogan's absence.

John Ford: "He had some hand in it, but the reason we lost that game is because the rest of us wanted to have a hand in it too. We all thought we knew what to do to win the game, and that wasn't good.

"Tom Conley had been the captain of the football team. He was doing graduate work at the time, and he went as our coach. Well, he knew nothing about basketball. 'Scrap-Iron' Young, who was our trainer, wanted to get his thoughts in as well, and that didn't help either. Jordan did have some say in the game with regard to substituting. But we lost because we had too many coaches at that game. We all thought we knew more than the other guy did, but it turned out that we didn't know as much as we thought."

Even with that inauspicious debut, the coaching bug had bitten Jordan hard. He returned to his alma mater, Mount Carmel High School on the South Side of Chicago, where he spent the next 14 years teaching history and basketball to students like Ed O'Rourke.

Ed O'Rourke: "I knew Jordan as a rugged individualist, but also as a terrific guy who had a great memory. He was very friendly, and a good coach. He was great for saying things like—and he repeated it all through high school and the years afterwards—'up on the boards and back on the defense.' I did some scouting for him, but no matter what I wrote up, the game plan ended up being 'up on the boards and back on the defense.'"

In 1950, Jordan abruptly pulled up stakes at Mount Carmel and traveled to the North Side of the city and the head coaching position at Loyola University. The sudden change of address caught some of his players like future Irish star Jack Stephens by surprise. But the move may have had a purpose given the announcement of Moose Krause's resignation and the need for an heir apparent as Irish coach.

Jack Stephens: "Jordan was like a part of my family. I remember one game we played at Mount Carmel in February where I went out afterwards with my buddies. I got in early in the morning, and Jordan and his wife, Irene, were in my kitchen. So here I am as a junior in high school at 1:30, and they're sitting there drinking beer in the kitchen having a good time while I went to bed.

"But in April, Jordan quit Mount Carmel and went to Loyola as coach. He's telling me I'm going to Notre Dame and I got my senior year in front of me. I'm thinking he'll want me to go to Loyola, and I wasn't going to Loyola. But he never put any pressure on me, because he already knew he was going to Notre Dame. Loyola fit on his resume."

After a year at Loyola, Jordan was hired as coach at Notre Dame . . . a job he wanted so badly that money was no object.

Jack Stephens: "Moose was interviewing Jordan for the job and he said, 'How much are they paying you at Loyola?' Jordan said, '$5,000 a year.' Moose said, 'You can't get that at Notre Dame. The assistant football coaches get $4,800. That's all I can give you.' "

Don Strasser: "When he went to Notre Dame, he had to take a pay cut. But Moose told him, 'You've got to come on down and take it. Because if you do, things will work out for you.' And evidently they did."

Jordan wasted little time getting to work and implementing his 1-3-1 offensive system.

Jim Gibbons: "He was all about high-percentage shots and beating the hell out of people on offense on the boards. He liked to play tough defense . . . he got that from George Keogan because I asked him about it several times. 'Up on the boards and back on defense' was all he ever talked about."

Leroy Leslie: "He never ran a zone defense. You played a straight switching man-to-man. You released. You got the ball down the floor. You didn't dribble it down the floor, you passed it. You didn't drive against zones, you passed around them."

Given his familiarity with Catholic League players who had gone on to Notre Dame like Strasser, Gibbons, and Norb 'Gooch' Lewinski, Jordan could have been forgiven a tendency to depend on and play them more often. But his players didn't see any favoritism, which endeared the coach to them almost immediately.

Dick Rosenthal: "John Jordan was the basketball coach to Jim Gibbons and Gooch Lewinski in high school. He coached in the Catholic League, and we had a number of Catholic league players: Don Strasser, Tommy Sullivan, Jack Stephens, Eddie Condon, there were a ton. But John gave everybody an equal shot at playing and tried to put what he thought was his best team on the floor."

Norb Lewinski: "He was well-liked by everybody, that was the thing. He found the hearts of the families, and they didn't feel like outsiders. They all felt like they were part of that Chicago contingent."

As Jordan prepared for the 1952 season, he had a strong roster to work with. Strasser and Leslie provided senior leadership. Future All-American Dick Rosenthal was the future in the low post, and he and Leslie were a formidable defensive (and fouling) combination. Because of the Korean War, freshmen were made eligible in a one-year "experiment," meaning Jack Stephens was available at guard.

But no one on the roster received as much attention as two sophomore guards who would be seeing their first varsity action. One, Joe Bertrand, was a silky-smooth scoring machine who would eventually receive a degree from Notre Dame and go on to a career in Chicago politics. The other, Entee Shine, a fireplug who played ferocious defense, would transfer to Tennessee State after a frustrating sophomore year. Both were tremendous players—who happened to be the first black basketball players at Notre Dame.

Fr. Ted Hesburgh: "I felt it was insane for a Catholic university not to have good black basketball players, especially considering that a lot of the good black basketball players at that time were playing at Catholic high schools. Ned [Joyce], while a South Carolinian, was in complete agreement with that.

"I don't think it was a big problem because they were good basketball players. People could be impressed by that and not the fact that they were black."

Being a black athlete on what was then an almost entirely white campus was certainly a change—for Bertrand and Shine, their coaches and teammates, and the university community at large. But no one on that team remembers any problems.

Don Strasser: "Where I grew up in Chicago, there was no such thing as prejudice or hatred. It didn't affect us in any way. We never even thought of them as being black."

Dick Rosenthal: "Entee used to always joke about some of his high school buddies who moved on to Michigan State and other schools. Lack of color was a little bit of a question for him. Joe Bertrand had a huge, huge following in Chicago. His high school coach came to virtually every game, along with a great many friends from St. Elizabeth High School. So Notre Dame was a very comfortable place for Joe Bertrand."

The Notre Dame administration, however, was concerned about the reaction of Southern opponents and their fans. So the Irish made no trips south of the Mason-Dixon Line during the time that Bertrand and Shine were on campus except the annual trip to Louisville. Those games just over the Kentucky state line provided a strong life lesson for a Notre Dame team possibly insulated from the problems of race in America then.

Leroy Leslie: "We were going down to play Louisville. We go to check in, and the clerk looks at us and says, 'You guys can't stay here. You've got two black boys here. We don't cater to black boys.' "

Jack Stephens: "The Knights of Columbus had a bar. We went to the second floor—the dance floor—and they put cots down. That's where we stayed. We were a block and a half away from the arena. We dressed at the Knights of Columbus, put a topcoat on over our uniforms, and then walked over."

Jim Gibbons: "After the game, Joe Bertrand and I went out to eat. We got into a restaurant and sat down at the counter. We sat there and sat there and sat there, until finally the guy that was the maitre d', so to speak, came up and said, 'Excuse me, but you'll have to leave. We don't serve blacks here.' Joe didn't say a word. He handled it like a champion. We got up and walked out and didn't cause any problem.

"That was my first experience with racism. It had never happened to me before, and I wouldn't have imagined it in a hundred years. It registered with me obviously and Jordan handled it with the team. But that was a wake-up call."

Notre Dame lost that game to Louisville, one of three losses the Irish suffered in their first 14 games. They spent several weeks ranked in the top 25 and probably would have been invited to a postseason tournament—although the ability to accept would be subject to the university's continuing policy against postseason play.

But after the first semester, the Irish experienced another "first" in their history: academically ineligible players. Strasser, Shine, and Stephens had not achieved the minimum grades Notre Dame required during the first semester and would have to sit out the rest of the season.

Jack Stephens: "That first semester I was on my own, and I didn't make it. I just wasn't ready and didn't grasp the whole situation. The second semester they started with tutors, and from that point on I had no problems."

Don Strasser: "I goofed up in Spanish. I just didn't hit the books as hard as I should have. It was probably one of the biggest regrets that I had by not applying myself a little more.

"We were playing Kentucky in the Chicago Stadium. I think they were trying to hold the grades off until after, but they came out before, and that was it. I was coming back to Chicago, and I couldn't play. It was a hard pill to swallow. I got through it, and it turned out all right. But it's something that I regret that happened to me."

Leroy Leslie: "My mom and dad came from Johnstown to watch the game, and they were with the Strassers. We were in a hotel, and all of a sudden we got a call from the athletic director saying Strasser, Shine, and Stephens couldn't play. And my mother and dad were sitting there with Mr. and Mrs. Strasser."

Dick Rosenthal: "Don Strasser, Jack Stephens, and Entee Shine were our three guards. So we had to go to the halls and get a couple of people who hadn't played, Tommy Sullivan being one of them.

"We had Kentucky on the ropes. Jim Gibbons played an incredible game. Late in the game, he fouled out and Tommy Sullivan came in. And twice Tommy Sullivan dribbled the ball inbounds instead of passing it. Both times, of course, we lost the ball.

"We were with them all the way in that ballgame and just got beat at the end. I remember Adolph Rupp came into our locker room and had some very complimentary things to say to our team. Leroy didn't want any part of it—he said, 'Yeah, get out of here.' But they were a good team, and who knows what would have happened if we had had those three people."

Without their top three backcourt players, the Irish lost seven of their last 12 to finish the season. But they managed an upset of No. 18 NYU in Madison Square Garden thanks to timely scoring by Rosenthal and Irish football legend John Lattner, a temporary replacement on the depleted roster, and were invited to play in a postseason tournament in Hawaii.

Although Moose Krause recommended they take the bid, the Irish administration declined, citing concerns about the expense and class time missed.

Dick Rosenthal: "Everyone would have loved to have the opportunity to do that. But missing school was not a very tolerable thing. Even the way we scheduled games, we'd play Tuesday one week and Wednesday the next so we wouldn't miss the same classes. We did a lot of flying out after class, play the game, and get right back. But as young kids, we would have played in a barn."

Missing a postseason reward had been frustrating for the team. But one year later, a similar invitation would be extended to the Fighting Irish. They would respond to it differently and usher in a new era of competition possibilities.

7

First Time for Everything
(1953–1954)

John Jordan's first season had seen its share of "firsts" for the Irish program, including the first black players and the first players lost to academic ineligibility. Jordan's second and third seasons would see even more, some more meaningful than others, but all contributing to putting the Irish squarely in the public eye.

The "firsts" started quickly. The Hoosier Classic—the two-day tournament in Indianapolis that featured Indiana, Purdue, Butler, and Notre Dame—was suspended, a casualty of an expanded Big Ten schedule. So Indiana University made its first trip to South Bend in 21 years. The Hoosiers owned a five-game win streak over the Irish and had a talented sophomore center named Don Schlundt.

Dick Rosenthal: "Don was the leading scorer in the Big Ten, and he was really a fine player. When we were getting ready for those games, Johnny Jordan used to come in and he'd say, 'Junior [Stephens], you are going to have Bobby Leonard, he's averaging 18 a game and you've got to hold him to 12. Bill Sullivan, you've got Charlie Crock, and he's averaging 11 and you've got to hold him to eight.' And he'd go down the whole team. And then he'd say something like, 'And Dick can't play Don Schlundt, so he'll score his usual on us.' I used to get so damn mad. Poor Don, I was ready to kill him. And he was the nicest guy in the world."

Jack Stephens: "The place was packed. Nobody could get a ticket. It was the first time Indiana had been to Notre Dame in what seemed like 100 years. We had an assistant coach who had just come down with polio, Marty O'Connor, and he was lying in a hospital bed. The game was dedicated to him, and we just played out of our minds.

"We fouled them with seven seconds to go down by one. They had two free throws and missed both. Rosenthal tipped the ball to me and I went down the length of the court. It was a three-on-two by the time I got to the other end; we had the advantage. And I'm looking to give it to Joe [Bertrand] on the right. Bobby Leonard, the Indiana player on that side, is a good friend of mine, and he knew me like a book. He moved to cover Joe. He didn't take me fully, so I had to go in and lay it up. And we won by one.

"Indiana went on and won the NCAA tournament. But when we played them at Notre Dame, it was one of their three or four losses for the year."

Two weeks later, the Irish went to East Lansing to participate in the Michigan State Classic, a two-day doubleheader. While they suffered their first loss there, 80-64 to No. 2 Kansas State, the trip was notable because the second day featured Notre Dame's first game against a team that would play a very large role in Irish basketball history: UCLA. While definitely not among the notable games in the series, Notre Dame's 68-60 win would be the last over the Bruins for quite a while.

Dick Rosenthal: "UCLA wasn't what UCLA was to become in those days. John Wooden, we had heard about. He had a great Indiana heritage and he coached in South Bend. But the game didn't have the significance the subsequent UCLA games had."

Jim Gibbons: "Why do I remember it? Only because I took the ball out of bounds after they scored a basket and instead of passing the ball inbounds, I dribbled the ball inbounds and got all the way past the free-throw circle still dribbling it. Neither one of the two officials had realized it. Jordan never realized it. But they finally did blow the whistle, and on the next change of possession or killing of the clock, I was on the bench."

As the season wound down, Jordan's crew took on a succession of ranked opponents—No. 6 Holy Cross, No. 10 DePaul, No. 17 Louisville, and No. 18 St. Louis. The last was always an interesting opponent for Dick Rosenthal, a native of the St. Louis area. Billiken coach and longtime Irish antagonist Eddie Hickey thought he had Rosenthal signed, sealed, and delivered, and losing the big man to the hated Irish was just one more source of South Bend frustration for him.

Dick Rosenthal: "Hickey and Moose were great competitors. They were exact opposites. Moose was a wonderful, gregarious, huge man, and Eddie Hickey was a small in stature, very intense, find-no-humor-in-anything kind of person.

"I remember when I was a freshman, St. Louis had won the NIT and they came out to Notre Dame. They had these wonderful white satin warm-ups. After a couple of lay-ups, they took off one jacket and they had another set of warm-ups under that.

"Notre Dame had a woolen warm-up uniform that almost looked like khaki. They were just awful. So Moose had Jack McAllister, the equipment manager, bring up sweats. Everybody took off their warm-ups and put on sweats. So there was a contrast of the Notre Dame team coming out in sweats and St. Louis University having all of the fancy things. Eddie Hickey was just beside himself—accusing Moose of demeaning the whole game. So there was a rivalry there. And it was a good rivalry."

With Hickey following Adolph Rupp's lead and not willing to bring his Billikens to South Bend, the Irish played them on Valentine's Day in Chicago Stadium, and came up short, 78-77. But they were given the chance to settle a score against a different old rival 10 days later in the cozy confines of the Fieldhouse.

Jack Stephens: "We went into Chicago Stadium and we played DePaul. To give you an idea of the time of year, we finished final exams on Thursday and played DePaul on Saturday. We hadn't practiced or done anything. I'm taking nothing away from DePaul—they cleaned our clocks. They beat us by 27 points. Ray Meyer was letting us have it.

"Arch Ward used to write for the *Chicago Tribune,* and Leahy used to use Arch Ward for football. If he didn't like something that was happening with the Notre Dame football team, he'd talk to Arch Ward and Ward would write it in his column. The next week in the *Tribune,* they said Notre Dame with all of its superstars from the Catholic League got beat by a couple of guards, Ron Fer, Jimmy Lampkin, and Bill Schuman, who had held me down to nothing. We just got blasted brutally by the *Tribune*.

"Well, the last week of February, they came back to our place. Again, it's a situation where you get yourself up. At halftime, we were up 58-31. The whole student body wanted blood, because they'd read the article, too. We were up something like 87-54. Jordan turned out to be the gentleman, because he called off the dogs. We would've scored 100 on them that night. Ray never tried to run up scores against us after that. I'm not knocking Ray—Ray's a good friend of mine. But that's what happened."

The 93-67 win set a Notre Dame record for points in a game and gave the Irish a 17-4 regular-season mark, their best finish since 1947. The selectors for the NCAA Tournament were bound to notice such a performance, and sure enough, they extended Notre Dame an invitation. Would the Irish accept?

The answer: yes. The postseason ban was now a football-only issue, and Notre Dame made its first of many appearances in the NCAA Tournament. There wasn't one particular reason the ban was lifted, although the fact that the NCAA had instituted a regional system that ensured teams would play opening-round games close to home certainly factored in. But Notre Dame also had plans in place that postseason revenues would help.

Fr. Ted Hesburgh: "I can't think of anything in particular, except we could always use more revenue, and the revenues today are incomparably better today than they were when we started doing these things. A lot of schools used those revenues to create dynasties and build up big affairs. But we added something many of the big schools didn't have: everything the university earned went to the university. It didn't go to any special interests. So the fact that they may have gone into postseason games and made some money created more scholarships, mostly.

"We went from one endowed scholarship to 60 to 70 percent of our students being on paid scholarships. That came about because of athletic money, which allowed us to upgrade the scholarships for black and Hispanic kids. When I became executive vice-president, we started to push for having scholarships for black youngsters, and today we have several hundred black students. Not as many as we would like, but several hundred more than nothing."

For their part, the players were delighted for the opportunity.

Jack Stephens: "Bids were so hard to get because at that stage, they only had 16 teams in. You would only have four teams from the Midwest. One would go to the Big Ten and one would go to the Southeast Conference, which meant Kentucky and the Big Ten champion. And there were two others who would have a chance.

"We felt we deserved it, and if we hadn't gotten it there would have been more of an issue. Getting it was not really a big issue at all. We were just happy."

Jim Gibbons: "To me, it was like we had won the national championship. It was a major accomplishment after a 19-5 record for Rosey, Bertrand, Gooch, Stephens, and myself.

"The reason it was so important to us was football at that time was king. They had gone from 1946 to 1949 with Leahy winning 38 straight games and three national championships. So basketball was just basketball. You've got to understand where you fit in. Football is number one, and it always is going to be. Jordan accepted it. He knew that. He lived off of it. He was never threatened by it."

The Irish were sent to Fort Wayne, where they had little trouble with first-round opponent Eastern Kentucky. The next two games would be played in a familiar haunt, the Chicago Stadium. Penn, No. 20, fell by 12 points, and then it was a rematch against old rival Indiana.

But this was a different Indiana team than the Irish had faced earlier that season. Don Schlundt had come into his own, and remembered the loss in South Bend well. His 41 points set an Irish opponent single-game scoring record and the Hoosiers cruised to a 79-66 win.

Jim Gibbons: "I thought we just ran out of gas against Indiana. We had played four or five games at the Stadium, which was a big plus for us. And we had already beaten Indiana at home 71-70 that same year when Jack Stephens took the ball off the board, dribbled the whole length of the floor and put in the shot at the buzzer."

Jack Stephens: "Schlundt had just improved immensely. We ran into him in the Chicago Stadium. When we played the first time, they were going to Schlundt maybe 25 percent of the time. When we played them next, the man I had, by the name of Dick Farley, didn't score. I didn't hold him score-less, he held himself scoreless. He was passing off to Schlundt."

But the Irish had improved for the second year in a row, and there were more improvements and "firsts" to come in 1954. Lewinski and Gibbons were gone, so Jordan moved Rosenthal back to the pivot from forward. Sophomore John Fannon moved into the starting lineup, while junior Bill Sullivan joined Bertrand and Stephens in the backcourt.

This lineup would prove to be prolific on offense, setting records with 1,896 total points and an average of 75.8 points per game. According to then-sophomore Lloyd Aubrey, good chemistry among the players was among the reasons why.

Lloyd Aubrey: "I didn't play much as a sophomore, but I had more fun that year than any of the other years I was there. They were just wonderful guys. There was a wonderful camaraderie among us. Rosey was very good. Joe Bertrand was there, and he was a wonderful player. Jack Stephens was very good. They were probably the best three players."

Dick Rosenthal: "I'm sure there is a certain camaraderie that exists in all uni-versities and perhaps on all teams. I know it's extremely true of our basketball team with the kids who played from 1950 to 1954. That's 50 years now, and for 50 years those people have been getting together. When Joe Bertrand died, there were eight of us there at the funeral plus Johnny Jordan. The guys were always close. I wouldn't have the slightest compunction to pick up the phone and call any one of those teammates and say I am in trouble or I need a favor or I'd like you to do something, and I'd be shocked if they wouldn't do it to the fullest of their ability. And I can guarantee you I would do the same for them."

The season started 4-2, with losses at defending national champion Indiana and at Bradley, which would advance to the NCAA title game at sea-son's end. But after that, the Irish ran off 18 straight wins, a streak eclipsed only by the 22 in a row that the teams in Jordan's playing days had won.

Dick Rosenthal: "We had a group of people who just wouldn't let us lose. Jack Stephens was a great competitor. Billy Sullivan was a great competitor. If we got outrebounded, John would have thrown us all in the lake. So it was five guys who just wanted to play."

John Fannon: "We won all those games from the Midwest to the East. Coach Jordan didn't like to fly, but he had to fly to the East Coast. Then he would take the bus back and forth. And so we played Holy Cross, Penn, NYU, Navy."

Notre Dame's game against the Naval Academy represented another program first: the first national television appearance by a Notre Dame basketball team.

Jack Stephens: "We had been on local television before, so cameras didn't bother us. It was a buildup for us, because I knew the game was going back to Chicago and across the nation. What Navy had was just like Notre Dame has in football now. They had all their games on television all over the country. It wasn't just because we happened to be coming there.

"So we went in there, and to be honest with you, I think they were scared of us. We beat Holy Cross at the Boston Garden by 20 or 25 points. The coach from Navy scouted us and he told them we were one of the roughest teams they were ever going to see. So he put [a jinx] on his own team."

The game turned out to be a serendipitous moment for Fannon. With his higher-profile teammates the focus of the Midshipmen defense, Fannon was left alone and led the team with 28 points. Such a performance in front of a national audience, Jordan reminded the sophomore, would probably be noticed.

John Fannon: "It was nationally televised, but there were only televisions in the bars around the country. I don't think too many people had their own set. This was 1954, and television still hadn't caught on. I just remember Coach Jordan saying at the end of the game, 'Fannon, you'll be a household name in all the Irish bars in the country.' This was the first time we'd been on television, and everybody was looking for Rosenthal and saying, 'Who's this guy?'"

The 20-2 regular-season record was the best Irish effort since the 1936 Helms national championship team. Once again, the NCAA came calling. Once again, the Irish accepted. And once again, they found themselves pitted against the Indiana Hoosiers.

But that's where the similarities ended.

Jack Stephens: "I mentioned before that Bobby Leonard was a good friend of mine. He was a scorer—he could shoot like hell. He killed us at Bloomington.

"On defense, we played a straight two-three, and I was back rebounding. Even as a guard, I always played defense on the forward. And I had Farley, who didn't score the year before. I knew Leonard. So I told Jordan to let me take Leonard and let Joe Bertrand, who usually took the guard, go back because all Farley was doing was feeding. Let me take Leonard and see if I can stop him.

"That was the only major adjustment, other than the fact that Rosey was possessed. Rosey played so badly the last time that he wasn't going to let Schlundt go. Rosey held Schlundt to nine points, and I held Leonard to 10. They couldn't score."

Dick Rosenthal: "At the end of the game we were up by three points. Bobby Leonard comes screaming down on a fast break, and I'm standing at the free-throw line. I literally had both of my hands holding my thighs and I was anchored to the ground. He ran right over the top of me and made the basket. They called a foul on him, but they awarded him the basket.

"Now we've got eight seconds or something to go, and I'm going down to the other side shooting one-and-one up by one. I had the heaviest arms I've ever had in my life. There was a timeout, you know, kind of icing things. And I remember John Jordan saying, 'After you make the free throws, don't anybody let him get it. Just let him go.' Both of them went in, and we were back up by three. We all went to the side. And Leonard ran at us, threw himself at us, and tried to shoot at the same time, made a harmless basket, and the game was over.

"The thing that's great about sports is here's a team with seven guys who had won the NCAA before and were clear favorites to win it again playing a team they had beaten. But we won the ballgame by one point.

"Obviously there was a lot of jubilation. When we got to the dressing room, Bobby Leonard and Dick Farley were both standing there with their hands out wanting to shake hands and urging us to go all the way. It was a terrific thing because it had to be a bitter, bitter defeat for them."

The Irish had knocked off the defending national champions and were one game away from their first Final Four in only two tournament trips. Their next opponent, Penn State, was unranked and not considered a threat.

But Rosenthal's "great thing about sports" could work against the Irish as well, and when they played the Nittany Lions it did. Penn State came out with a zone press, the first the Irish had seen all year. They found themselves in an early hole and proved unable to climb out, falling 71-63.

Jack Stephens: "The problem with the NCAA then was you played the next night. We were wired after beating Indiana. You couldn't get to sleep that night if you wanted to. We were flat as a dog. The next night, Penn State came out and pressed us and beat us."

Dick Rosenthal: "We came out and they threw the zone trap press on us. I think we were down 17-2. We spent the rest of the game trying to catch up. Of course, at the end, we started fouling and trying to get the ball back. We never quite climbed over the hill.

"Penn State had a good team; you can't take anything away from them. But we were way, way down starting off the ballgame. Jack could really handle the ball. But he tried to dribble through the zone press, and he got caught."

Even with the upset, the Irish had finished an impressive two seasons. Jordan became Notre Dame's first Coach of the Year, receiving the honor from the New York Metropolitan Basketball Writers Association. Rosenthal's 20.2 points per game for the season was the first time the 20-point mark had been reached, and he was named a first-team All-American. Moose Krause was quoted as saying his first good move as athletic director had been firing the basketball coach.

But all good things must come to an end. Bertrand and Rosenthal were getting their diplomas and would be taking their scoring and playmaking abilities with them. It remained to be seen if Jordan could successfully reload the Irish cannon.

8

"The Butkus of Basketball"
(1955–1956)

With three starters gone from the 1954 team, Jordan had some work to do getting the 1955 lineup acclimated to the limelight. His habit of sticking with a shallow rotation meant he would be dealing with a roster short on experience.

Don Strasser: "One thing with Jordan was if you were one of the top seven players, you had it made. If you were below seven, you practiced and that was it. He just played five guys. There would be a sixth occasionally, but he was strictly a five- to seven-man coach."

John Fannon: "He knew how to motivate players. His philosophy was if you got a scholarship and got on the starting five, you played the whole game. Today's philosophy would not be analogous to that, so from that perspective, maybe he could have done more. But he knew what we had to do against each team."

Jordan tried to get the newly minted starters up to speed as soon as possible while riding his returning horses, including Stephens—the go-to guy in the offense—and Fannon, as far as they'd take him.

Jack Stephens: "As a freshman, I played forward. As a sophomore and junior, I played point guard. As a senior I was playing both post positions. It depended upon whom we were playing.

"I guess the big difference was the fact I really didn't have to pass off. We didn't keep records, but I would have led the team in assists. That year I just shot a little bit more. And I wasn't shooting from one spot—I would move anyplace I wanted to."

Lloyd Aubrey pitched in immediately in Bertrand's role of scorer, averaging 17 points per game. But the major hurdle would be replacing Rosenthal's imposing low-post presence. That job fell to a sophomore whose physical style of play allowed him to set a career personal fouls record that would stand for many years. Those on-court practices would be contrasted, however, in his post-Notre Dame years by wonderful acts of charity in the aid of neglected children. Those children would know him as Father Smyth. His teammates just called him John.

Lloyd Aubrey: "John was an outstanding rebounder. He was not an exceptional passer, shooter, or defender. But when he put it together he was special. The whole was greater than the sum of the parts. When you ran into John Smyth in the post, it was like running into a tree. He was really strong."

Jim Gibbons, newly returned to the team as an assistant coach, saw two sides of Smyth—the off-the-court gentleman and the on-the-court roughhouse.

Jim Gibbons: "My first impression was he was just a big, nice, quiet guy. But after watching and coaching him, I felt he was one of the toughest and meanest players ever at Notre Dame. He had an unbelievable passion to win and play hard. He should have been in the National Football League. John could have stepped right in and played in the NFL. He was the Dick Butkus of basketball."

Smyth had played football in high school, but a shoulder injury had ended that career. He brought his football demeanor to the basketball court, where John Jordan threw him right into the mix, starting him as a sophomore.

Fr. John Smyth: *"I was very, very aggressive. I felt I could put my elbow on any part of anybody's body at any time I wanted to. I did break a lot of noses, and I look back and I feel bad about that. But what can I do? Everybody grows up, and everybody has a second chance in life."*

The team did a good job of camouflaging its weaknesses early, and season-opening wins over Wisconsin and Northwestern earned the Irish a top-10 ranking. But their third Big Ten opponent was Indiana and their old friend, Don Schlundt. In front of the first national television audience ever to see a game played in the Fieldhouse, the Irish blew an early lead and fell 73-70.

Jack Stephens: *"Rosey and Bill Sullivan and Joe Bertrand had been three starters, and Jordan played his starters 99 percent of the time. So we had three inexperienced starters [that season], and early in December we weren't ready to play. They weren't ready to play us, either, because all they had back was Schlundt. But he was 7 foot 2 inches.*

"It was a lot of fun, though. At halftime, the ROTC came out and did a drill with rifles. They formed a circle or a star at halfcourt. We were just coming out for the second half, and they were out there trying to go through the precision drills in the last minute and a half. I never felt so sorry for somebody. The student body stood up and started making noise, so the ROTC guys couldn't hear the next guy give a command. They're trying to go shoulder left or right, and they can't hear a command, and they are on television."

As the youngsters gained experience, the results were predictably unpredictable. The Irish were unable to sustain any positive momentum and finished the season 14-10. But they upset 18th-ranked Holy Cross to win the Sugar Bowl Tournament in New Orleans. They closed out a 22-year series against NYU with green jerseys and a 19-point spanking. And for their last game of the season, they went to Milwaukee to play No. 4 Marquette, which had won 22 games in a row.

Jack Stephens: *"Roughly three weeks before, we'd played Marquette at Notre Dame and they beat us by about 10 points. We stunk. I stunk. Everybody stunk. They held me to nine points. This was my last hurrah, so I wasn't going to leave anything on the table.*

"At halftime I had 25 points, and we were ahead by 20. Then Lloyd Aubrey got hot in the third quarter and ended with 25 points. My anxieties were down at that point—I just wanted to win the game and achieve what I wanted to achieve. I didn't know how many points I had. People were hollering at me to shoot. But the game was over."

The 85-64 wipeout ended 1955 on a positive note, giving the players and fans hope the team could continue that momentum in 1956. But those hopes were soon derailed, as the Irish finished a frustrating 9-15, their first losing season in 33 years. Of the 24 games played, 14 were decided by six points or fewer, with five of them going into overtime.

Lloyd Aubrey: "For some reason we didn't get any better. In fact, we got worse. My senior year was our worst year. We just couldn't get it together.

"I remember playing up in Providence in a real close game. We were ahead one point with about three seconds to go, and a guy threw in a 75-foot shot. Things like that were happening to us. It was just one of those years. The chemistry and whatever were fine; there was no tension on the team to speak of that I remember. Obviously we didn't have the talent we needed."

Fr. John Smyth: "Frustrating. Frustrating. We had leadership on that team, but it just didn't seem to take off. I probably fouled too much, which didn't help. I had to learn how to control my method of fouling too much, but that was part of my game."

A bright spot amidst the disappointments was the development of two sophomores, forward John McCarthy from Chicago's Catholic League, and guard Bob Devine, who, if you talk to him today, is almost surprised he was offered a scholarship.

Bob Devine: "I was about 5 feet 10 inches and 135 pounds, and was not a major rebounder to say the least. They flew me out and I was met by John Smyth, who was 6 feet 5 inches, 240 pounds. And I'm thinking, 'Why would they send a football player out here to pick me up?'

"They took me back to the campus and out to dinner that night, and then the next day I was going to meet with Johnny Jordan. So I put a couple of sweaters on under my coat to make me look like I was 140. I went in and, in hindsight, I knew he was thinking, 'My God Almighty, he's a midget.' So he casually said, 'Would you like to work out while you are here?' And I said, 'Sure.' John Smyth and I went down to the Rock and we played. I'm sure Smyth was reporting on me, and obviously he said, 'Get him.' "

McCarthy's recruitment would indirectly bring into the fold one of Jordan's old students at Mount Carmel, Ed O'Rourke. Over the years, O'Rourke would become a program fixture and friend to Irish coaches and players alike.

Jack Stephens: "In 1953, Johnny Jordan took John McCarthy to Notre Dame to play basketball. His brother, Emmett went down there on scholarship two years later. Peg, the mother of the family, was a great fan and she loved to go see her sons play. But John Senior was a very dedicated banker, and he was hardly available all the time to go to the games.

"At that time of the year, traveling back and forth between Chicago and South Bend can be dangerous with the snowstorms. She didn't want to go by herself. So she took one of the neighborhood ND graduates, a lawyer who was doing well and was a good fan of basketball, down there to be a co-driver. That man's name was Eddie O'Rourke.

"After Emmett graduated in 1960, Mrs. McCarthy didn't need a driver anymore. But Eddie was very attached to John Jordan. Jordan had great followers, both in South Bend and Chicago. So he just went there. There was always a party after the game. And when Jordan gave coaching up, Eddie got with Johnny Dee, and it just continued from that point on. That's how it started."

As he had with Smyth the previous year, Jordan didn't hesitate to put his talented sophomores' feet to the fire. But like the overall effort that season, the results were mixed.

John McCarthy: "My strongest suit was I always was an intense player. So at practices, I would guard people very aggressively and I would work. But I didn't have one critical element, which is game confidence. So I would say I was a very unsteady, uncertain entity in my sophomore year."

Bob Devine: "Well, I was a little scared the first game. I didn't know I was starting until we got to Detroit, where we played our first game. And then when we got to the Fieldhouse, I jumped to the roof. I was ready.

"It took me a little while to adapt to the college game. I knew how to play the game. I saw the court really well. I knew I had the talent. I just wished I was 6 feet 8 inches. But I wasn't. So I couldn't do much about that."

Nor could the team do much about the 1956 season. But 1957 would be a horse of a different color . . . literally and figuratively.

Hawk Meets the Men of the Cloth
(1957–1958)

Fr. John Smyth: "He could jump higher than anybody from a standing position. He would go up and he would come down. I'd go up and come down, and he'd still be going up."

Jim Gibbons: "I had coached Carl Yastrzemski in baseball when he was here, and people keep asking, 'Did you know how good he'd be?' No, I didn't know. I just knew that he was head and shoulders above anybody I had ever seen here. And I knew this guy was in that same category—head and shoulders. He was also one of the nicest human beings that you'll ever meet in your lifetime."

Fr. Theodore Hesburgh: "He was a first-rate player, and a guy who has maintained his good character and attitudes. Sometimes guys get out there in that rough-and-tumble pro world, and they get disreputable in a sense. He was always a guy who I felt I could uphold, quote as an example, and be proud of as he got out of here and got into professional life."

The object of those accolades was a 6-foot 5-inch sophomore forward on the 1957 team who had been one of the most coveted athletes nationwide in his high school class. His coach at Chicago's Parker High School, Ed O'Farrell, had grown up with John Jordan. So it was no surprise that O'Farrell wanted Tom Hawkins to give the Irish strong consideration.

Tom Hawkins: "O'Farrell came to me my junior year and asked, 'How would you like to go to Notre Dame?' And I said, 'You've got to be kidding.' Growing up in Chicago, Notre Dame just loomed as the ultimate place to be. How fortunate you would be if you became a student at Notre Dame. He says, 'No. If you're interested, I'll set something up for you so you can meet Johnny Jordan.' I said, 'Wow, this is incredible.'

"So Notre Dame came to town my senior year to play at the Chicago Stadium, and Coach O'Farrell set up a meeting between me and Johnny Jordan. I put on my Sunday best suit, got on the bus, and took my grade transcripts to Johnny Jordan. I met him at the Conrad Hilton Hotel, we talked, we hit it off, he gave me tickets—I guess you could do that without being penalized back during that time—to come to see Notre Dame play against DePaul at the Chicago Stadium, which I did. And he said, 'At the end of the year, we want you to come to Notre Dame and visit.'

"My mom and I put together a list of 10 universities that I would consider, and Notre Dame was No. 1 on the list. During the spring football weekend, I went down to Notre Dame to pay a visit, and as soon as I walked on campus and started talking to people, I asked to be excused, went to the phone, called my mom, and I told her, 'Tear up the list, this is it. I don't want to see anyplace else.'"

"Hawk" came aboard with a strong love for the Irish, and his teammates and Jordan certainly loved him. Beyond his personal magnetism, it was hoped Hawk's talent would be the salve that would heal the wounds of 9-15 the previous season.

Off the court, however, there were potential issues that would have to be dealt with. Hawkins would be only the second black starter in Notre Dame history, and as with Joe Bertrand, there were questions about how a black man would feel playing for a predominantly white school.

Tom Hawkins: "Of course, being a black kid and thinking about Notre Dame, I knew that there were very few blacks attending the university.

Everyone said to me, 'Why are you going to Notre Dame? You know, there are only 10 blacks in the entire university. Why do you want to put yourself through that ordeal?'

"Notre Dame received an invitation to play down South at the Sugar Bowl Tournament in New Orleans. They asked the university to come but also asked that the Irish abide by their segregation laws. Father Hesburgh, who rates No. 1 on my list of all-time great men, in a press conference in 1956 when he was asked what he was going to do, said to the nation, 'Anywhere that Tommy Hawkins isn't welcome, Notre Dame isn't welcome.' In the mid-1950s, that statement was huge. He was the ultimate leader. That's the kind of backing I got from everybody at Notre Dame.

"If my being black was a problem to other people, it was their problem. I had an education to get, I had basketball to play, and I enjoyed myself and the city of South Bend. I became a two-year All-American there. So I can't say enough for those four years at Notre Dame and the hundreds of people who made my stay so memorable."

Hawk's support came from sources other than the university administration. Like Joe Bertrand before him, Hawk was almost unanimously accepted and liked by his classmates—classmates who were not shy about going to bat for their fellow Notre Dame man when the situation required.

Tom Hawkins: "I walked into a downtown South Bend pizza parlor with a date one night. And a guy said to me, 'Do you have reservations?' And I said, 'Reservations? In a pizza parlor? You've got to be kidding.' He said, 'Yeah, you can't come in unless you have reservations.' Well, all of the Notre Dame students there knew what was going down, so they simply discontinued eating and got up and walked out. When the university heard about the situation, the pizza parlor was put off limits to Notre Dame personnel and students until I got a public apology.

"There was a knock on my door one day. I opened the door, and there stood Paul Hornung. And Paul said, 'Hawk, we're going down to the pizza parlor, the owner wants to make a public apology to you.' We went down to the pizza parlor, I got the apology, it was open to Notre Dame personnel and students again, and we went on from there. And I'm thinking, you know, this is the Golden Boy, this is Paul Hornung. This was the type of treatment that I received.

"Fast forward to years later, when Paul Hornung was named to the Pro Football Hall of Fame. I was sports director at KABC radio in Los Angeles at the time, and I called him to offer my congratulations. We were on the air discussing our days at Notre Dame and his days with the Green Bay Packers. I said to him, 'Paul you really didn't have to do what you did.' And his reply was, 'Yeah, I did. It was the thing to do and it remains one of the most memorable things I've ever done, football or otherwise.' When I think of things like that and the backing I received, I can't help but feel very good about myself and others.

"So I was never made to feel like a minority. I was never made to feel like I was a second-class citizen. I was a valued and respected Notre Dame student-athlete—their All-American. They were proud of me and I was and remain proud of them."

Hawkins's teammates were as loyal and supportive as his classmates.

Tom Hawkins: "When we traveled in the South, anywhere I couldn't stay, the team would not stay. Anywhere I couldn't eat, the team would not eat. Anywhere I couldn't go, the team would not go.

"When we were in Lexington, Kentucky, for the NCAA Tournament, this hotel had integrated for the first time to accommodate the NCAA teams. We went downstairs to go to a movie and we were told, 'Fine, you're all welcome, blacks in the balcony and whites on the main floor.' So my guys said, 'We're not going to do that.' And the manager said, 'Well, you can't come in here.' Ed Gleason, from Chicago, said, 'Where is a place we can all go?' The manager gave us the name of a theater that was black-owned. We got cabs and went to that theater. It was absolutely an incredible taste of humanity. I'll never forget it."

Fr. John Smyth: "That's why we didn't go down to New Orleans as returning champs. Jordan brought to us that if we went down there, Tommy Hawkins could not be in the same hotel. I was the captain, and I said that wasn't going to fly. I said, 'If that's the case, either we stay at Tommy Hawkins's hotel and we all stay as a team, or we don't go down there. Tommy is the No. 1 player on our team. So he's going to be the No. 1 player in our dressing room and the No. 1 player in our hotel.' So we didn't go down there—we went to New York for the Holiday Festival tournament."

John McCarthy: "He came from such a fine family, a family with strong religious beliefs of their own. Tommy was not a Catholic, but I think there were ministers in his family. And everybody in the family, the mother and father and the whole family, respected and loved him. You knew Tommy came from very, very good people. And in fact, that was his strength."

With no off-the-court distractions, the team was free to focus on improving from the 1956 disaster. Unfortunately, things didn't look good early. The Irish opened 2-2, with the two losses of the blowout variety to Northwestern and Purdue. It was after the latter defeat in West Lafayette that the team captain, John Smyth, decided to assert himself.

Bob Devine: "Our sophomore year was awful. I had never lost nine games in a season since I was 10 years old. It was the worst year of my life in basketball. There was just a disorganized group of guys, and there was no way of getting together.

"When we came into my junior season, we weren't coming off a lot of success. When we went down to Purdue, we lost. John Smyth got on the bus for our trip back and asked everybody to get off the bus except for the players. Now when John Smyth spoke, there was no argument. Nobody would ever challenge him because he was enormous to start with. And he loved to play and he was just so tough. I don't remember anybody tougher than him.

"And that's how we turned it around. Jordan eventually put in John McCarthy and Gene Duffy. We came in to New York, and we won two games in the Christmas Holiday Festival losing to Manhattan in the final. And then from there on we didn't lose until we lost in the NCAA to Michigan State in double overtime."

Well, it wasn't quite that good—there were three other losses during that time. But Jordan's move of Duffy into the starting lineup proved to be the spark the team was looking for.

John Smyth: "Gene Duffy was terrific. He was extremely fast. He and Bob Devine seemed to play very well together. It was almost like a mismatch when you went out there. He was the type of person who could set anybody up for a good shot."

John McCarthy: "I can remember going down on fast breaks with Gene and not even realizing the ball was in my hands. He was such an incredible passer and an incredible playmaker that he was just a joy to play with. He was only about 5 feet 6 inches, but very strong."

Tom Hawkins: "Duff was our man. Eugene Raymond Patrick Duffy, my roommate on the road. A 5-foot 6-inch All-American in three sports in high school: football, baseball, and basketball. Little All-American in basketball in college, All-American in baseball for the Irish. Just one of the most incredible people I've ever met. I was probably more coordinated with Duff than anyone with whom I have ever played. Gene and I knew each other's thoughts, we knew each other's moves, and we just worked magic on the court."

That magic was good for 13 wins in the team's last 15 regular-season games, and a return to the national rankings and the NCAA Tournament. Although they fell short in the aforementioned loss to Michigan State, which avenged a 10-point loss to the Irish during the regular season, the late-season run also provided good momentum going into 1958, when only John Smyth would need to be replaced in the starting lineup.

Replacing a talent like Smyth was difficult, but made easier by the offensive firepower of four returnees. With Duffy directing traffic, Hawk, McCarthy, and Devine were all capable of pouring in points. For the fans, eclipsing the 100-point mark for the first time in Irish basketball history was almost a given, though the players didn't give it much thought when it eventually happened at Marquette in February.

Tom Hawkins: "That was a high-scoring team. With Duff, we had five guys on the floor who could put up double figures. We were fast-breaking, and we were capable. If everything was clicking, we were going to be 80-plus, especially against Marquette. There was no love lost between Ed Hickey, who was then coaching Marquette, and our coach, Johnny Jordan. Marquette and Notre Dame was a huge rivalry during those days."

John McCarthy: "It was really a nonevent. I don't think we even reflected on it. It was just a really good game. Marquette had beaten us earlier that season, so we came out fired up because we knew we never should have lost that game. We just wanted to put a beating on them."

The 106-74 win over Marquette would be one of the last for a while. Ed Hickey, newly moved over from St. Louis, would do at Marquette what he'd done at his previous stop—drop the Irish series in a fit of pique. The contracted games in 1959 would be the last between the old rivals until 1970, after Hickey had left.

But Eddie Hickey didn't rate a lot of attention for the 1958 Irish. They were on a roll, winning 18 of 20 games to end the regular season, including a 19-point drubbing of defending national champion North Carolina at the Chicago Stadium.

Bob Devine: "They had won the title with an undefeated team the previous year when they beat Wilt Chamberlain in the final. Then they came into Chicago to play us the next year. That was probably the best game I remember us playing ever during my career. We were really, really ready for them.

"I had played against Tommy Kerns in high school, and he taught me a couple of lessons. He was grabbing my pants and stepping on my feet, knocking me all over. So I was ready. I really wanted to play them because I wanted him. That was the game I started thinking we could win the whole thing if we got hot."

Tom Hawkins: "Going back to the Chicago Stadium, to me, was like going back to Mecca. As a prep player in Chicago, I was the city's leading scorer and most valuable player. North Carolina had won the national championship the previous year, and this was the second game of a college doubleheader. The place was packed—20,000-plus, standing room only.

"I was having just a heck of a year in the Chicago Stadium that year. I think we played three games, and I think I averaged over 30 points a game. I think I had 35 against North Carolina that night, and we beat the defending national champion. The place was roaring and that big organ was playing. . . . I had about 50 tickets. My family was there, and it was absolutely incredible.

"When I think of games I played during three years of varsity at Notre Dame, I had some exceptional nights. But that was a crowning glory night. That year I was named Chicago Stadium player of the year. I still have the trophy in my study."

Confidence was high as the seventh-ranked Irish stormed into the NCAA Tournament. They blew away Tennessee Tech 94-61, and a seven-point win against Indiana was their second against the Hoosiers that season. Only No. 9 Kentucky stood between Notre Dame and the Final Four.

But the game was being played in Lexington, where the Irish didn't have a good track record. That trend would remain unchanged—the Wildcats shellacked them, 89-56.

John McCarthy: "This was the game where we were not only outplayed but also outcoached. Man for man, they were a better team. We got stomped. But we could never get on track offensively because Adolph Rupp did something we were totally unprepared for: he made Gene Duffy and whoever else was bringing the ball up start the offense as close to midcourt as possible. That lengthened all the passing lanes, and we could never get anything started. Also, they called three fouls on Tommy Hawkins in the first five minutes. That hurt us a lot."

Jim Gibbons: "The game wasn't five minutes old and Hawk was on the bench with two or three fouls. He made one move and they blew a whistle on him. He couldn't move. He was paralyzed. I thought they were out to get him. It was calculated. It was one of those things—a black playing in Lexington—and the fans were going absolutely crazy, because they didn't accept that. He just never had a chance."

Emmett McCarthy: "They blew three fouls on Hawkins in the first eight minutes of the game. That just killed us. It was an instance of prejudice against black Americans in 1958 that you could see, feel, understand, and not be able to do a damn thing about."

Tom Hawkins: "I don't know if we were a little drained coming out of Indiana or not. I picked up three fouls really quick, and two of those fouls were for backing in. The coaches couldn't believe it. They thought we were jobbed. Of course I had to go to the bench. They went on and they creamed us.

"That was probably the most difficult night in my college career. I can remember walking off the floor with Jim Gibbons, who was freshman coach and assistant varsity coach, and he said, 'We've had a good run. We've had an exceptional year. I can see that you're crying, and I know you're feeling bad. But pick your head up and walk off this floor with some dignity.' I'll never forget him saying that."

The 1958 season had ended strong, and the camaraderie of that team and the one that had preceded it was obvious. So strong was it that three of the best players from those two teams, Smyth, McCarthy, and Devine, all ended up in the seminary and were ordained Catholic priests. Coincidence?

John McCarthy: "It was largely coincidence. None of us ever talked to one another about it. All of us came from religious families. All of us had priests who were mentors to us. All three of us were very idealistic. That was the late 1950s, before idealism sort of turned secular with the Peace Corps and everything like that. It was a natural thing to do in those days—at least it felt that way to us."

Regardless of how it had happened, the Irish now had three more men of the cloth in their alumni group. That was probably a good thing, because tough times were coming for the Notre Dame basketball program, and the players needed all the prayers available.

10

Winning One for Bridget Ann (1959–1962)

L ed by John Smyth, Bob Devine, John McCarthy, and Tom Hawkins, the Irish had gone 44-13 in two seasons and came within sniffing distance of their first Final Four. Within four years, however, Notre Dame hardwood fortunes would plummet. Three of those four seasons would result in sub-.500 records, and the team eventually bottomed out with a 7-16 campaign in 1962.

How could what was going so well suddenly go so badly? According to the players, recruiting and game philosophy didn't keep pace with the game itself.

Emmett McCarthy: "Tom Hawkins was a senior when I was a junior. He was hurt a good bit of the year and didn't play some of the games. My senior year, we had a winning record, but not a distinguished team.

"Then it hit the fan. Jordan ran out of luck in getting Chicago players, and the people who were advising him about the quality of the players had made critical mistakes. By the time it was over, it was chaos."

The recruiting game was also being played differently, although Jordan's adherence to "old-school" methods didn't necessarily sit badly with his players.

John Tully: "When I was a senior, I was asked to escort a very sought-after 6-foot 10-inch recruit from Pittsburgh around campus. We had a nice time going around. We went back to Jordan's office in Breen-Phillips Hall, and Jordan said to this guy that we were impressed and we were prepared to offer our standard scholarship: room and board, books, tuition, 10 bucks a month for laundry, whatever it was. This kid leans back in his chair and says, 'Oh, that's terrific. Let's start with that.'

"Jordan just exploded. He had a big, florid, Irish face, and he came right up out of his chair, put his hands on his desk and said, 'Get out of here! I'm sick and tired of you shoppers! If you don't want to come to Notre Dame, we don't want you!' He loved Notre Dame and he felt that the best thing anybody could ever get would be a free ride to Notre Dame.

"In 1961, things were starting to change. Television was just starting to be interested in covering college basketball. People coming out of high school were more sophisticated. Instead of the father-figure coach, the arm-around-the-shoulder coach was starting to appear on the scene. And Jordan was definitely the father-figure coach."

The decline started slowly. In 1959, his last season, Tommy Hawkins was elected the first black captain in the history of Notre Dame basketball.

Tom Hawkins: "To be a Notre Dame captain carried such weight and such prestige. I still have my letter sweater: three gold stripes, one white stripe—three years varsity, senior year captain.

"I shared that captaincy with Gene Duffy, and we felt so good about that because you look at all the people who had been captain at Notre Dame, that's an honor roll. That was a position of pride, dignity, and responsibility.

"I remember I would be a little nervous because after the pregame meal, the captain always led the team in prayer and the Litany of the Blessed Virgin. I wasn't Catholic—I grew up a Methodist, and my grandfather was a Methodist minister all of his life. Still, I led the prayer.

"It was a distinction—it was an honor—to serve as the first black captain of the basketball team and the first black captain of a major sport at Notre Dame. I didn't bathe in it but it was a badge of courage and honor."

Along with the captaincy, however, came injury to an ankle, which kept Hawkins from playing at his full potential. Coupled with the loss of McCarthy and Devine, it proved too much for the 1959 team to overcome, and it struggled to a 12-13 record.

Jim Gibbons: "Hawk was still 10th in the nation in scoring with 23 points per game. We lost McCarthy, who was a rock. We lost Devine. Our road record was very bad again—10 of the 13 losses were on the road."

Tom Hawkins: "We were lucky to achieve the success we did my sophomore and junior years with a starting lineup of guys who averaged 6 feet 5 inches. Senior year, we were still operating at 6 feet 5 inches, but without the elements of McCarthy and Devine to give us what we needed. I averaged 23 points, but it's not about who averages what. It's how well you work as an integrated unit. And we didn't have that."

John Tully: "It was putting together a group of people who hadn't played together that much. We didn't really have scorers. Tom Hawkins was a scorer, so people double-teamed him a lot, and we weren't really good at adjusting.

"John Smyth and Bob Devine and John McCarthy had played together for a number of years, and Tom Hawkins had played with them for a couple of years, too. Chemistry probably just wasn't as good as it had been in the previous years. Plus the talent level overall was not as high."

In that season of discontent, things even went wrong when they seemed to be going right.

John Tully: "John Jordan loved children. Because of health problems, he and his wife were unable to have children, but John was always in great form around young kids.

"After his wife died, he met a widow from Kalamazoo, and after a period of time they were married. She became pregnant in 1959. Late in the pregnancy she fell and broke a hip, and because of her age and the injury, it was a precarious pregnancy. She was very popular with the team, and so there was more than the usual concern you'd naturally feel for a development like that.

"We had a traditional game on New Year's Eve with Northwestern, and Eileen was due at just that time. The team took the bus to Chicago without Coach Jordan, who stayed behind to be with Eileen. We stayed at the Sheraton

Hotel on Michigan Avenue and went through the scouting report, pregame meal, got on the bus—still no John Jordan.

"Just as the bus was about to pull away from the curb, a car screeched to a stop ahead of it. Coach Jordan jumps out, leaps up the stairs, and from the front of the bus, with an even more florid Irish face than usual, booms out, 'It's a girl, Bridget Ann!' Wild cheering broke out on the bus.

"We took our usual warm-ups, and as we went back to the locker room for the final words before tip-off, Coach Jordan said, 'I've asked you to win one for your parents, I've asked you to win one for Notre Dame, and I've asked you to win one for yourselves. But I've never asked you to win one for me. Let's go out and win this one for Bridget Ann!'

"We left the locker room like troops going over the top of trenches in a major war. But our enthusiasm didn't quite measure up to our first-half ability, and we came down at halftime losing by 20 or some ridiculous deficit like that.

"Our pep talk consisted of the same florid face appearing briefly behind the open door, screaming, 'You stink', and slamming the door. We got ourselves all charged up again, determined to make up the deficit and win one for the new Jordan heir. But the final score was 102-67—the worst defeat in ND history up to that point. In years afterward, when I'd visit with Coach and his family, I had trouble looking little Bridget in the face, and I'm sure the same was true for other members of that team."

With Hawkins's departure after that season, things seemed poised to go from bad to worse. But they didn't immediately. The 1960 squad had good senior presence with Tully, Mike Graney, Bob Bradtke, and Emmett McCarthy. The sophomore class of Armand Reo, John Dearie, Karl Roesler, Eddie Schnurr, and Roger Strickland came in with some fanfare. The hope was that the youth would mesh with the senior talent and get the team back to the NCAA Tournament.

The season started well, with the team winning seven of its first eight, and a 75-63 win over Detroit bumped its record to 9-3, good enough for a top-20 ranking. But that game also saw Bob Bradtke injure his knee, which left him out for the season. With the inexperienced Schnurr running the offense, the team went 8-5 the rest of the way. The 17-8 record was good enough for an NCAA berth in an era where only one team from a conference was allowed to go and some otherwise-deserving teams that had beaten the Irish during the regular season like North Carolina, Indiana, and Illinois had to stay home.

Some believed the Irish had got into the tournament on a technicality. Notre Dame went out for its first game against Ohio and played like it.

John Dearie: "It was a disaster. If my memory serves me correctly, our next stop in that tournament was going to be Ohio State and Jerry Lucas. We got caught in that worst of all diseases, and that is looking ahead. We could have and we should have beaten them."

The bubble of 1960 burst the next two seasons. The senior-dominated team was no more, and departing with those seniors was a lot of playing experience. As it had in 1955, Jordan's penchant for sticking with his starting lineup left him with unproven talent to take him through that period.

Ed O'Rourke: "Jordan put five guys on the floor, and the sixth guy didn't get in until the first guy fouled out.

"I remember when Monk Malloy was first made the president of the University, Bill Gleason was doing an article about not only Monk the new president but also Monk the former basketball player. Jordan had agreed to sit down for an interview about him since he had been Monk's coach.

"The day of the interview, John called me first thing in the morning and said 'Gleason's coming over in a little while. When did Monk play for me?' I was still half asleep, and I said, 'I don't know, John, somewhere around 1963.' 'Was he any good?' Jordan asked. 'How the hell should I know?' I replied to him. 'You only played your first five.'"

Also problematic, according to the players of the time, was Jordan's reliance on his 1-3-1 offense, which by then had become somewhat archaic and didn't necessarily fit the talent that Jordan had recruited.

John Dearie: "The system that we played under was a very structured, slowed-down 1-3-1 offense. If it was executed, and you had the players who fit into that system, it could be effective. During that period with big John Smyth underneath and Tom Hawkins on the side and Gene Duffy and Devine and McCarthy, it was a perfect offense.

"But when it got to the talent we had, we were, in many ways, restricted. It was very structured and slowed down. With fellows like Armand Reo and Eddie Schnurr, we had the potential to be a more wide-open, moving, fast-breaking kind of team. It was trying to squeeze the proverbial square peg into the round hole by taking the talent that didn't really fit that offense and not having the flexibility to be able to play otherwise."

Fr. Edward Malloy: "Most people would say that John Jordan was a nice person who was not state of the art, and that his perspective on basketball was a little behind the curve. For example, he insisted that everyone shoot underhanded foul shots. One year he told us we weren't going to have any fast breaks the entire year. He had an offensive system that, for a team that played us regularly, was so predictable I don't think they even scouted us anymore."

John Andreoli: "My freshman year, they made us—*made* us—shoot free throws underhanded. Even though I was an 80 percent free-throw shooter, I had to shoot them underhanded because the ball comes off softer and our big guys could tap it in. This was 1930s thinking in the 1950s. But after they saw me shooting 40 percent of my free throws and John Matthews hitting the back of the basket, they said to forget it and just shoot them the regular way."

With team discontent growing at the same rate its winning percentage was dropping, the Irish finished 1961 with 12 wins and 1962 with a mere seven.

John Tully: "The chemistry wasn't good. There was some dissension on the team. The younger players weren't playing as much as they thought they should. They said Jordan had favorites. He played me and he played Bill Crosby maybe more than he should have. Jim Gibbons and John Dearie and Eddie Schnurr and Armand Reo were very close. Conspiracy is too strong of a word, but Jordan definitely felt there was some rumbling in the ranks that he didn't appreciate. I don't think our chemistry was really good, and I'm not sure our talent was all that good."

John Dearie: "We had high hopes for that year. I remember going out to California. We played two good teams, UCLA and USC, back-to-back, and we got blown away by 25 or 30 points. We never recovered from that. That trip set the tone for us, and I don't think we recovered.

"It's very painful for me to talk about some of the aspects of it. You had a situation for the next year and a half where you didn't have strong coaching leadership. Jim Gibbons would go down and scout and drive five hours back for practice the next day with a 25-page detailed, hand-written scouting report that was never really analyzed, in many ways never really shared, and never really taken advantage of.

"It was a very stressful year. It was certainly a disappointing one. I guess, as you're a senior, and you know that by and large these are the remaining games of your college career. There was a lot of disappointment, and probably some bitterness. Time has a way of melting that stuff away, but it was not a fun year."

But that's not to say the team lost any toughness.

John Tully: "We had a game at the Fieldhouse against St. John's. There was a guy named Boo Ellis who was a center. He had his hands all over me; he'd pull my pants going for a rebound. And I got pretty mad at him. I was in the pivot, leaned way over after taking what I thought was an undue amount of abuse, brought my elbow up and caught him right in the solar plexus, and then spun across. As I spun, he swung at me—which the referee saw—and then fell down on the floor because he was out of breath. The referee called the foul on him. He got up, came out to the foul line, and was threatening me. Those were the days when it was harder to get thrown out of a game for that sort of thing.

"In the second half, they had a guy named Tony Jackson, who was an All-American. Bill Crosby had this habit—which refs weren't wise to at the time—of either poking someone in the stomach or putting one hand up as though to try to block a shot, and with the other hand maybe nicking the guys elbow so the shot would go off. Well, Jackson went up for a shot on the far side of the Fieldhouse. The ball went nowhere, but no foul was called. He came down and swung at Crosby. I ran over and grabbed him from behind. Crosby thought this was a great opportunity to plant one, so he threw a punch at Jackson while I was holding him. I didn't see the punch coming. Jackson ducked his head to the side, and Crosby wound up punching me on the side of the cheek.

"Our bench cleared, and I mean cleared. We had a guy named Ted Romanowski, who was a tackle on the football team. Ted took about five people into the second and third row of the bleachers over there, and the fans started pummeling the St. John's players. It was just pandemonium."

The 64-63 win over fifth-ranked St. John's was one of the few highlights of those two seasons. It seemed Jordan had little time left to right the ship. But coming in was a class of sophomores who, he hoped, would do just that.

The Whiz Kids
(1963-1964)

s he had in 1957, Jordan needed a strong class of sophomores in 1963 to pull out of a multiseason slump, and the one he brought in seemed as though it would fit the bill.

John Andreoli: "Walt Sahm was total enthusiasm and idealism. He had the best attitude you could hope for in a player. He loved coming to Notre Dame; it was like his dream. He was a very hard worker and a good rebounder. He was a great ball-handler for a guy who was about 6 feet 9 inches. Back in those days, that was big.

"Ronny Reed had a body that God built for basketball. He had the prettiest looking jump shot. He was 6 feet 7 inches, but his arms stretched down to his calves, and he had big hands. When he went up or got a rebound or played defense, he just looked like the prototype body for a basketball player.

"Jay Miller was 6 feet 4 inches, and he could jump higher than anyone I'd ever seen. He was a little more of a mechanical player, but really good. He saved our butts lots of times that I can remember—against Boston College and NYU when we played them here. He really came through for us.

"Larry Jesewitz was a bruising rebounder. He was a great defender in the middle who had a nice hook shot and set good screens for us.

"But the most talented player in that class was Larry Sheffield. He was 6 feet 1 inch and a great ball-handler with a great jump shot—an Elgin Baylor, one-hand type of thing. He could definitely play one-on-one. I was watching the films the other night, and even in our static offense he made one-on-one plays even though there wasn't a lot of room to do it. He was the most talented player on our team, including John Matthews, who was a great guard himself."

Talent, however, doesn't always win championships . . . or even right the ship. The problems that had manifested themselves as the 1960s began could have continued very easily, even with the youth and enthusiasm of the new arrivals. Those sophomores would also be displacing established players, which could ruin team chemistry.

How did it work out? Just fine, according to the players, who were quick to cite the leadership of Andreoli and Matthews as the main reason.

Fr. Edward Malloy: "The sophomores who played were the most talented I'd seen at Notre Dame. They had a lot of potential as a group. It was a much more athletic team than we'd had before then. That, of course, required from the people who were older a willingness to recognize it was going to be a different kind of team. It wasn't going to be the kind of team where seniority was going to count as much. John Andreoli and John Matthews probably played the biggest role in terms of trying to adjust to the new reality."

Andreoli prefers to credit the coaching staff.

John Andreoli: "We had the same coach when we were seniors, and we could have had the same problems. But the 'Whiz Kids' came in. That was one thing the coaches handled really well.

"In that 1-3-1 offense, we had Matthews, two forwards, a high post and a low post. For a right-hander, the preferred place to play is on the right wing, where [Armand] Reo played, because you'd come around and you'd be facing the basket. I really liked it there because it squared me up better, and as a senior, I felt I should be over there. We tried it for a while. Then Jordan finally said, 'Look, I'm going to put Miller over there because you shoot better from all sides, and he needs to be there.'

"Other than that, it was a total acclimation and acceptance. It blended beautifully. I can't remember ever having an argument or any kind of altercation at all. But why would we? We got our butts kicked the year before, and we picked up great players. Why not win some games?"

The results spoke for themselves. An 11-3 start to the season, including an upset of No. 4 Illinois at the Chicago Stadium, and 78 points per game quelled the doubts and problems from the preceding campaigns and got the Fighting Irish back into the top 25. After only one postseason bid in the previous four seasons, the team was positioned not only to be invited to the tournament, but to make some noise once it got there.

But problems have a way of flaring back up when least expected. The good vibrations of the season were quashed when the university declared Reed and Sheffield academically ineligible for the second semester.

Fr. Edward Malloy: "You can't give up players of their talent in the middle of the season without paying a huge price. I don't think we had the caliber of players left over to replace them. As I remember it, it was a case of shifting responsibilities. But it made us less powerful, especially on the offensive end."

Walt Sahm: "We had to switch everything. They had to move me out to a wing because Reed was gone. We still had Andreoli and we still had Matthews. And then they brought in Larry Jesewitz. He played a high / low with me."

Larry Jesewitz: "When Ron and Larry became ineligible that second semester, I got a little bit more playing time. Instead of being the first man off of the bench, I'd be starting. So there was a feeling-out process as to how we were going to fill the two voids. We felt like we did fairly well, but it was a shock to their teammates that they were attending Notre Dame— a school for a higher education—and all of a sudden you got a problem with grades."

With the two sophomores and their point production benched, the team limped down the stretch 6-5. But a 17-8 record was good enough for an NCAA Tournament invitation.

The question was, was it good enough for Notre Dame? Jordan realized the current team was a shadow of its potent first-semester self and considered refusing the bid. But the players, confident in themselves and their ability to overcome, made it clear they relished the challenge.

Walt Sahm: "A lot of teams like Indiana were pissed off because they didn't get to go. In those days, if you didn't win the conference, you didn't go. So it was tremendously tough to make it.

"Jordan didn't feel we were really going to be competitive. He told us, 'Well, I don't know, fellows, if we really feel we want to do it. What do you think?' And it was Miller who said, 'Coach, what do you mean? Are you kidding me?' We worked hard. Sure we lost Reed and Sheffield, but we were still competitive."

John Andreoli: "There was some discussion about whether the team that was going was the same team that had been selected. But I don't think it was much of a democratic thing. I don't remember the discussions that went on, or how involved we were, but I do know there was some discussion."

The Irish were sent to Northwestern to face a Bowling Green team that featured Nate Thurmond and Howard Komives. They had lost to Bowling Green earlier in the season without Reed and Sheffield, and when the Falcons completed the season sweep with a 77-72 win, the Irish were left wondering how much of a difference their ineligible teammates might have made.

Fr. Edward Malloy: "Komives was the leading scorer in the country that year. Thurmond was a dominating rebounder and shot-blocker. We had a difficult time playing against that combination."

Larry Jesewitz: "Nate Thurmond was probably one of the biggest individuals I've ever played against. Talk about pushing and shoving—they say I was pretty rough under there, but it seemed like for every action there was a reaction."

John Andreoli: "Komives was one of the best college basketball players I ever saw, and I don't think anybody could have stopped him. Thurmond was, well, Thurmond. If we had [Reed and Sheffield], would we have beaten them? We might not have, but we could have."

Jordan had kept the wolves at bay thanks to the Whiz Kids and the leadership of his seniors. Those solutions were not permanent, which meant Jordan would have to work the same magic in 1964. That team, on paper, would be one of his strongest. But Andreoli and Matthews's leadership had been a strong catalyst in the previous season's success, and the Whiz Kids had not proved themselves from a maturity standpoint.

Other upheaval quickly destabilized the program. Jordan had dismissed some of his assistant coaches during the off-season, which did not sit well with the sophomores who had been coached by them the previous year. Problems from his personal life began to affect Jordan's coaching performance. The offense was still perceived as being behind the times, even with the talent available. And one of the junior stars was hobbled by a back injury.

Walt Sahm: "I always worked construction in the off-season and I just hyperextended it. When we played Illinois in Champaign right before Christmas, I couldn't even bend over it was so bad. The following Monday when we got back from Champaign, I couldn't even get out of my bed. I somehow got out of bed, went over to the hall phone, and called the infirmary.

"Jordan wouldn't let me play because I couldn't bend over. I said, 'Coach, let me. It's going to affect the team.' He said, 'I don't care.' So we lost five out of six and essentially it cost him his job."

Losing Sahm didn't make a season that started out 4-5 any better. The loss to Illinois was the second in what would become a six-game losing streak. The players weren't playing good defense, evidenced by the fact they lost three games despite scoring over 100 points.

Larry Jesewitz: "Losing Monk and John Matthews and John Andreoli shouldn't have affected us that much. There were some sophomores like Bucky McGann who came up and were able to fill those gaps the seniors had left, and we should have had enough maturity as juniors to do the same. But that never happened, and I believe it was the loss of leadership."

The fans, who had come into the season expecting great things, were disappointed and frustrated. By the time DePaul came to town, the students chose to voice their displeasure with chants of "Jordan must go" and other expressions of their desire for a change—expressions that shocked and dismayed the players.

Larry Jesewitz: "You're pretty much immune when you're on the court or on the bench. You're focused on the game. But yeah, it was heard. Was it proper by the students? I'm not sure. But at that time, they were hanging the football coaches in effigy—Joe Kuharich, Hughie Devore—and that attitude might have been carrying over."

Tom Bornhorst: "The team was upset about it. They didn't feel it was appropriate. Most of them were pretty upset that the student body would treat him that way. It affected Coach Jordan quite a bit."

But the Notre Dame administration didn't need prompting from the students to know it was time for a change. The decision had already been made.

Walt Sahm: "Moose Krause called Jay Miller and me into his office and asked us point blank what was going on. Jay Miller said, 'We are not getting coached. Sooner or later, there's got to be a change. We've got to change our offense.' And I said, 'I think the world of Coach Jordan. But I don't know what to do, Mr. Krause. No matter what we say, no matter what we do, we are going to be bad guys.'

"That night I was out with an injury, and DePaul beat us in the Fieldhouse. And the crowd was yelling, 'Jordan's got to go.' It broke my heart.

"Our freshman year, we were told by the senior players that we ought to leave right now. When we asked why, they said, 'You'll understand.' And then my freshman year, Jim Gibbons, who truly cared about the team, was caught in the middle between the players and Coach Jordan. Jordan saw Gibbons as a threat, and Jim couldn't stay on.

"John Jordan truly loved Notre Dame. But John Jordan couldn't recruit. And when they made the decision, we were seen as these disloyal people. The saddest thing for me will be that as much as I loved John Jordan—and I remember him every day in my prayers—I'll be the guy in some people's minds who cost him his job when all I did was tell the truth. He had to go. We were hurting big-time at that point."

Ray Meyer: "I was told before our game at Notre Dame that Jordan was out. I felt so sorry for him. I called Chuck Borowski—we were teammates and very close friends—and I asked Chuck whether I should tell Jordan he was out or not. He said, 'Don't worry about it, because it's already in the papers.' So that relieved me of a difficult thing."

On January 10, two days after the DePaul loss, John Jordan announced his resignation as coach of the Fighting Irish, citing health reasons. He finished one victory short of 200, but had won 60 percent of his games. And he left behind a legacy of players who, whether they played for him in good times or in bad, take pains to profess their love for the man as a person.

Dick Rosenthal: "Johnny Jordan was absolutely a beautiful, beautiful man. John was a great person and a great leader of people. He believed in the kids."

Bob Devine: "I loved him. He was a very kind man. He had his own personal problems, but he was a good man to me."

John Andreoli: "John was a committed Notre Dame man. He loved the place. He gave it his all."

Walt Sahm: "He was a wonderful man and he loved Notre Dame. He was like a father to me."

The love his players had for him got Jordan to come back to Notre Dame 11 years later, a practice he continued until his death in 1991.

Don Strasser: "When Leroy [Leslie] and I would be in the Chicago area, we'd go down to the Monogram Club golf outing every year. Jordan wouldn't go back to Notre Dame after coaching until one year I said, 'Come on, Coach, you've got to go down there. Everybody is asking about you.'

"So he came back, and we went to the banquet—his first time back to Notre Dame since he left as coach. And Digger got up and gave one of the best talks I ever heard in my life about Johnny Jordan. He was saying how it was great to meet him. He said, 'I thought he was a phantom, because every place I went it was Johnny Jordan, Johnny Jordan, Johnny Jordan. And I never knew the man existed until meeting him.' After that, Jordan never missed another one.

"That was my responsibility every year when we went down there. I was working with Budweiser. I would usually get the Budweiser van. I'd pick him up and then pick up Leroy, and the three of us would drive down with Leroy sitting in the back seat."

Ed O'Rourke: "John stayed away for a lot of years, but once he did start going back, he would go to one or two games a year in South Bend with me.

"John was sort of a shy man in a lot of ways. He really didn't enjoy a lot of public acclaim while he was coaching at Notre Dame. But we made sure when he was there that [Sports Information Director] Roger Valdiserri would introduce him to the crowd. And John loved it. He'd stand up and wave to everybody."

The
Johnny Dee
Years

(1965–1971)

12

Reconnecting
(1965)

In 1965, Irish fans probably knew Johnny Dee better for his football career than for anything he'd done in basketball. Because of injuries and a war-depleted roster, he was pressed into service as a quarterback in 1944, literally going from selling programs in the stands one week to starting against Georgia Tech the next. But his play on the hardwood certainly got him noticed, not to mention varsity letters in the 1945 and 1946 seasons, and was remembered fondly by his teammates of the time.

Frank Gilhooley: "Johnny Dee was a digger—a real battler. He was very quick, and he was tougher than hell. I was always glad he was in there."

Leo Klier: "He was a tough little guy. He wasn't very big, but he was a great guy and a good friend. I was always amused with him because he had a nature about him that reminded me of the good old days."

Although he did not graduate from Notre Dame—he had left Loyola University in Chicago when the war shut down its basketball program, and returned there after the war ended—Dee's Irish connections didn't stop there. After serving in the Coast Guard, he accepted a job as one of John Jordan's assistants for the 1952 season. He then became the youngest head basketball coach in NCAA history up to that time when he accepted a job at Alabama in 1953 at the age of 28.

After averaging 17 wins per season in Tuscaloosa and winning the Southeast Conference title in 1956, he went on to coach Denver's D-C Truckers AAU team, winning one league title. But the league folded in 1962, which left Dee available on March 7, 1964, when he was named Notre Dame's seventh basketball coach.

The program he inherited was in disarray and in search of an identity. With only two postseason appearances and no victories to show for its previous six seasons, Notre Dame basketball did not resemble the proud program of the Keogan, Krause, and early Jordan eras. So Dee set out to reconnect the program to those days of success while bringing a more modern look to the place. He hoisted banners in the Fieldhouse commemorating past accomplishments. He updated the uniforms and shoes to a more contemporary style. But most important, he discarded Jordan's 1-3-1 in favor of a more up-tempo, motion offense that would take advantage of the athletes he had at his disposal, and he expected those athletes to get up to speed quickly.

Walt Sahm: "He put us in a very strong conditioning program—what I would almost call brutal. We had a boxing program run by the guys who trained for the Bengal Bouts, who were the best-conditioned athletes on the Notre Dame campus. I went from 238 pounds down to 217 for my senior year. He had us in shape.

"He put us in black Converse All-Stars—the Boston Celtics' shoes. Half the time we wore green uniforms like the Celtics. In that respect, he brought a whole new freshness. He was the right guy at the moment in the sense that he did bring us, with a limited budget in a limited facility, into what I would call a more promotion-oriented era for basketball."

Larry Jesewitz: "Johnny Dee was a breath of fresh air for somebody like me, the sixth man coming off the bench. We were going to be in a different type of offense and we were going to run. We went to a 2-3, and he wanted us to fast break as much as possible, get the ball off the boards, and get down the court as quickly as we could. This fulfilled the wants for almost everybody on the team."

Jim Monahan, entering the Dee regime as a sophomore, remembers the coach's plan to create the camaraderie that had been missing.

Jim Monahan: "A finance company in South Bend had a conference center up on Lake Michigan. He took the whole team up there for four days, and we all got to know each other, hung around and played cards. He took us to a Cubs game. We spent a lot of time together in those four days before school started. He did a lot of psychological things to bring us together as a team."

But change does not affect all people the same way. Dee's fiery personality and offensive strategies were almost 180-degrees different from Jordan's. A clash was inevitable, and he had one with Walt Sahm almost from the season's start.

Jim Monahan: "That whole class was the great recruiting year that Johnny Jordan had. They were all individuals. Walt was the type of individual—maybe a 'free spirit' back then—who was different. Not in a harmful way. His personality was just a little bit different. Dee was trying to figure out how to motivate Walt a little bit better. Maybe he needed to be more like Phil Jackson or something."

According to Sahm, the problems started off the court.

Walt Sahm: "The first thing Dee ever said to the team when he came in was, 'Wally Sahm, I know you cost John Jordan his job.' That's the first thing he said to me, right in front of the whole team. So we got off on that note.

"He spoke with a lot of cockiness, and he was the kind of man who was a sharp dresser and streetwise. The exact opposite of Coach Jordan."

The two men had their differences, but that didn't stop Dee from making Sahm a captain. And it didn't stop the Irish from getting off to a strong start. Four wins in a row got the team a national ranking and a feature article in *Sports Illustrated*. The offense was certainly capable, scoring over 100 points seven times that season.

But that Irish team would end up being known more for its inconsistency than anything else. The players were still getting used to Dee's style, on and off the court.

Larry Jesewitz: "The offense did well with our talent. Bucky McGann was maturing and was able to bring the ball down. His knee was hurting him but he would get down the court as quickly as he could. Larry Sheffield was an excellent ball-handler and could dribble the ball down as fast as anybody else could run, so he wouldn't lose any speed with the ball in his hand."

Jim Monahan: "Johnny Jordan ran a 1-3-1 offense, and he had the perfect five guys to run that offense. Dee came in and kind of went to a more pro-style offense. Ron Reed, Jay Miller, and Larry Sheffield fit right in, but the big guys—Jesewitz and Sahm—had a little more problem fitting into Dee's system."

Inconsistency became the watchword for the season. Big wins over Kentucky and Michigan State were offset by losses to Evansville and Bradley. Jesewitz and Sahm found their way into Dee's doghouse and watched the Irish loss to Illinois from the bench.

Notre Dame sat at 14-11 going into the final game of the season against Creighton at the Fieldhouse and seemed out of the running for postseason consideration. But there was a lack of capable contenders for at-large bids that season, and the NCAA announced before tip-off that the winner of the game would be the last team invited to the tournament. The seniors wanted to make sure that bid ended up in the hands of the home squad.

Jim Monahan: "Jay Miller was pretty much the team leader, and Ron Reed was a bit quieter but everyone respected him for the athlete he was. I remember Jay getting up and saying this was the seniors' last game and he wanted to make sure they won and had an opportunity to extend their season and go to the NCAA Tournament. The seniors were going to do everything they could to make sure it continued and wanted everyone's support."

With Miller's charge ringing in their ears, the Irish overwhelmed the Jays 92-74 and earned a date in the first round with the University of Houston. The Irish had defeated the Cougars by 30 on the road in January, so it seemed an easy matchup. But the players remember the Cougar-friendly environs of Lubbock, Texas, and a puzzling lack of intensity.

Jim Monahan: "When we played them down in Houston and beat them by 30 points, we played our best game of the year. Going down to Lubbock, we were concerned because everyone knew that had been one of those nights that everything we did just worked out great. We shot well, we played well, we had very few turnovers—it was just our night to click. We knew the rematch would be different, unless we had two nights like that."

Larry Jesewitz: "Unfortunately, the urgency we built up in the Creighton game was reversed in the first NCAA game. They pretty much ran with us, they gunned with us, their shots were falling, ours weren't."

Walt Sahm: "I had 20 points and 18 rebounds in the first half, and we were up by 24 points. Even with about 15 minutes to go, we still had a 12- or 13-point lead. Then our entire starting lineup fouled out. If you even breathed on their players, you were gone.

"They beat us 99-98 in overtime. By that time the entire team was gone. Poor Bucky McGann was so crippled that when they were trapping him, he'd stop. He couldn't balance. So he'd throw the ball in self-defense just to get rid of it because he knew his bad leg was buckling."

The Whiz Kids had finished their run and had served as the bridge between the end of Jordan's era and the beginning of Dee's. Now it was up to the fiery 41-year-old coach to make his own mark on the Irish program.

13

Priming the Pipeline
(1966–1968)

The departure of the Whiz Kids left the Irish in a depleted state. Dee's late arrival after the 1964 season precluded a recruiting solution for 1966, and the talent that did return was hamstrung by or lost to injury. Kevin Hardy injured his back playing football and did not return. Bucky McGann struggled with an injured knee.

The 1966 season had little chance of being memorable, and it wasn't. The 5-21 record included a losing streak of 13 games. But no one associated with the team hangs his head when discussing it.

Jim Monahan: "The main factor was inexperience. Bucky and I were the only two who had played. I played a lot as a sophomore, and Bucky was a senior. No one else in our classes had really played much.

"That team worked hard, but we were out-talented by a lot of other teams. Then we had some key injuries that really slowed us down. We probably were not a very good shooting team.

"We played some tough teams and played a lot of teams very well. But mentally it was hard. You get down and lose three or four or five in a row, it's hard to be positive coming down to the last two or three minutes. You start thinking, 'How are we going to lose this game?' "

Tom Bornhorst: "When we had all those losses, we still hung together and approached practice and the next game with some enthusiasm. I don't remember it being one of those things like 'God, what in the world is going on?' Everybody realized that in most games, we were in over our heads talent-wise."

John Tracy: "Everybody who could see the roster could see it was going to take a while. When Johnny Dee came in, it was clogged up with guys like me. We were, quite frankly, outmanned. There was no other way to look at it. We didn't have enough players, and we were playing the Dukes and Kentuckys of the world.

"We took some lumps when I was a sophomore. We really got the hell kicked out of us. But we were scrimmaging those guys every day, and we knew we'd be good the following year."

"Those guys" were freshmen players who were going to try and turn Irish fortunes around the next season: Bob Arnzen, Dwight Murphy, and Bob Whitmore.

Tracy described Arnzen, a 6-foot 5-inch forward from Kentucky, as "a marquee player we didn't get all the time." An athlete with a national pro-file, Arnzen hadn't grown up a Notre Dame fan, even with 12 years of Catholic school education. But like many before him, he had been captivated by the place during his visit and decided Notre Dame was where he wanted to go. Murphy, a quiet guard from Kansas City, was a good complementary player, contributing 12 points a game, and was an excellent defender, usually drawing one of the opponent's forwards.

But it was Whitmore's recruitment at center that heralded a new era for the Fighting Irish. Whitmore had attended DeMatha High School, a basket-ball powerhouse in suburban Washington, D.C., and was the first recruit from what would come to be known as the "D.C. Pipeline." The Pipeline's success was mostly due to the efforts of Frannie Collins, an old friend of Dee's. Collins had met Dee when the two were in the Coast Guard, after which he had returned to his native city and knew where the basketball tal-ent could be found.

Roger Valdiserri: "Frannie was a great guy and a great friend of Johnny Dee's. I bet he and John talked almost daily on the phone. He was very helpful in recruiting. He would scout that area and let John know who the best players were. Frannie had great relationships with some of the high school coaches in the D.C. area. Nothing illegal, of course."

Bob Whitmore: "I can't say anything about Frannie without including his wife, Helen. Outside of my family, they were probably the biggest influences in my life. They'd send me articles from the paper at home when I was lonely that first year. They attended both of my parents' funerals. They still call me today and treat me like a member of their family, making sure that everything is all right with me. You could always talk to them. And they never got anything out of it other than maybe coming to see us play a couple of times. I have so much love for them, it's hard to find the words. They're classics."

Frannie Collins: "I looked at recruiting strictly as a hobby. I never got any rewards out of it, except the personal satisfaction of watching those kids grow. These guys are my close friends now. They're part of my extended family."

Over the years, Collins's Notre Dame "family" became extensive, as he helped recruit some of the biggest names in Fighting Irish basketball history: Whitmore, Austin Carr, Sid Catlett, Collis Jones, Adrian Dantley, Donald "Duck" Williams, Tracy Jackson, and Tom Sluby. Collins's efforts would become a key component in making the Irish program the powerhouse it would become.

Whitmore and Murphy represented another change in recruiting strategy for Notre Dame: targeting and signing black athletes. One of the criticisms of John Jordan had been that he seemed unable to recruit talented black players, other than those he'd known from his time as a Chicago high school coach like Bertrand and Hawkins. According to Jack Lorri, now the radio voice of Notre Dame basketball, Dee took it upon himself to reverse that perception.

Jack Lorri: "John took over in the 1960s, which was a different time in America, especially regarding the black athlete. And Johnny Dee was at the forefront. He brought terrific black players in from the East Coast."

With Arnzen, Murphy, and Whitmore now eligible as sophomores for the 1967 season, Dee decided to cast his lot with them. All three started in the first game against Lewis College, and one of their classmates, Jim Derrig, joined them in the lineup soon afterwards. Captain Jim Monahan was the only upperclassmen starting, but no one remembers any tension.

Bob Arnzen: "We didn't think a whole lot about it. They'd finished 5-21 the previous year. The only thing tough about it was most of the players who had started the year before were benched when Whitmore and myself and Dwight Murphy and Jim Derrig came in. I remember thinking how hard it would be if it would happen to one of us. But we expected to play right away, and we did."

Bob Whitmore: "I know when I was recruited out of DeMatha, Johnny Dee told us that he had a plan to return us to competitiveness on the national scene. He said, 'We're not very good right now, but with you and some of the people we're planning on bringing in, we're going to be back to national prominence very, very soon.' "

"Soon" didn't seem to be a good description early. The sophomore-dominated team struggled to a 2-9 start, including a blowout loss to a UCLA team led by superstar sophomore Lew Alcindor, who would later be known as Kareem Abdul-Jabaar.

John Tracy: "UCLA played Fridays and Saturdays. So on Friday, we saw the game after we practiced, and the same officials had the game Friday night and Saturday night. Dee went up to them before our game and said, 'What, do you two guys got an office in this building?' They almost T'd him up before the game."

Jim McKirchy: "The night before, UCLA was playing Bradley or someone like that, so we watched that game. And after we watched, Dee said to us, 'Forget all the strategy, just go out there and do the best you can.' "

Jim Monahan: "In high school, Bob Whitmore's team, DeMatha, had defeated Power Memorial for Alcindor's only loss in high school. So the morning we were supposed to play in Los Angeles, there were headlines in the paper saying 'Lew Alcindor to face the only man to beat him in high school.'

"Alcindor was very motivated that night and they beat us by 20 or 30 points. I remember Johnny Dee coming back in after the game saying,

'Don't worry about that one too much. We lost that one when Mr. and Mrs. Alcindor decided to have a baby.'

"He was just fantastic. It took you out of everything you did. You started thinking about where he was and whether he was going to block your shot. The other players for UCLA were good players, but with Alcindor. . . ."

Bob Whitmore: "He was the most talented ballplayer I ever played against. When Sid [Catlett] and I first played against him, it was the time when we were going to the moon. Sid was saying, 'This guy is like Neil Armstrong . . . he just keeps going up and up and up and up.' I said to Sid, 'Well, if he's going up, then my heart is going down.'"

Even with the poor start, the Irish got the sense that the desired improvement was right around the corner. And as the calendar moved to 1967, confidence and experience started leading to better results on the court.

John Tracy: "Johnny Dee never went into a game where he didn't think we could win. He always let us think there was some way we could do this. It might have involved their team bus getting lost on the way to Notre Dame, I don't know. But he always thought we could.

"We were coming back from playing Indiana in Ft. Wayne, and they'd beaten us pretty good. We were getting something to eat after the game, and as we were waiting to get on the bus, someone in the university party said to Dee, 'Don't worry, Jack, nobody expects you to win these games.' John decked him. He just put him on the ground. And boy did that hit the bus real quick. After that, it seemed like we got better and better and better."

Jim Monahan: "We had some real tough games early. We played Kentucky, we played California in our first game at the Rainbow Classic, and they were a highly ranked team. Then we played UCLA. We were starting four sophomores and myself. It took a while for us to jell and become comfortable with each other. After we got some confidence from winning a couple of games, it really started to snowball, as evidenced by the Houston game."

The fifth-ranked Houston Cougars came into the Fieldhouse on February 11 looking for an easy win against the sophomore-heavy Irish. Led by Elvin Hayes, the team was a precursor to the basketball style prevalent today—quickness and lot of play above the rim.

Jim McKirchy: "At that time during warm-ups, you could stuff the ball. So we were going through our standard warm-ups, and the crowd was oohing and aahing. We thought it was unusual, because they saw us warm up all the time. We looked down at the other end and the rim never stopped moving. It was unbelievable. I'm sure it didn't happen this way, but it seems like we all stopped our warm-up and stared at theirs."

Bob Whitmore: "It was an unbelievable show. All of their guys could reverse-stuff and all that. I tried not to look, but I couldn't help checking it out."

Once the game started, it was the Cougars who were in awe—of the manic Fieldhouse crowd and Bob Arnzen's coming-out party.

John Tracy: "We were supposed to get there about an hour and a half before the game. There couldn't have been a roll of toilet paper left on the campus. The kids were already packed in there with toilet paper flying all over the place. They had to clean it up before we could even come out."

Jim Monahan: "Johnny Dee solved their defense. I was out on the wing and as soon as I got the ball, I knew Arnzen was sitting in the free-throw lane with nobody on him. I couldn't catch that ball and throw it to him fast enough. Arnzen got a lot of open looks, and if you gave Bobby Arnzen open looks, they usually became baskets."

While Arnzen was taking care of things on the offensive end, Bob Whitmore's job was making Elvin Hayes's life as difficult as possible on both ends of the floor.

Bob Whitmore: "He was probably the second-best player I ever faced behind Lew Alcindor, and luckily I was able to contain him for a while. There are ways of beating people to the spots they like to be, and I was beating him to that post area that he liked to use. I was trying to deny him the ball, and if he got the ball, I used position to try and force things on defense or block his shot."

With Arnzen hitting from everywhere and Hayes a nonfactor because of Whitmore's defense, the Irish grabbed an early 19-point lead. Getting the lead was one thing, though. Keeping it was something entirely different.

Jim Monahan: "We were way ahead of them at halftime. In the last couple of minutes, they started to make a run at us. Jim McKirchy came in from the bench and ignited us. McKirchy was always a really high-activity player, so good things or bad things happened when McKirchy came in. Dee put him in because we were tired, and McKirchy got some long lay-up passes. He picked us up there when our lead was down to six or eight points."

Jim McKirchy: "I got in the game and ended up with five field goals. Trouble was three of them were goaltending by Hayes. When we had our reunion last November, one of the guys thought I never scored an actual basket in that game and Hayes goaltended on all of them."

The clocked ticked away to the 87-78 upset, and the crowd reacted in typical Fieldhouse fashion.

Roger Valdiserri: "I was sitting at the scorer's table. The table was down below, and when it was over, I stood up and got on the floor in front of the table. The students rushed down and knocked me over the table backwards. My feet were up in the air; my head was on the floor. It was scary. But that was one of the great games of all time."

The 12-5 turnaround wasn't enough to offset the early-season troubles and the Irish remained home during the postseason. But a corner had been turned, and the Irish players knew it.

Jim Monahan: "That was one of the first big upsets Notre Dame had in many years. It reinforced that Notre Dame basketball under Johnny Dee was coming back strong from the previous years, and that Coach Dee was going to put us back on the map. We were starting to play top 10 teams, and it's good when you start beating a few of those teams."

Although it would take a while before those teams started falling consistently, the 1968 season dawned with the hope the Irish could carry forward the attitude and talent that had been on display against Houston and get the NCAA bid that had eluded them. Those hopes appeared to be realized with a 13-3 start to the season, but were quickly dashed as five losses in the next six games moved them out of NCAA Tournament contention.

John Tracy: "We did have some bad losses, but the coaches never let us think that. The first day we found out we weren't in the NCAA, [assistant coach] Gene Sullivan had these things figured out. He told us we could win the NIT and show them.

"But we did it to ourselves when we lost to Illinois down here. We had a bad stretch for Illinois and Michigan State. We could've ended up 20-6, which meant we were clear, but 18-8 doesn't get you there."

An 18-8 record might not have gotten Notre Dame to the NCAAs, but it did prompt the administration to break with tradition and accept a bid to the NIT. Having been given a surprise postseason opportunity, the Irish took advantage of a long stay in New York City.

John Tracy: "We had a blast. We beat Army and Bob Knight. We beat Long Island in a very good game against a local favorite. And the third day, we lost to Donnie May and Dayton in overtime. They had been second to UCLA the year before, but they didn't make the tournament.

"On Friday night, we went to Toots Shor's for dinner and went to see *Hello Dolly* with Pearl Bailey. They let the five seniors sit up front. Pearl Bailey comes out and says, 'What are you five guys doing here?' We told her, and then we all went out.

"We had to play at eleven o'clock the next day so the other game could be on at one o'clock on TV. I don't know how long those guys stayed out. I know how late I stayed out, but I didn't have to play. Nobody showed up for the pregame meal. I heard Dee was waiting in the lobby when Sullivan got in there. We played at eleven o'clock with not too many people there. Guys were sick. But we beat the St. Peter's team that had beaten Duke. I don't know how we did it. I don't know how THEY did it. I know I didn't have to do it."

A good showing in the NIT was a long way from the hell of 5-21 two seasons before, and Notre Dame rewarded Johnny Dee with a three-year extension to the four-year contract he had originally signed. But Arnzen, Whitmore, and Murphy closed 1968 still not having made the NCAA Tournament. Unlike Dee, they only had one more shot before graduation. It remained to be seen whether a new arena—along with a spectacular sophomore class—would do the trick.

14

New Digs

Johnny Dee had come to South Bend with change in mind. He had modernized the offensive scheme, nationalized the schedule, created a recruiting pipeline to the East Coast, and raised the profile of Irish basketball. But first on his list of priorities was a new home for the Irish. And in that goal, he had partners in a Notre Dame administration that realized it was time to bring Irish basketball into the 20th century.

The Fieldhouse had a well-earned reputation as a snake pit. The raucous and (sometimes) ribald student body was the predecessor to Duke University's "Cameron Crazies" of today, making things impossible for visiting teams.

John Tully: "There was always a crowd that wanted to be under the scoreboard at the East end. They would get there early, and they were kind of 'trouble' fans. Before the days when people started waving handkerchiefs when people took free throws, these guys—of course, it was all males at the time—would be screaming and yelling every time the opposition took a foul shot."

John Andreoli: "If a player from the other team fell into those stands, it was like falling into a sea of piranha. I remember one game when I was a freshman we played St. John's, who had the great coach, Joe Lapchick. Tony Jackson was an All-American forward. He went for a ball, threw it back on the court, and fell into the stands. It was almost like, 'Is he going to get out alive?' It was so bad playing there for other teams that Joe Lapchick, we were told, was the only major coach who would bring his team in there."

The gym also had quirks that the home team learned to use to its advantage.

Leo Klier: "They had metal backboards, and I kind of liked those because there are some plusses hooking the ball on a metal backboard as opposed to glass. When the ball hits glass, it's inclined to slide, and a hooked ball has some spin on it. So it would come off the metal and you could use it to good advantage.

"They had a canvas surrounding the entire floor, and you were on display there. The scores were posted by hanging the points on a hook. There wasn't an elaborate, lighted scoreboard—just names and points."

Bob Whitmore: "I loved that floor. It was the best floor that I ever played on because there was so much spring in it. The Chicago Stadium had a floor like that, and they don't make them that way anymore. I was kind of disappointed when we opened up the new place because the floor wasn't as bouncy. I asked Johnny Dee if we could go get the old floor and put it in there."

John Tracy: "The floor was better than the floor is now, because it was elevated like Minnesota's is. You actually sat below the floor when you were on the bench. And the people were two feet away."

Richard Kluck: "There weren't too many outsiders or visiting team fans in the place. We probably always filled it up with students. The football team sat at one end and tried to intimidate anybody who came that way."

As much of an advantage as it gave Notre Dame, the lack of "outsiders" at games was part of the Fieldhouse problem. Because there were now more students at Notre Dame than seats in the Fieldhouse and students saw the games for free, that meant a drastically reduced gate for Notre Dame to split with visiting teams. So it was no surprise that John Jordan had played most of his games on the road and Johnny Dee was following suit.

Jim Gibbons: "The teams that could afford not to come here like Kentucky and St. Louis might have come once. But they were never going to come back because we put the band right behind the visiting bench. It was a bandbox, and you couldn't hear yourself think. The coaches couldn't communicate with the players at timeouts. They said, 'We don't have to put up with this.'

"It was a very, very, very, tough place to play, and it surprised me that anybody would do it. I guess I'm talking about Kentucky where we won seven in a row and then lost in 1943 in Louisville. We had lots of home-and-home games with teams like DePaul and Butler. But the St. Louises and Kentuckys didn't come in. There wasn't any way that they were going to be a part of it."

Because the Fieldhouse was also the only major indoor athletic facility on campus, Irish basketball coaches sometimes had to yield to more "pressing" athletic needs.

Don Strasser: "If football had a bad day with the weather outside, we'd have to cancel our practice so Leahy could take his guys in the Fieldhouse. The quarterbacks would be on the basketball court doing their drills, and we'd cut short practice for them, because football was the No. 1 priority at the time at Notre Dame."

John Andreoli: "I can remember practicing many times and having the door swing open and the football team come in. Jordan would go over and talk to Kuharich, and the next thing John would say is that practice was over. He'd say, 'Well, the football team needs to practice here. They've got a big game on Saturday. Sorry.' So we'd just get dressed and leave."

Dee started campaigning for a new arena the moment he arrived. Fortunately, he found the tracks greased in his favor, with the university administration having decided that the Fieldhouse had seen its best days.

Fr. Ted Hesburgh: "We didn't have a decent place to play, and we were playing more and more teams from the top leagues. It was a disgrace bringing people in to what we had. We had Bob Hope out here, and the Fieldhouse was the only place on campus we could get 2,000 people inside. As we finished the program, he said, 'Well, I think it's time to get all you guys out of here and let the cows back in.' "

The Challenge II capital-raising program in 1964 included a provision for a state-of-the-art athletic facility to be built across the street from Notre Dame Stadium. The next step would be paying for it—a project athletic director Moose Krause and university executive vice-president Fr. Ned Joyce spearheaded.

Fr. Ted Hesburgh: "At the time I decided to build the library, Ned and Moose came over and said, 'We think it's high time we got money together for a new athletic center.' I said, 'Well, I think you do need it, but you're going to have to raise the money. I've got all I can do to raise $12.5 million for a library. And the athletic center can't cost more than the library.'

"We were planning simultaneously and raising money simultaneously. They raised the money for that, and I raised the money for the library."

Roger Valdiserri: "Moose Krause and Fr. Joyce, who was always a big basketball fan anyway, ran with it. We formulated teams and we would go out to alumni clubs, talk about it, and try to raise money for it. But Moose was the motivating factor. He was so good at rallying alumni. Johnny Dee wanted it for recruiting purposes. They were originally going to open it up a year later than they did, but John wanted to be able to tell his recruits that they'd play there their senior year."

The designs were finally completed—after a little bit of tweaking on Krause and Joyce's part.

Fr. Ted Hesburgh: "When we came down to the final approval, which is when the foundations were going in, it turned out that their place was a little bigger than ours and was going to cost a couple hundred thousand dollars more. So I said, 'You're going to have to cut something out. I'm not going to have it said that our library cost less than our athletic center.' So we cut out the swimming pool."

The Rolfs of West Bend, Wisconsin, would eventually provide the funding for a pool for the new Athletic and Convocation Center. Ground was broken in 1966, and 29 months and $8.6 million later, it was ready to host its first basketball game. The Fieldhouse was spared demolition by the need for a headquarters for the university's art department, a purpose it served for 14 years until the art department found new quarters on campus.

The Fieldhouse met the wrecking ball on March 12, 1983. The Irish had won an astonishing 84 percent of their games in the old building. It had hosted Irish games for 63 seasons and had built a level of lore that would be tough for the Irish to duplicate in their new home. But that didn't mean they weren't going to try.

15

A.C.(C.)
(1969)

With the new Athletic and Convocation Center well on its way to completion, Dee needed a quality product to draw fans to it. The addition of players like Arnzen, Whitmore, and Murphy got him most of the way there. But the trump card was the sophomores who became eligible in 1969, a recruiting class that is considered the greatest in the history of Irish basketball: Austin Carr, Sid Catlett, Jim Hinga, Collis Jones, Jackie Meehan, John Pleick, and Tom Sinnott.

Carr, Catlett, and Jones were Frannie Collins's latest contributions to Irish recruiting. While all were highly sought, Carr was in particular demand. Collins had to make sure the young man's commitment to ND held firm, especially when high-profile coaches like Dean Smith of North Carolina came calling. In Smith's book, *A Coach's Life*, he remembers being thwarted by "Father Collins" in an effort to make a recruiting visit, an incident Collins also recalls vividly.

Frannie Collins: "It was getting close to signing time, and I got a call from Austin's father saying Austin was going to talk to Dean Smith. His dad was from North Carolina, and I think he always wanted Austin to at least take a look at it. I said, 'When is he supposed to come?' and Mr. Carr replied, 'I think he might stop by tonight.'

"I hung up the phone and went over to Austin's house. I went upstairs and said to Austin, 'Pack some clothes, you're coming with me.' Then I called Jimmy Jones, Collis's dad, and told him I was going to bring Austin over and I wanted him to pull every phone line out of any bedroom he would think about putting them in. I didn't want him talking to anybody. The next morning, we signed them in the Statler Hotel coffee shop, using the same gold pen we used to sign all the D.C. recruits."

Thanks to the combined efforts of his staff and Collins, Dee seemed to have the product he needed to fill his new arena. Now he needed to get the word in the streets. Seeing an opportunity to showcase his freshmen and make a difference in the South Bend community, Dee created a program called Operation Reach-Up, where Irish basketball players went into the South Bend community to help mentor young people threatened by a life of violence. Operation Reach-Up was a resounding success for the three summers it ran, having an impact on young lives that continues today.

Austin Carr: "It gave us an opportunity to get involved with the community. We did a lot of things with little kids. We had basketball clinics at all the different playgrounds. It was a good situation—something that really has stuck with me. I've been involved with the community in Cleveland ever since I came here."

Bob Whitmore: "It was revolutionary in that I knew of very few teams at that time that were doing things like that. As a result of that, when we came back to D.C. after graduation, we put on the same kind of program, and it had a great effect."

Collis Jones: "It was one of the greatest things we did up there. The community knew us, and we got a lot of community backing. There was a tremendous amount of community involvement while I was there.

"I felt we helped the community tremendously going in there and talking to the kids. I run into guys in their forties now who talk about how that helped them. When I go back, I go into the city to see some of the people we knew."

Dee now needed an opponent to christen the new arena, and he found one in UCLA. Knowing what a draw the Bruins would be, Dee agreed to play the first two games of the series on the road at Pauley Pavilion. To him, the two lopsided defeats by John Wooden and Lew Alcindor were well worth what the Bruins' presence would add to "Performus Maximus," the name given to the opening weekend of the A.C.C. And thanks to assistant coach Gene Sullivan, Dee felt he had the team (ranked No. 5 in the preseason polls) and the strategy (called the "Grand Plan") to surprise the heavily favored UCLAns: use the team's depth and speed to outrun the press-happy Bruins, substituting freely to ensure fresh legs.

December 7, 1968, was designed to be a day that lived in UCLA infamy. And when the Irish jumped out to a big lead in the first half, it seemed it would turn out that way. But it was not to be. According to some players, the "Grand Plan" wasn't followed the way it was supposed to be.

Collis Jones: "Our guys got tired. Dee only played six guys. We were beating their pants off the first half, but they got us tired out. UCLA played about 10 or 12 guys. Wooden was running guys in and out of the game trying to get the right combination. They finally caught up, and by that time the other guys who had been out there too long were tired and weren't able to perform."

Bob Whitmore: "When you're going up against guys like Sidney Wicks and Curtis Rowe and Lew Alcindor—we're talking about guys who played 10 years in the pros. You've got to have fresh legs when you're playing guys like that, and we really didn't have it."

Such a result was emblematic of that 1969 team. The talent was obvious. The friendships were strong—many team members still keep in close touch today. But that team on the court was less than the sum of its parts, never developing the proper chemistry to succeed at the level the players had hoped.

Bob Arnzen: "We had a lot of problems senior year, but I don't think it was because of the sophomores. We all went to summer school that year and we really got to be pretty close. We did a lot of clinics up there for the South Bend kids, we all lived together in the dorms, and we really got to know each other a lot before the season started.

"Then Sid Catlett got sick, and I got hepatitis. When I came back, I wasn't able to practice. And then when I did practice, I had tendonitis in my Achilles for the whole season, which slowed me down. Then Austin broke his foot. So injuries just killed us completely. That more than anything else ruined our senior year."

Bob Whitmore: "All the guys loved each other, that was the strange part. We had a camaraderie that you don't always see in a basketball team. We still call each other now, 30 years after the fact. But when we went on the court, it just wasn't there."

Injuries and illness couldn't completely offset the level of talent the team possessed. The Irish won 11 of 12 after the UCLA loss and managed to stay in the top 25 for most of the season.

But team chemistry sat on the razor's edge. On February 11, the Irish hosted unranked Michigan State. The 71-59 loss should have been considered no more than a minor upset in the annals of Irish basketball. But it gained notoriety because of an incident in the second half that brought home the racial unrest that troubled the nation in the late 1960s.

Bob Arnzen: "We were not playing very well. Johnny Dee took me out and put one of the other black players in, and it just happened that there were five black players on the court at the same time, which none of us—or the blacks—realized. Some people in the crowd started booing. We thought they booed because Johnny Dee took me out."

Collis Jones: "We were getting beat, and Johnny Dee inserted five black players in the game for the first time. People started booing. I could see people counting and booing. I have never felt that way before or since. Dee quickly took two black players out."

Austin Carr: "All five of us were on the floor, and it was just an eerie feeling in that arena that day. It hurt that it happened. It was something a lot of us were always a little bit afraid of because it was such an eerie feeling. I didn't really know how to deal with it. But I knew it happened, so we felt the way to deal with it was the way we did."

Bob Whitmore: "Once we walked off the court after the game, if we had any question about whether or not there was booing, our girlfriends and other people close to us that we trusted reinforced that it really had happened. As a result of that, we felt we had to make a stand."

Notre Dame, neither a particularly diverse campus nor team before Dee's recruiting efforts, now had a situation on its hands. The black players, stung by this apparent display of racism by their classmates and other fans, considered a boycott of Notre Dame's next game, a televised contest against Utah State.

Jim Hinga: "I remember the next day vividly. Collis came to me and said, 'I think we are going to boycott.' I said, 'What for?' And he said, 'Well, because we got booed, the five of us.'

"I was sort of the liaison, if you will, to smooth that over. I remember going to Austin and Collis's room and just talking with them for 45 minutes to an hour. It was really Collis and, I think, Bob Whitmore who brought Sid Catlett and Dwight around. Dwight was insulted, and so was Sid. But Collis and Bob really brought them around."

Roger Valdiserri: "The following day we had meetings with the players. With the racial situation in America at that point, you had to be careful. I don't blame the players for feeling the way they did because to them, it seemed like they were being booed. In a situation like that, perception really has to be allowed for because if they feel like that's what happened, you have to show them that it's not and respect their feelings and address the fact that they feel that way."

Bob Whitmore: "Johnny Dee was a very persuasive guy, and as a result of talking with him and our teammates and some of our classmates, we felt that we had made our point and decided to play the game."

The black players wanted an apology from the students, and they got one from the student body president. But the incident illustrated the tough situation black athletes had to deal with at Notre Dame—and in college athletics in general—at that time.

Bob Whitmore: "It was the first time that I know of that black players had stood together and said, 'This is something that we're not going to tolerate.' No one could tell us how we felt—it was something we had to deal with. I've been lucky to have been in a lot of integrated situations and seen it happen since then, but that was the first time I ever had to face it.

"Some of it probably built up over the years. There were not many blacks on campus. When we went out into the community at first, we didn't know too many blacks there—although we got to know them and became a part of the community through Operation Reach-Up—and sometimes they'd call us 'Uncle Toms.' Some of that might have contributed as well."

Collis Jones: "I'm not going to go into what it was like to be a young black person from Washington, D.C., on a college campus in Indiana that was less than 1 percent black in 1969. There were five of us, and we stuck together. We had the support of our families, teammates, and members of the school administration.

"But it was not an easy experience to go through. Some of the letters we got were pretty explicit and ugly. I still have some. We were not Jackie Robinson, but certainly we had some of the same experiences, which all black athletes went through on the campuses in those days.

"But we didn't leave school. We all got our degrees. And some of my best friends today are my former teammates at ND, both black and white."

The incident seemed to galvanize the players, who went out and thrashed Utah State by 14 to start a five-game winning streak punctuated by a victory at eighth-ranked St. John's. With 20 wins for the season, the quest for an NCAA bid by the Arnzen-Whitmore-Murphy class was finally achieved, and the Irish went to Carbondale, Illinois, to take on Miami of Ohio.

But just as it seemed the season goals were within reach, they were snatched away by a combination of factors. The new student newspaper, *The Observer*, started a series called "The Black Athlete at Notre Dame," which raised the specter of Michigan State and its aftermath. The heavily favored Irish probably didn't take Miami seriously enough. And Austin Carr finished the 63-60 upset loss on the bench, the victim of a broken foot suffered during the game.

Bob Arnzen: "By that time we were in disarray. We went down to Carbondale, and we weren't together as a team. I still remember the walk-through practice the day before the game—there were almost fights between a few of our players on the court.

"Miami was a pretty scrappy team, and we weren't doing anything. Austin broke his foot in the first half, which really left us shorthanded. In the second half they got up on us and they held the ball. We kept fouling them and they kept making free throws. We just couldn't get ahead of them. But that was probably the point where I was glad it was over because that season was miserable."

Austin Carr: "I thought that would have been one of our best opportunities to advance. But when I broke my foot, it threw us out of kilter. And that's what really hurt us. It wasn't so much that I was out of the lineup, because we had other guys who could fill in. But we had gotten into a rhythm with five guys starting and five guys coming off the bench, so it threw us out of whack when I got hurt early in the game."

The 1969 team was probably one of the most talented in the history of Notre Dame basketball, but it never achieved the level of play that coaches, players, and fans had hoped for. Four players finished among the top five in career scoring at the time: Austin Carr (1), Bob Arnzen (3), Bob Whitmore (4), and Collis Jones (5).

Bob Whitmore: "The talent on that team got us to 20-6, which says something. But Sid was going through his problems in his freshman year, Arnie and Collis were playing the same position, Dwight was left out of some pictures . . . all kinds of little things that people who were aware of the program looked at and said, 'Things are not right there.' "

Collis Jones: "Of all of the teams I played on, that was the most talented. But we never really lived up to that. You've got your returning five from a team that came from third place in the NIT. Then you have seven sophomores coming up who have beaten the varsity eight or nine times without Sid Catlett, who didn't get to play his freshman year. And then you've got Johnny Dee telling everybody they were going to start instead of telling people, 'Hey you might not play as much, but if we work together, we can really do something great.'

"So we had a lot of problems. There were a lot of chemistry issues. And not a lot of people were happy. That was a very sad occasion. We had a lot of talent, and we went out."

16

Records
(1970)

Ed O'Rourke: "Austin Carr was, by far, the best player ever to play for Notre Dame."

This comes from a man who has watched Notre Dame basketball up close for more than 50 years, and that praise is echoed by many others who admire Carr for his work ethic and his ability to improve the play of his teammates.

Jim Hinga: "Austin remains to this day a fabulous human being. He was almost always the last one to leave practice. Usually he was the first one there. He worked his ass off to graduate. It was a struggle for him, but he worked his ass off."

Jackie Meehan: "If you want to put a tag on Austin, he would remind you of a John Havlicek—he was in constant motion. He was a point guard's dream. I could always find him open. If you were playing defense on him, you'd play him hard for a quarter or 10 or 15 minutes, and then you'd get tired because the guy never stopped. By the end of the game you just didn't want anything to do with him."

Collis Jones: "One of the things that helped me was we were out there every summer playing. Austin and I would play full-court one-on-one for six or seven hours a day. That helped me get better because I had to work against him, and it helped him, too, because I was a bigger guy and he had to work on getting his shots off. It got to the point where I felt comfortable doing anything myself after playing with him."

One aspect of Carr's game that impressed his teammates was his strength. While not always part of a shooting guard's repertoire, he used that strength to augment his already deadly shooting.

Jim Hinga: "He had a combination of absolute brute strength and a finesse and fluidness you don't see very often. I remember there was this guy by the name of Hill who was from Indianapolis. He was guarding Austin up at Minnesota in 1968. Austin was running down the court elbowing him, and you could see the grimace on Hill's face.

"Austin would just pound people to death. He was a hell of a natural athlete and a wonderful shooter. But it was his brute strength that set him apart from almost every other guard."

Given the respect Carr had among his teammates, it's no surprise he was elected captain for his junior year—the first black captain since Tommy Hawkins and the first black player at Notre Dame to hold the position solo.

If Carr's game had a weak point, it was his inability to take his man off the dribble in an isolation game. Knowing how important Carr would be to the 1970 team, assistant coach Gene Sullivan devised an offense called the double stack, which would play to Carr's strengths.

In the double stack, the point guard stayed at the top of the key while the remaining players "stacked" on each side of the lane, two per side. While the point guard demanded attention with the ball at the top, the other players set a variety of picks, with the eventual goal of getting a shooter open on the wing and one or more players positioned for the rebound. This strategy posed problems for Irish opponents no matter what defense they tried against it.

Austin Carr: "We used it against zone, against man-to-man, against box-and-one—we used it against everything. And that's what really forced me to learn how to play without the basketball, because I had to use the picks properly. It set up the inside game and the outside game and Jackie Meehan was a master at running it."

Jackie Meehan: "When you have a double stack, if they were playing man-to-man, they really couldn't guard him unless they were knocking people over. So Austin was getting the ball in an open lane. If opponents started to overplay the big men, they would step toward the basket where a lot of times they would get a lay-up. If not, then the two big guys would come out and play at the top of the key right alongside the foul line and I could give the ball to Austin on the side. I would go down, take my man off the big guys. I could continue in if he wasn't playing me trying to get the ball back for a lay-up, or I would come back out and get the ball where I could take a shot, or if the guy came in on me, I could dump it inside. It created many passing lanes and many opportunities. It was a nightmare for anybody playing man-to-man."

Jim Hinga: "Our double-stack was really more to get Austin free for 10- to 15-foot shots and leave somebody in underneath to rebound. If you look at the way Bobby Knight plays today, it's a double-stack. It originated with Jimmy Walker in Providence in the mid-1960s. Gene just took it to the logical conclusion. It was a bona fide meat grinder. We chewed people up."

Collis Jones: "You had John Pleick and Sid Catlett, who were the really big guys, and they would have to put bigger guys on them. So I would come up with the small forward, and I could usually dominate the small forward. I was taller than them and usually stronger."

With the Irish using the double-stack, Carr opened the season with 37 points against Michigan. A week later he was good for 42 against Northern Illinois, and the Irish cracked the top 10 in the AP rankings as they prepared for one of the toughest weeks in the program's history: road games against No. 1 Kentucky, No. 2 UCLA, and No. 3 West Virginia.

They went 1-2, with Kentucky and UCLA scoring in triple digits. That proved to be a problem with the Dee-coached teams of the time—while they had no problem scoring points, they had no problem giving them up, either.

But a team with a scoring machine like Austin Carr could afford defensive deficiencies in the short term. As Carr continued to score, the Irish record books were being rewritten almost every game. He eclipsed Larry

Sheffield's single-game scoring record against DePaul with 51 points, broke his own record a month later by two against Tulane and not even a week later, bested it again by two more against West Virginia. The 135 points Carr and company scored against St. Peter's remains the school record.

Jackie Meehan: "There was a lot of talent on the team. When Austin was on—which was most of the time—he was just a shooting machine. I could tell the minute Austin released the ball whether I could turn around and run back, I knew his stroke so well. I knew he had his stroke that day. Collis was automatic underneath. Big John and Sid were very good players when they focused, and they really went in hard to the boards. When everybody went together, there was a lot of offensive firepower there."

But Carr's scoring records were coming at a public relations price. Dee would reinsert Carr late in an already-decided game if he had a chance to break the scoring record. While Irish fans loved it, the coaches of opposing clubs did not, and some muttered darkly about Dee running up the score.

Jim Hinga: "I remember Gale Catlett in West Virginia just stomping down at Dee and screaming at him. We were up 20 points, and he put Austin back in. I'd be pissed too."

Austin Carr: "The only time I had any awareness of it was when I broke the NCAA [Tournament] record. Johnny Dee came to me and said, 'Look, I've got to get you out of the game. You've got two minutes and forty seconds to break the record. If you don't break it, I'm still taking you out.' Other than that, I was never aware he was putting me back in to break any type of individual record."

Jackie Meehan: "No. I disagree with that. Austin was a very unselfish player. The only time I saw Dee purposely put him back in was in the NCAA tournament. But in other games, no. He'd put him back in at various times for whatever reason, but not to run up the score. I never saw him do that."

Collis Jones: "Johnny Dee was trying to elevate Notre Dame basketball, and he had a player like Austin Carr who was a scorer. He was trying to have Austin break records. I don't think he tried to run up scores per se. But he was trying to get scoring records."

Carr and company rolled inexorably toward an NCAA Tournament berth and, for the second year in a row, a first-round game against the Mid-American Conference champion, this time Ohio University. Carr torched the Bobcats for 61 points—a total that remains the single-game record for the NCAA Tournament and the single-game record at Notre Dame.

Austin Carr: "I remember there was a guy named John Koenine. He hit his first six shots. Coach Sullivan, at the timeout, came to me and said, 'Well, AC, are you going to stand there and let him score all night long, or are you going to guard him?' After that it was all history."

The Scoring Express derailed, however, in the next game, a rematch against Kentucky. Once again the Irish couldn't stop the Wildcats, and 52 points by Carr went for naught as the Irish bowed out 109-99. Their disappointment was evident, as Iowa demolished them in a lackluster effort in the consolation game.

Carr's performance was good enough for second-team All-America mention on a lot of lists, although playing in the same era as "Pistol" Pete Maravich made his scoring totals slightly less impressive. But these were not the days of early exits for the NBA, so Carr and his supporting cast would be back for another go-around in 1971.

17

One-Man Band?
(1971)

The 1971 Notre Dame basketball team seemed destined for greatness. The members of the acclaimed recruiting class of 1967 were now seasoned seniors. Austin Carr had attracted national attention with his scoring and overall play, and his supporting cast appeared to have talent to spare.

But did it? And with such an imposing presence on the squad, were the Irish too physically and psychologically dependent on their star? Had they become a one-man team?

Thirty years after the fact, opinion is split.

Austin Carr: "A little bit, yes. We would try to get more guys involved in the scoring. Our center position was one that we really needed a little more production from. But it was tough sometimes, because teams would play triangle-and-two or box-and-one on us, just to cut our scoring down."

Collis Jones: "Yes, that seemed to happen. You can't just rely on one person. You need somebody else. So I felt that if I was getting all the rebounds, then I could take my shots. And I was doing all right. I wasn't afraid to shoot the ball. But the plays were designed for Austin.

"Nobody on the team felt jealous of Austin. He was a great player, and we felt we were part of all those records he set. We rebounded, set picks and assisted, all of which helped him to score."

Jackie Meehan: "How do you win 20 games a year with the schedule we had depending on one guy? How do you get a guy like Collis Jones, who was a first-round draft pick in the ABA and the NBA? Sid Catlett was a third-round pick. Big John had played over in Europe.

"Were we dependent on Austin? No. Did it look like it was Austin's team? Absolutely. This guy was the best player in America. But when you win 20 games, one guy can't do that. So we never looked at it. We all realized our role. And when we did realize our role, playing within the system, we were very tough to beat."

This would be an issue the team would have to deal with that whole 1971 season. With Carr a preseason All-America pick, the players went into the season feeling good about themselves and their chances, but losses to South Carolina and Indiana preceded the game with Kentucky in Louisville. Dee, perhaps seeking to shake the team out of its funk or wanting a chance to tweak an old rival, decided to apply some good old-fashioned gamesmanship.

Roger Valdiserri: "John would really have liked to win more games against Kentucky. He had an adversarial relationship with Kentucky during his days at Alabama. In fact, he got a technical before the game one time. When they were warming up, he'd line his players up at halfcourt and just let them watch Kentucky warm up. Well naturally, the teams got in a fight, and I think he ended up getting a technical."

Jim Hinga: "He loved to piss Rupp off. Johnny coached in the SEC at Alabama, and he was put off at Rupp being so condescending. So he'd tweak in every shot he could."

In this situation, Dee noticed that the ball that was going to be used in the game was an Adolph Rupp–autographed model. So he stopped the game just before tip-off and demanded that another brand of ball be used. The ball remained the same, but the result didn't—Carr dropped 50 on the Wildcats, and the Irish had their first win in Louisville since 1964.

Two weeks later at No. 2 Marquette, Dee went to that well again.

Jackie Meehan: "When they introduced the Marquette players to come out for the TV, they would come over and shake his hand first. Johnny Dee thought that was sort of a hotdog move. So before the game, he got about 10 packets of mustard. When they came over to shake hands, he put a packet of mustard in their hand. It wasn't opened. But just to let them know what he thought."

The move backfired as the fired-up Warriors held Carr to 22 points and won by five.

Collis Jones: "When Gary Brell, a Marquette starter, went over to shake Dee's hand, Dee handed him a packet of mustard, as in 'Hey, you hot dog.' Brell went back to the huddle, and the whole team was visibly upset. We lost that game in a real close one. And of course we were thinking, 'John, why did you have to do that?'"

The Irish were left with little time to lick their wounds. UCLA was coming to town, and the seniors had one last chance to defeat the heavyweights from California and avenge the four defeats that had started the series.

But the team still struggled with the "one-man" perception, and in the days preceding the game with the Bruins, that struggle came to a head. During the last practice before the game, Johnny Dee put tape on the floor in an arc about 16 feet around the basket, saying he didn't want anyone other than Carr or Jones shooting from outside that arc.

Collis Jones: "Our sophomore year when we went to play UCLA, Dee didn't want anybody other than Austin or Bob Arnzen shooting the ball. And everybody got all ticked. We ended up losing that year.

"But then our senior year, Dee did the same thing. And we had a meeting. We said, 'Wait a minute, if you get a shot, you've got to take the shot.' We decided that we were going to shoot no matter what Johnny Dee said."

Sensing the tension on the floor, Gene Sullivan took the "Blue" team—the top eight players—into the locker room for a chat. Before it was over, Dee and the rest of the team had joined in the conversation, and the frustrations the players were feeling came out into the open.

Jackie Meehan: "Gene Sullivan closed the door and said, 'Get it out.' So we all got it out. And Gene being the coach that he was, said, 'Show me how Austin wins 20 games by himself with this schedule.' As I said, we were a very close team. Austin said, 'Hey, I don't go anywhere without you guys. I depend on you guys to get the ball to me or for rebounds or for helping out on defense when I take a chance.' It all came out. It was positive. It was constructive. We came out and we were ready."

With the frustrations and anxieties dispelled, a very loose Irish squad took the floor against a UCLA team that had won its last 48 games. But on this afternoon, the Bruins didn't have a prayer. The Irish dominated the first half, shredding UCLA's vaunted zone press. Carr went for 46 points, scoring 15 of ND's last 17, and the Irish held off numerous Bruin runs in the second half for an 89-82 victory.

Austin Carr: "We changed the way we attacked their press. Instead of having me take the ball out and throw it to Jackie, Collis or someone else would take the ball out and I would be in the back of the press. So when I received the ball, I would always be attacking the back part of the zone. The way their zone was set up, the back end was very vulnerable. The front end is where they would always beat you if you didn't focus on the back end. Sullivan came up with a great game plan, and it worked."

Jim Hinga: "I remember Austin taking Sidney Wicks and just schooling him. Wicks tried to guard him, Curtis Rowe tried to guard him . . . nobody could stop him. He would get the ball high left and just take them to the hoop. It was a thing to see. He was on a roll."

Jackie Meehan: "They had tried different guys on Austin. Sidney Wicks was their last resort. Austin went by him like he was standing still. Wicks turned around and looked at Johnny Wooden, and just put his hands up like, 'What do you want me to do?' That's when I knew we had them."

Jack Lorri: "People say the biggest game in Notre Dame history is the UCLA game with Walton. But in my opinion, the game before they started their 88-game win streak was the biggest game in Notre Dame history because it was Sidney Wicks and Curtis Rowe and those guys. They were unbeaten, and went on to win the national championship. It was UCLA's only loss that year. And Notre Dame didn't beat them by scoring the last 13 points of the game. They BEAT them. That was not a fluke. The game in 1974 was a fluke."

Unfortunately for the Irish, the calendar still said January and the NCAA Tournament was more than a month away. They still couldn't shake the up-and-down nature that had been practically a team staple under Johnny Dee. About a month after the UCLA victory, they went to play Fordham in Madison Square Garden and got their doors blown off by a psyched-up team coached by a fiery youngster named Richard "Digger" Phelps. According to many program insiders, that loss would be the death knell for Dee's coaching tenure at Notre Dame.

But that tenure wasn't over yet. The Irish closed the season with five wins in a row and went into Austin Carr's last NCAA tournament with some momentum—momentum that stalled in the second round with a five-point overtime upset by Drake.

Carr scored 47 points in his last game in an Irish uniform but was on the losing end of a 119-106 decision to Houston. He became Notre Dame's first consensus All-American since Kevin O'Shea in 1948 and would be the first player selected in the 1971 NBA draft. But his class had not achieved the on-court success that had been envisioned when they first arrived in the fall of 1967. Someone would have to take responsibility for those unmet expectations, and that person would be Johnny Dee.

Jack Lorri: "That team was supposed to win the national championship. Father Joyce was very disappointed that they didn't do very well in the tournament. And John Wooden said something very interesting after their game. He said, 'They won't go anywhere in the NCAA tournament. Teams that rely on one player to score can't win the national championship.'"

The knock on Dee had been that, while he was a fantastic recruiter and a good motivator, his X-and-O acumen was lacking. There were reports of friction with his bosses, Moose Krause and Fr. Ned Joyce. So with Dee's contract extension finished, he and Notre Dame parted company. The details of said parting remain sketchy, with opinions differing as to who decided what for whom.

Frannie Collins: "There was an article in one of the Alabama papers that said he was thinking about throwing in the towel. He was trying to get them to come to grips with whether or not they were going to renew his contract. That played a role in the situation."

Collis Jones: "All during the season, people were trying to get us to say something negative about him. But how are you going to come out and say something bad about your coach? In those days, we didn't go around bad-mouthing our coaches.

"Johnny Dee was a good promoter. But I don't think he knew basketball that well, as it turned out. So I wasn't surprised."

Jackie Meehan: "My understanding was that when we were freshman he basically told the administration that when these guys go, I go. I thought they knew all along that they had a two- to three-year window to try to find some up-and-coming coach that they could bring in who was young and at a lower level and would work with the team and grow with the team. At least that was my understanding. I thought he left on his own."

Roger Valdiserri: "I don't think anybody decided to let him go. He really resigned. He and I talked about it. Johnny Dee went to Fr. Joyce and told him that he wanted to resign because he had his law practice—he had been sworn in before the Supreme Court. He had a little business on the side. He went to Fr. Joyce and told him, and Fr. Joyce called me and told me that John was going to resign and that they would be looking for a new basketball coach."

Regardless of the circumstances of his departure, Johnny Dee had a strong influence on Notre Dame basketball in his seven years.

Jim Monahan: "Johnny Dee really started Notre Dame basketball on a new path. I know Jordan had done a lot for Notre Dame basketball and had been there a long time, but Johnny Dee was the coach who took it from being a good basketball program to being a national program. He scheduled a lot of these tougher teams and got us traveling into new areas of the country and got us known. The quality of the teams rapidly improved under him. Digger took it from there and made the program a national power. Before Johnny Dee came, the program had its moments, but those were few and far between."

Jim Hinga: "My brother, who graduated in 1974, loves Digger. But the players who played for Johnny Dee don't particularly care for him. Because if you listen to him, Notre Dame basketball didn't exist until he showed up. And that's just not the case. Johnny Dee put Notre Dame basketball on the map by recruiting the classes he did, getting the players he did."

With Dee gone, the question was who would replace him. To the players and other people close to the program, that decision was a no-brainer. Assistant coach Gene Sullivan had been the brains behind the double-stack offense and many other innovations, and he wanted the job very much. But it seemed the administration had already decided to look elsewhere.

Ed O'Rourke: "I was surprised he didn't get more consideration, but apparently it was a done deal even before he applied for the job. Still, Gene knocked himself out trying to get that job. He even got Ara Parseghian to back him."

Austin Carr: "I thought he would get more of a chance because he deserved it. He was the mastermind behind a lot of things we did. And I was surprised they turned their back on him."

Jack Lorri: "Gene Sullivan told me, 'They cannot keep it away from me.' Every person in the athletic department, including Ara Parseghian, signed a petition urging that they hire Gene Sullivan. But I know Roger Valdiserri wanted Digger Phelps. And Fr. Joyce wanted basketball to win. Although this was a football school, he had great concern about basketball. He thought they should have done a lot better in Austin Carr's senior year because it was the No. 1 recruiting class in the country."

Jackie Meehan: "They were looking for someone who was attractive, who was young, who would be more of a representative at the alumni dinners. And that might be shallow. But as for coaching ability and knowledge of basketball, I don't think they could have found anybody better than Sully."

The exit door from the Irish program was crowded that spring, with Dee and Sullivan following Carr, Jones, Hinga, Meehan, Pleick, and Sinnott through it. The cupboard seemed rather bare for 1972 . . . a fact that Dee's successor would learn quickly.

The Digger Phelps Years

Part I— The First 10

(1972–1981)

18

Style Points
(1972–1973)

I t is, by now, a well-established part of Irish basketball lore. A young basketball coach at St. Gabriel's High School in Hazelton, Pa., dreaming of
one day being the head coach at the University of Notre Dame, wrote
a letter to Irish football coach Ara Parseghian asking what is required to
coach at the college level in the hopes that someday that letter would help
him achieve that dream.

But the series of events that brought Richard "Digger" Phelps to his
desired destination in South Bend was probably influenced more by a less
famous letter he wrote to Irish sports information director Roger Valdiserri
after Phelps had become the coach at Fordham.

Roger Valdiserri: "The week before we went to the Garden to play
Fordham, we were playing Marquette at Milwaukee. Digger was there
scouting, and he sat next to me at the table. We got to talking, and he said
how much he loved Notre Dame, which I knew right from the start. When
he got back, he sent me a handwritten note saying how great it was to
meet me."

Valdiserri enlisted the help of former assistant coach Jim Gibbons, who had moved into public relations with the university.

Jim Gibbons: "We have an office in New York. I was there on business and Roger called. He asked me if I could go over to Madison Square Garden to watch a game that night between Marquette and Fordham. There was a guy coaching at Fordham named Digger Phelps, and he wanted me to watch him. I didn't have a clue about Digger, didn't know they were looking at him. Roger obviously talked to the Powers that Be and asked if we could do that. To this day, Digger credits Roger and me with getting him the job at Notre Dame."

Phelps, in the midst of a Cinderella 26-3 first season at Fordham, got an opportunity to impress Notre Dame administrators directly when Johnny Dee brought Austin Carr and company into Madison Square Garden. According to Frank McLaughlin, his assistant coach at Fordham and at Notre Dame, Phelps pulled out all the stops to take advantage of that opportunity.

Frank McLaughlin: "I can remember going out to scout Notre Dame when they played Illinois at the Chicago Stadium late in the year. Illinois beat them because they played a zone. So I came back to Digger and told him that we should really play zone because the only teams they had lost to had played zone against them. We hadn't played zone all year—we were a pressing, man-to-man team. But he begrudgingly agreed to it.

"We ended up upsetting Notre Dame in Madison Square Garden before a sellout crowd. Some people knew Digger Phelps, but what this did was bring him to the forefront."

Although Phelps had only been at Fordham for one season, he wanted to pursue his dream of coaching at Notre Dame. His enthusiasm for the place sold him to Fr. Joyce almost as much as his coaching acumen did. So in May of 1971, the 29-year-old son of an undertaker left New York City for South Bend.

Phelps came on the scene with a bang. His professed love for the Irish, coupled with his youth, enthusiasm, and sartorial flair, drew attention from all over. Lou Somogyi, now an editor at *Blue and Gold Illustrated*, remembers the first days of the Phelps regime and the parallels drawn to another young firebrand coach of the era.

Lou Somogyi: "People viewed Digger in basketball the way Ara was when he came in for football in 1964. He was an energetic, fiery, 'shake down the thunder' type of guy. That is such a big part of Notre Dame—having that figure you look at as 'Wow, I'm glad he's on our side.' "

That intensity carried over onto the court as well, and the players used to Johnny Dee's more laid-back style noted quite a difference in their new coach.

Gary Brokaw: "He was demanding—demanding, tough on his players. He was as prepared as any coach in the business. As a player, there was so much information for us.

"But there were times you know. . . . I remember going through weeks not speaking to him. Just saying, 'Let me play and let me get out of here.' We got into it several times, like he did with all players.

"He treated us all differently, which probably was a little bit ahead of his time. But as you see now, that was the right way to treat people. His ability to read people and be able to push certain buttons with certain people was a good attribute."

Dwight Clay: "Digger was an excellent coach to play for between the lines—very astute, very prepared. You wouldn't get a better coach to coach you on the court. Off the court, he was brash and braggadocio and ego. He was a young coach coaching a big-time basketball program and sometimes he rubbed people the wrong way."

Phelps and McLaughlin soon found that they had used up all their luck getting in the door at Notre Dame because things quickly went south on the personnel front. Doug Gemmell, one of only two returning letter-men, ruined his leg in a motorcycle accident. Sophomore John Shumate developed life-threatening blood clots in his leg, leading to a missed season. And NCAA rules still prohibited freshman participation, meaning star talents Gary Brokaw and Dwight Clay were unavailable. The end result: a forgettable 6-20 season that saw Phelps scrambling to field a team, let alone compete.

Frank McLaughlin: "Early in the year we played Indiana in the dedication game at Assembly Hall in Bloomington. I wasn't at the game because I was out recruiting. I went to see Mike O'Connell, who was a high school All-American. He was a very good player, but we had Dwight Clay and Gary Brokaw as freshmen, so we weren't really looking for a guard. I was staying with an alumnus named Paul Kelly in Cincinnati, and he was really upset at me because I would not offer O'Connell a scholarship that night.

"We were driving home to his house where I was staying, and they were doing all the scores for the day. They announced very quickly 'Indiana 94, Notre Dame 29'. I just assumed the score was inverted and was supposed to be 94-92. So now I'm upset, thinking jeez, that's a game we could have won.

"Then the guy gets back on the radio and says no, that's an accurate score. We had lost to Indiana 94-29. Paul turns to me and says, 'And he can't play for you?' "

The goal for the 1972 season became holding on for 1973 when Shumate, Brokaw, and Clay could make a difference. But 1973 seemed to be more of the same: a 1-6 start that included a blowout loss to UCLA in Los Angeles.

Slowly but surely, however, Phelps got the team believing in itself. A thrilling overtime win at home against Kansas kicked off a winning streak. And the first sign of things to come came two weeks later in Milwaukee against No. 3 Marquette, a team that had won 81 games in a row at home. A shot by Clay in the final seconds gave the Irish a 71-69 win, ending the first of many streaks.

Lou Somogyi: "Digger's first great victory was not UCLA in 1974. It was at Marquette in 1973. They had lost one heartbreaker after another. They lost by two to Indiana, which went to the Final Four that year; they lost by two to Kentucky; they lost by two to St. Louis on the road; they lost in overtime at home to Ohio State. They were 1-6, but they were knocking on the door.

"They went into Marquette, which had an 81-game winning streak at home, with a 3-6 record. They were down 10 in the second half and they made a great rally. Dwight Clay made a corner jumper with about two seconds left, very similar to the shot at UCLA. That was a spectacular victory on national television, and that quickly elevated them."

Four days later, Clay replicated his feat, canning a last-second jumper to send the game against Pittsburgh into overtime and helping the Irish to the eventual win. The man with ice water in his veins quickly earned the nickname "The Iceman" and, eventually, a role among his teammates.

Dwight Clay: "I didn't see that as my role, and they didn't start looking for me until a little later. But at that point, since I was the point guard and the ball was in my hands, it was up to me whether to pass it or shoot."

Gary Brokaw: "I knew I could get almost where I wanted to go with the ball, and a lot of times they'd run another guy at me to enable Dwight to get an open shot. He was such a good perimeter shooter. He always had a scorer's mentality. I had so much confidence in him, and obviously the coaches developed the same kind of confidence in him."

The Irish won 10 of their next 13 games to get back into contention for a postseason berth. But before they could get there, there was a trip to Madison Square Garden to face Phelps's former charges at Fordham. The hosts were bound and determined to take out their frustration at being "abandoned" by Phelps on the resurgent Irish.

Frank McLaughlin: "Digger had gotten permission from the president at Fordham, Fr. Michael Walsh, to pursue the Notre Dame job. But that was not publicized. So when Digger left Fordham, there were very hard feelings that continue even to today. When we came back to play in New York, it was very difficult because the fans unfairly felt they were betrayed.

"The first year we played them was at Notre Dame, and we were not good. All their players would come by our bench pitying us because Fordham won that game pretty handily. The next year we came to the Garden. I remember a kid we recruited for Fordham, Darryl Brown, tipped the ball in at the buzzer to beat us."

After that loss, the Irish put together a four-game win streak to end the season, including victories over No. 11 St. John's and No. 19 South Carolina. Their 15-11 record in the regular season was sufficient for the NIT selection committee, who knew the drawing power of the Fighting Irish name in New York City.

The win streak continued in the NIT, with USC, Louisville, and No. 12 North Carolina falling. All that stood between Notre Dame and its first postseason championship was Virginia Tech. But the Hokies' Bobby Stevens took a page from Dwight Clay's book as overtime ended.

Dwight Clay: "Stevens took a shot from the top of the key. It touched at least three of our players' hands and ended up in the corner. I don't know how in the world he got in the corner and got his hands on it and threw it up at the buzzer, but it went in."

Gary Brokaw: "It was like a helpless feeling. We thought we had a better team. We played that way most of the game. But they came up with the breaks. Like in football, the team that doesn't turn it over has a good chance of winning. And when they got an offensive rebound like that, that was the equivalent of a turnover. So it was an empty feeling. That was one championship that would have been particularly special if we would have won."

They had fallen short of the championship, but Phelps and company had acquitted themselves well. The 17-6 finish after a 7-26 start to the regime seemed to bode well for the future. But it would be in the next season where Digger Phelps would truly put his mark on the Notre Dame program and usher in a Golden Age of Irish hardwood success.

19

71-70
(1974)

Having weathered the initial season and established momentum in season two, Phelps and his staff could turn their attention to improving things while maintaining the pace they'd set for their program. First on that list was to continue what Johnny Dee had started: use the schedule and the medium of television to market Irish basketball to the nation.

Lou Somogyi: "Back then, you didn't have ESPN and Big Monday. It was once a week with TVS and Eddie Einhorn and the Saturday Game of the Week. As an independent, Notre Dame had a great luxury and a national name where it could afford to be on every weekend. So his scheduling ideology was to get UCLA, South Carolina with Frank McGuire, Marquette with Al McGuire, and all these teams into weekend spots. North Carolina State wins the national title in 1974? Get North Carolina State on a weekend game on the schedule. San Francisco had Bill Cartwright and the best class in the country in 1974–1975? Get San Francisco on the schedule. Lefty Driesell said, 'We are going to make Maryland the UCLA of the East'? Get Maryland on the schedule."

At the top of the list of those marquee games sat UCLA. The Bruins continued to dominate college basketball and represented the best opportunity for the Irish to gain the notice Phelps sought.

Going into the 1974 season, Notre Dame had two new weapons in its quest to bag the Bruins. First, the rules prohibiting freshman eligibility had been rescinded, and as luck would have it, the Irish were positioned to exploit this rule change with a dynamite class of newcomers . . . who, of course, had to be integrated into the lineup carefully.

Frank McLaughlin: "We had all five starters coming back, and we had a great recruiting class come in: Adrian Dantley, Toby Knight, Billy Paterno, Ray Martin, and Dave Kuzmicz. We had really good players who happened to blend in well together. Dwight Clay was a great point guard; Gary Brokaw was a great second guard.

"They were good, solid players, and the team really didn't have many weaknesses. Gary Brokaw had a sprained ankle and we beat Indiana at Indiana. Everybody was capable of stepping up. We had great players, but it was always a team effort."

Dwight Clay: "You know Digger. He made us compete against one another very thoroughly. And the chemistry started to develop from a competitive nature. Everyone was very competitive in practice. We all respected one another's playing ability."

Coupled with their talent was a growing reputation for "streak breaking" and coolness under pressure. Notre Dame went to Bloomington and stopped Indiana's 19-game home winning streak, and stopped South Carolina's 34-game streak with a 72-68 victory. The Iceman picked up right where he had left off the previous season, sending the game at Ohio State into overtime, where the Irish eventually prevailed 76-72. Knowing a good thing when he saw it, Phelps made sure to push the "streak-breakers" perception to the maximum.

Gary Brokaw: "It evolved because there weren't a lot of teams that had the exposure we had with television. TV coaches in my era like Al McGuire, Digger, Jim Valvano . . . they were all big on 'moment' games. And we just said hey, let's fall into that aura. If it helped or hurt us, it was just something we accepted. But we kind of enjoyed it because we knew we had targets on our backs most of the time we played."

Adrian Dantley: "Digger talked about upsetting teams and keeping it close. We would always practice taking the last shot. We would have drills with two minutes left on the clock. It prepared us for those types of games, and it worked out well against some of the teams we played."

Bill Paterno: "Digger lived and died for these games—to be in the spotlight, to create media hype. If he had started coaching nowadays, he probably would have been king of the world with all the media attention. He lived and died to beat the best, and that's what he prepared us for."

All this was enough for the No. 2 ranking behind UCLA when the Bruins came to town on January 19, 1974. Led by superstar Bill Walton, the Bruins had not lost a game since their visit to South Bend in 1971. They continued to mow down opponent after opponent, and had their win streak up to 88 games when they arrived at the Athletic and Convocation Center, with TVS on hand to bring the game live to the nation.

Phelps, with his knack for showmanship and preparation, knew exactly how to get the team set psychologically. At the close of practice in the week before the game, he got out ladders and had the team practice cutting down the nets as they would after a monumental victory.

Dwight Clay: "I don't know where he got that idea. I think that was the first time he employed that with us. In practice he said, 'Let's cut the nets down.' So we would practice cutting the net down. We got the ladder and everything. And it continued after practice a couple of times. I guess it was spontaneous."

Gary Brokaw: "Yes, it was a surprise. We had one group down at that end and another group down at this end. It was like 'OK, what's he doing?'

"But it just exuded the confidence he had in his staff, because they had prepared him so well and then us as a team. He knew UCLA's weaknesses as well as anyone, and he knew what our strengths were. This was the crowning moment of saying, 'Hey guys, you should be as confident as I am.' And when you get a coach to do that, it kind of takes you to the next level. It was one of the great motivational tools in practice."

Bill Paterno: "We were sitting in the locker room before the game. The entire time, Dantley was there at my locker, and he said to me, 'Bill, the first time I get the ball, I'm going to go down the lane, and I'm going to elbow Walton right in the face.' If you go back and look at the film, the first play of the game, Dantley went up the gut, scored, Walton fouled him, and he broke Walton's lip open. That's how we prepared for the game. We had to be physical with them and we had to play good defense. That's where we had to beat them. We couldn't stop Walton, but we tried to stop everybody else."

But preparation and execution are two different things, and as the game progressed, Phelps's plans seemed to be going for naught. The Bruins got out to an early lead, and though the Irish made numerous runs at them, UCLA wouldn't relinquish the advantage. With 3:21 left, Phelps called time-out with the Bruins holding a 70-59 lead.

Frank McLaughlin: "There was a guy I knew named Lee Williams, who was the director of the Basketball Hall of Fame in Massachusetts. I sat in the first seat next to the scorer's table. Lee leaned over to me when we were down 70-59 and said, 'Frank, thanks for everything, but I'm going to leave early and beat the crowd.' And he left the game."

Lou Somogyi: "I remember thinking, 'Man, the magic is just not there.' Notre Dame never had the lead. And when it was 70-59, all you were thinking was maybe they could make it look respectable. UCLA seemed to be invincible.

"And then the magic just happened."

In the huddle, Phelps decided to go for broke. He instructed the team to increase the pressure on UCLA, hoping to force a frenetic pace and not allow John Wooden to stall his way to victory. He also subbed in Ray Martin for Paterno and put John Shumate at the top of the press in place of Brokaw, who moved back down the court.

Dwight Clay: "We put Shumate at the top of the press. When one of their guards was taking the ball out, Shumate smothered him so he couldn't see where he was throwing it. Ray Martin was quick and long-armed. I used to tell Ray that when he opened his arms, he covered the whole foul line area. We knew when Ray came in the game it was press automatically. Ray got his hands on a couple of those passes and deflected them, and that started a couple of baskets in the rally."

Gary Brokaw: "My thing was anticipation. I always enjoyed playing deep more so than at the front of the press because they thought I was better at being a 'center fielder.' Digger made a game adjustment that UCLA wasn't prepared for. I was really comfortable going there, and it worked out well for us."

As the clock wound down, so did the Bruin lead. Shumate scored, then stole the UCLA inbounds pass and scored again. Dantley picked Keith Wilkes's pocket and went the distance for a lay-up. Tommy Curtis was the victim of a questionable traveling call, and Brokaw cut the lead to three with a jumper over Wilkes and then to one with another from the free-throw circle.

With less than a minute remaining, Martin drew a charge on Wilkes, nullifying a basket and giving the Irish the ball and a chance for the win. Needing a last-second shot for a big victory, the Irish turned to the man who had done the job for them so many times before.

Dwight Clay: "I took the ball and I passed it to Ray Martin. I told Ray to pass it to Gary and clear out the corner, and I was going to the other corner. Gary was killing Wilkes—he had his number. If Gary and Shumate could work a two-man game, I'm quite sure we could have got a score."

Gary Brokaw: "In the last three minutes, I had to make two or three key jump shots. Shumate had scored one. Adrian had a steal. And again, I was getting ready to take this last shot. It was either going to be me or I was going to give it to Shu inside. I was in a comfort zone coming through the middle there. But I had so much confidence in Dwight as a shooter, I didn't care whether I scored or made the assist."

Dwight Clay: "As Gary was trying to make a move on Wilkes, Tommy Curtis started cheating toward Gary to help out. Curtis knew if Gary got near the foul line, he was going to get that shot off. So as Curtis started cheating, I started waving my hands at Gary. We had played together so often that when he would see my hand in the air he knew I had to be open. It took him a while, but he finally threw the ball."

Gary Brokaw: "In basketball, when you've got an open man, you pass the ball. And when an open man could make shots like Dwight, it was just fun to watch. So I said, 'Dwight, you go on.'"

With 29 seconds remaining, Clay's high-arcing shot swished through the net, giving the Irish their first lead of the game, 71-70. Pandemonium reigned in the A.C.C. stands as John Wooden called timeout and the Irish prepared their last defensive stand.

The Bruins wanted the ball in Walton's hands, and after missed shots by Curtis and Dave Meyers, they got it. But the normally dead-eyed big man missed only his second shot of the game. Pete Trgovich and Meyers couldn't get putbacks to go before Shumate corralled the rebound. The bedlam in the stands spilled out onto the court. Notre Dame was No. 1 for the first time since 1949.

Ed O'Rourke: "The thing I remember most about that game is the people streaming out onto the floor when it was over. I was sitting in the front row, and I can remember trying to get back into the locker room afterwards and feeling like my life was in danger from the crush of people."

Dwight Clay: "After Shumate grabbed the ball and threw it in the air, I fought through the crowd. My mother was sitting in the second row. I ran up there and gave her a hug and a kiss and told her that shot was for her. I wish I could relive those moments. After that I ran in the locker room. I didn't even take part in cutting down the net. I got the hell out of there because there was so much pandemonium. I wish I could have stayed up there and relived that moment."

Lou Somogyi: "One scene you can see in the television replay shows a Notre Dame student tearing off a shirt that says 'God made Notre Dame Number One.' And that's the feeling that permeated the campus—ND was unbeatable now. The football team was 11-0 and had won the national title, and here's the basketball team 10-0 and they've just knocked off No. 1. It was the most magical time in the world then."

That "magical time" lasted all of one week—the time between that game and the rematch between the two teams in Los Angeles. Looking to avenge his first loss in 139 basketball games dating back to high school,

Bill Walton poured in 32 points and sent the Irish to a lopsided 94-75 defeat.

Bill Paterno: "That was the first time I had been to Pauley. There's no seating for the students. They just open the doors and they play the 'Charge' thing on the trumpet. The students come flying in and dive down rows and rows of stairs to get to their seats.

"We didn't have a good game at all. The feeling I got out there was that they needed to win that game big time. If they had lost that game, it would have been the season for them."

Adrian Dantley: "We knew when we defeated them that they would be ready the next week at UCLA. It's too bad we didn't have any separation between the games because we were only No. 1 for one week."

Defeat didn't get the Irish down. They took down fifth-ranked Marquette at home by six points three days later, and they would taste defeat only once more during that regular season—an inexplicable 15-point loss at Dayton in the last game of the season that might have been a case of Irish players looking ahead to an NCAA Tournament in which they were a definite Final Four aspirant.

After dispatching Austin Peay in the first round, the Irish were off to Tuscaloosa, Ala., to face Michigan, an upset winner over Indiana for the Big Ten championship. But they soon found that the Wolverines had picked up some extra fans for the game.

Dwight Clay: "The atmosphere was all against Notre Dame. The football team had just beaten Alabama in the Sugar Bowl, and all those Tuscaloosa fans, the Michigan fans—anybody else that hated Notre Dame was rooting against us that day."

Of greater concern to Phelps and the Irish was Michigan forward Campanella "Campy" Russell and his 23 points per game. Stopping Russell would be the key to the Irish advancing to the regional final. The good news was that Russell didn't score 23 points. The bad news was he scored 36.

Gary Brokaw: "For me, Campy Russell was the early Larry Bird, but he didn't get the exposure. He didn't have quite the career that Larry did, obviously.

I played against him in some of the All-Star games. He was such a good player. And in this game he was such a dominant player. He was Magic Johnson for Michigan in this game."

Michigan's 77-68 win ended the team's Final Four hopes. It didn't matter that the Irish destroyed Vanderbilt by 30 in the consolation game or that Michigan fell to Marquette two nights later or that three of the teams that went to Greensboro, North Carolina, for the Final Four—Marquette, Kansas, and UCLA—had been Irish victims that season. They had fallen short of their goal. And it hurt.

Bill Paterno: "That was definitely our year, no question about it. It was really the best chance I had of the three years to go to the Final Four. We did make it to the regional finals a couple of times, but there are a lot of 'what ifs' there because we were definitely the best team in the country at that point."

Gary Brokaw: "Our 'moment' games were so big. But the only ones that ultimately count for championships are the ones that you win in the NCAA Tournament. We thought we were one of the best teams in the country. That's why the Michigan game was so tough. We thought that was our year. We thought we had the confidence and the momentum to win it all."

There were some consolation prizes for the 26-3 finish. John Shumate became Notre Dame's eighth consensus All-American, and Brokaw was named to the UPI third-team. Phelps was named UPI's Coach of the Year. And with a powerhouse lineup eligible to return for the next season, things were looking bright.

20

A.D.
(1975–1976)

The 1974 team had tremendous talent, and on paper, most of it looked to return the next year. But 1974 hadn't even ended before attrition took its toll on the potential for 1975.

There were some who hoped consensus All-American John Shumate would stay for the year of eligibility he had remaining even though he had received his degree. Those hopes were slight, however, and few were surprised when Shumate decided to forego that extra year and graduate with his class. More of a surprise was the decision of junior Gary Brokaw to enter his name in the hardship draft. But a unique combination of circumstances dictated a move for the young guard.

Gary Brokaw: "Probably it was the timing of not having Shu. My last year, I knew he wouldn't be there. And the other thing was the ABA and NBA were still two separate entities. So I thought the leverage and the bargaining for players such as myself was high. I thought the big moments we had that year meant my value was as high as it ever would be.

"My dream was to go on to the NBA. I wanted this dream when I was 4 years old. I went to Notre Dame with the goal of graduating and then going to the NBA. And I said, 'What if I get hurt and I can't ever reach that dream?' I was 17 or 18 years old. I just said, 'You know what, I'm going to take the opportunity while it's there.' "

Brokaw's decision surprised his teammates, but they understood.

Adrian Dantley: "It didn't surprise me Shumate was leaving because he was a senior academically. He had a good year and he was a first-team All American. So it didn't surprise me he didn't come back.

"Gary kind of surprised me because he wasn't drafted high. Usually when you weren't drafted high, you'd come back to school. But he didn't go until the late first round. So that kind of surprised me."

Dwight Clay: "I was disappointed in one way and happy for them in another way. I knew they were going to the next level, but I knew if they had stayed, we would have definitely been a shoo-in to win the championship. So that was kind of disappointing. But then again, it gave me the opportunity I thought I would have as a shooter to have a great season."

Going into 1975, the coaching staff had to replace two All-Americans. The pain was mitigated by the talent in an excellent sophomore class and the arrival of freshmen Dave Batton, Donald "Duck" Williams, Jeff Carpenter, and Randy Haefner. But with Dwight Clay and Pete Crotty the only seniors, the pressure would be on the youngsters to produce, especially on the team's newest star, Adrian Dantley.

Frank McLaughlin: "Adrian Dantley was the kind of guy who when he was in grammar school, he was so big and physical a player, people said, 'Well, he'll be a good high school player, but he'll never make it in college.' He had to re-prove himself in college and became a great player, but then people said, 'Ah, he was lucky in college, but he won't make it in the pros.' "

Bill Paterno: "Adrian Dantley was probably one of the nicest people I've met in my life. He was a professional, and he taught me a lot about being professional. He worked hard. He just lived and died to play basketball."

Lou Somogyi: "The best 6-foot 5-inch presence I ever saw inside. He had the best head-fake I ever saw here. He got about four or five offensive rebounds a game where he'd head-fake the defender into the air, draw the foul and either get a three-point play or two points from the foul line. He would get 10 or 12 points at the foul line almost every game. Yet he could also take you outside and beat you off the dribble."

Notre Dame was originally not high on Dantley's list, but the tradition of Frannie Collins's D.C. Pipeline and the players it had sent to South Bend ahead of him eventually swayed him to choose the Irish.

Frannie Collins: "When Johnny Dee left, I cut off all my recruiting ties with Notre Dame. After all, I had a job and a family. I don't know who it was Digger asked, but he said he wanted to get Dantley. That person told him there was only one person who could get Dantley, and that was me.

"I was on my way to a brunch down the street, and my youngest boy hollered to me that someone was at the door. I went back, and Sid Catlett was there with Digger, asking me to get involved."

Adrian Dantley: "What really got me started at Notre Dame was the Washingtonians who had attended Notre Dame—Austin Carr, Collis Jones, Sid Catlett, and Bob Whitmore. That's what got me interested in Notre Dame when I was in high school. When I was a young kid, they were always on TV, so everyone knew about Notre Dame and everyone thought about attending Notre Dame.

"My senior year, though, I really wasn't that interested in Notre Dame because they'd had a pretty bad season the year before. But Digger wanted me to come out for just one day."

Frank McLaughlin: "He came to visit Notre Dame as a courtesy to Bob Whitmore and other players from the D.C. area. He was only coming out for one day, but Sid Catlett and Collis Jones and Austin Carr had said if he stayed an extra day, they'd come out.

"At the end of that day he said, 'Well, I think I'll stay an extra day.' So Sid, Collis, and Austin drove out to see him in South Bend.

"I'll never forget coming to pick Adrian up at the airport when he decided to come to Notre Dame. He had these two big steamer trunks. I said, "A.D., I remember when you were only coming here for a day. Now you look like you're moving in for life.""

Collis Jones: "I don't remember driving out there, but I do remember we did a lot of hand-holding back here in D.C. I remember a number of times leaving the Dantley house at 12 or 1 o'clock in the morning with Bob Whitmore and Digger and other folks. They pursued Adrian very hard."

Bob Whitmore: "We knew his mother, Virginia, and Rose, his aunt. As a result, they were very comfortable with us and they were very impressed with us as examples of the 'finished product' Notre Dame represented for Adrian both athletically and academically. I was in banking, Austin was a high draft pick, Collis was playing in the pros, Sid was doing things in marketing for Motorola, and Dwight was working in Denver. It's hard to turn your back on something that is obviously successful, and it certainly appeared that Notre Dame had 'polished' us."

Dantley quickly impressed his coaches and teammates with an indefatigable work ethic.

Gary Brokaw: "The first two weeks of school, we were still playing pickup games. He went up for a lay-up, and Billy Paterno went up to try to block his shot. Adrian just kind of put a stiff arm up there, held it there, and shot a regular lay-up. Billy landed on the floor. That was the moment where I could see his strength, his ability to score on bigger opponents."

Frank McLaughlin: "One time during the summer, I saw Adrian and asked him how everyone was doing. He said to me, 'You know, Toby Knight's not working hard.' I was surprised at that. Then I saw some of the guys who had graduated already like Bob Whitmore and Sid Catlett, and I asked them about Toby Knight. They said, 'You don't understand. If you don't play six hours a day like Adrian does, that means you're not working hard to him.' But that was Adrian Dantley: very focused, very hardworking."

Youth is youth, though, and a schedule that featured more than a dozen games against opponents that had played in a tournament the previous postseason would tax even a veteran squad. So the 19-10 record wasn't surprising or disappointing, especially when the young Irish had to face an early four-game gauntlet of No. 7 Kansas, No. 3 Indiana, No. 3 UCLA, and No. 15 Kentucky.

Bill Paterno: "Playing down at the so-called 'neutral' court in Louisville was always a nightmare. I never won down there. I don't know what it's like to win down there."

Adrian Dantley: "It was pretty grueling, because we were playing against the toughest teams in the country. But that's what Notre Dame talked about when they recruited me—playing the best teams. As a player, you wanted to play the best teams because it would prepare you for the next level if you made it there. Playing that competitive schedule definitely helped me when I was a rookie in the NBA."

Dantley was a star, even against the arduous schedule. He finished second nationally in scoring with just over 30 points per game. He attempted and made more free throws that season than anyone in Irish history. He became Notre Dame's second consensus All-American in as many seasons.

Given Dantley's explosive success that season, there were concerns he would follow Brokaw into the hardship draft, even though he was just a sophomore. He entered his name originally, but to the relief of everyone in the program, he decided he wasn't ready and withdrew before the deadline.

Adrian Dantley: "I thought I needed another year. It didn't change my eventual position in the draft—I expected to be No. 5 that year, and I ended up being No. 6 the next year. I just thought I needed another year to get closer to my degree."

Dwight Clay: "He lost about 30 pounds that year. He stayed in school and his ball-handling skills got better. His offense and shot got much better. Staying really benefited him in the long run."

Bill Paterno: "He was very close to his mother, and she wanted him to stay in school and finish four years. I wasn't surprised, because she was always there."

Having decided to stay, Dantley was determined to make the most of that decision. Clay and Crotty were gone, but the Irish had reloaded again with a class that included two big men, Bruce Flowers and Bill Laimbeer. The youngsters of the previous season had another year of maturity under their belts, and the schedule featured 16 home games, which seemed quite a bounty for those used to the 9 or 10-game slates in the old fieldhouse.

Bill Paterno: "Laimbeer gave us two big guys who could shoot, and they could shoot from anywhere. Laimbeer and Bruce Flowers had great years. Toby Knight was still the sixth man, but he should have been starting, and he eventually did start in his junior year.

"Three big guys who could shoot the ball opened it up a lot for Ray Martin and me. It gave us a different look. When Laimbeer got hot, he could hit 10 in a row. We had a unique team."

Duck Williams: "Everyone got along on that team. When you're on a team and the expectations are not high, but you have a group of guys who are close-knit, it's like someone telling you that you can't do something. All you want to do is do that thing. We knew we had some good young ballplayers on our team, and we pulled together and surprised a lot of people."

Bruce Flowers: "We had strong players in each class, and I felt I could come in and contribute right off the bat. If any team is going to do well, it has to go deep, and that team went really deep."

Even with depth, it was clear Dantley would once again be the straw that stirred the Irish drink. So Phelps and his staff came up with an offensive strategy to take advantage of Dantley's abilities in the open court.

Lou Somogyi: "This was the era when the Four Corners with Dean Smith came to the forefront. Digger had a kind of offshoot of it called 'Four to Score.' Not to delay, but to score, with the strategy being putting four guys into the corners—two on the wings and two at halfcourt—and Adrian Dantley dribbling to the middle and taking his man to the hoop. They were not going to stop him. Here is this 6-foot 5-inch, 241-pound locomotive with good dribbling skills just taking it to the basket. And he would either draw the foul or get the basket and a three-point play."

Using the Four to Score, the Irish won 12 of their first 15 games, falling to eventual undefeated national champion Indiana and No. 4 UCLA along with the usual bump in the "neutral site" game against Kentucky. But any success in the latter part of the schedule would have to be achieved without Bill Laimbeer.

Bill Paterno: "He didn't show up for exams, and that's something you didn't hear of. You may have had a bad year in school, but you went to class and you went to your exams. That was expected of you. Since he didn't do that, I kind of figured we wouldn't see him again. And I didn't, because he sat out my senior year.

"He really hurt us, and you figured he did it because he didn't want to be there. But his father made him come back. His father said, 'Get your ass into the community college and make up the grades and get back.' So good parenting kept him in school."

Frank McLaughlin: "Laimbeer was a great, great athlete. He's a scratch golfer and a very good tennis player. A fierce competitor. I think he's the only male in the Laimbeer family not to go to Harvard.

"It was tough losing him. I remember him coming over to my house when it happened. It was a difficult thing because he was very bright. It was totally unexpected. For some reason, he wasn't motivated academically, although he was very capable."

Duck Williams: "He was our main guy clogging up the middle, and any time you lose a guy with that kind of size, it affects you. But Bruce Flowers and Dave Batton pulled together and held down the middle, with Toby Knight helping out."

And A.D. continued to be A.D. He remained in the top five nationally in scoring with almost 29 points a game. He led the Irish to a 10-point win over UCLA in the rematch at home. And when the Irish received an NCAA bid at the end of that season, he, along with Knight, Kumicz, and Paterno joined the class of 1971 as the only Irish players to play in the NCAA Tournament three years in a row.

But once again, the euphoria of making the NCAA Tournament was dampened by a poor performance. The Irish barely survived against Cincinnati when a five-second violation in the closing seconds went their way, and were upset in the second round by their old nemesis Michigan. This time when the draft rolled around, Dantley, who had become Notre Dame's first two-time consensus All-American since Leo Klier in 1946, followed through on his decision to leave.

Adrian Dantley: "I went into that season thinking that it *might* be my last year. I had attended summer school every summer, so I was pretty ahead of the game. But I didn't go in thinking it was *going* to be my last year.

"But when the season was over, the decision wasn't that tough. I was a two-time first team All-American, so there wasn't much sense in me coming back. I felt I was ready."

Duck Williams: "I thought after that year he'd probably be gone because of the year he'd had, being an All-American and one of the leading scorers in the country. To me, it was a foregone conclusion because of who else was out there and where he'd go in the draft."

Dantley's position in Irish basketball history was secure. He was No. 2 in career scoring behind Carr, the career leader in free throws made and attempted, and was among the top 10 in career rebounds. Replacing him would be quite a task, and some believed the team would need a sixth man to pick up the slack.

George Keogan. Photo courtesy of Notre Dame Sports Information Department

Ray Meyer. Photo courtesy of Notre Dame Sports Information Department

Eddie Riska with George Keogan, 1941. Photo courtesy of Notre Dame Sports Information Department

Leo "Crystal" Klier. Photo courtesy of Notre Dame Sports Information Department

Kevin O'Shea. Photo courtesy of Notre Dame Sports Information Department

Edward "Moose" Krause. Photo courtesy of Notre Dame Sports Information
Department

John Jordan. Photo courtesy of Notre Dame Sports Information Department

The 1957 squad was one of John Jordan's strongest. Pictured left to right are Bob Devine (g), Tommy Hawkins (f), John Smyth (c), John McCarthy (f), and Gene Duffy (g). Photo courtesy of Notre Dame Sports Information Department

(from top to bottom) center Dick Rosenthal, forward Joe Bertrand, and guard Jack "Junior" Stephens. Photo courtesy of Notre Dame Sports Information Department

Johnny Dee is credited for bringing a more modern feel to the Irish program. Here he is pictured with his first big recruiting class (from l to r), Dwight Murphy, Bob Arnzen, and Bob Whitmore. Photo by Laughead Photographers

Richard "Digger" Phelps coached the Irish for twenty years, leading them to their only Final Four appearance in 1978. Photo by Cheryl Ertelt

Austin Carr remains the greatest player in the history of Irish basketball, and his name still pervades the Notre Dame record books. Photo courtesy of Notre Dame Sports Information Department

Final Four pic from other disk here betweeb 12 and 13]] 1978 Men's Final Four. Photo courtesy of Notre Dame Sports Information Department

With 29 seconds left in the game, Dwight Clay launches the most famous shot in Notre Dame basketball history while Adrian Dantley (under basket) and John Shumate (34) look on. Photo courtesy of Notre Dame Sports Information Department

Two-time All-American Adrian Dantley was only the second Irish underclassman to declare himself eligible for the NBA draft. Photo courtesy of Notre Dame Sports Information Department

Kelly Tripucka's effervescent personality made him a favorite of Irish fans while his athletic ability made him the bane of Irish foes. Photo courtesy of Notre Dame Sports Information Department

John Paxson was nicknamed "The General" by Gary Brokaw for his take-charge attitude. Photo by Karen Croake

David Rivers recovered from a horrific automobile accident to lead the 1987 team to the Sweet 16. Photo by Steven Navratil

John MacLeod guided the Irish during one of their most rocky periods, but didn't get to experience the subsequent success. Photo by Brian Spurlock

LaPhonso Ellis set new standards for shot-blocking at Notre Dame. Photo by Greg Kohs.

Pat Garrity used determination and hard work to make himself an All-American. Photo courtesy of Notre Dame Sports Information Department

Matt Doherty's fiery personality helped jump-start the Irish program.
Photo by Lighthouse Imaging

Troy Murphy accepts the 2001 Big East Men's Basketball Player of the Year award from conference senior associate commissioner Tom McElroy. Photo by Tom Maguire

Under Mike Brey's leadership, the Irish returned to the NCAA Tournament after an 11-year absence, reaching the Sweet 16 in 2003. Photo by and courtesy of Joe Raymond.

21

The Sixth Man
(1977)

Long before the "Cameron Crazies" came on the scene, raucous crowds were a mainstay of Notre Dame basketball. And in no season was their nature as prominent as it was in 1977.

The atmosphere at games in the old Fieldhouse was conducive to fan fervor of all types. Since "The Barn" only accommodated about 5,000 people, there was precious little room for opposing fans, which made the crowd quite partisan in its support of the Irish.

John Smyth: "I was a sophomore playing against Michigan State and Johnny Greene, who was very, very good. But it was his first game out of the service. And he'd never witnessed anything like that. When you ran down the court, the fans could hit your legs, they were that close. And, of course, they did hit legs. Johnny Greene froze, and we beat him."

Tom Hawkins: "It was the most incredible place to play. It seated only 5,000, and the fans were right next to the floor. As a matter of fact, when you threw the ball in from the sidelines, the fans behind you could pat you on the back.

That's how close it was. There were St. Mary's women and a big section of priests—you saw all of those black robes and white collars in the stands as the band blared the Victory March near the visitor's bench. I don't know how many we lost during my three years, but not many at the Fieldhouse."

The change in venue and a move to coeducation did nothing to dampen the crowd's enthusiasm. The A.C.C. quickly matched its predecessor's reputation for sound and difficulty for opponents.

Going into the 1977 season, Phelps and his staff weren't concerned with crowds. They had to replace Adrian Dantley's 30 points and 10 rebounds per game and deal with the loss of Bill Laimbeer to grades and Bernard Rencher to transfer.

Replacing Dantley's production would be a group effort, with contributions from all the players, including newcomers Rich Branning and Bill Hanzlik. But the philosophy was definitely more conservative than it had been in Phelps's previous years.

Bill Paterno: "We really didn't have a scorer, a guy who could create baskets. Dantley could score at will. We had the big guys, so we ran a lot of motion. Digger went conservative defensively because we didn't have the speed; he went conservative offensively because we didn't have the great scorer."

Also missing was Dantley's attention-grabbing "star quality." Some of the players believe Phelps looked in a different direction for that solution.

Bruce Flowers: "There was definitely a change when Adrian left. Adrian was the star of the team, and Digger was propping him up as the All-American who was bringing prestige to the school. When Adrian left, Digger decided that was going to be his role.

"In his office during those days, you saw photographs of Digger and all the dignitaries who came through ND—the Pope, Gerald Ford, Ronald Reagan. . . . His whole wall was just plastered with those pictures. He'd go off to Aspen for Christmas break and come back wearing a big cowboy hat. He was a young man who was getting a lot of exposure via the ND program, and he was living large and loving it."

The Irish opened the 1977 season with a seven-game win streak, including a one-point overtime upset of No. 8 Maryland in the season opener and an attention-grabbing win at No. 3 UCLA. The Irish not only were the first ND team to win in Los Angeles, they also were the first nonconference team to defeat UCLA at Pauley Pavilion in a record 115 games.

Duck Williams: "That was a great experience. To think about all the teams that had played at Pauley Pavilion, and we were the ones who went in there and won. Back in those days, the rivalry between UCLA and ND was huge, and just to participate in it was a big thing for me. I still have those nets at home, because we cut them down."

It was a colossal achievement for the players, and the student body, which had become the team's sixth man, expressed its appreciation. Assistant coach Danny Nee remembers the reception awaiting the Irish on that snowy night.

Danny Nee: "It was insanity. The bus turned up Notre Dame Avenue, and it seemed like every damn student in the world was out there. And it was snowing. I know I had never experienced anything like it. It was big. It was just fun."

Bruce Flowers: "We pulled up to the Main Circle, and there were 200 to 300 hundred people waiting for us just going crazy. A platform had been put up, and Digger got up there to say some words as everyone was chanting 'Dig-ger, Dig-ger.' I had brought a palm leaf back with me, and I held it up while he was speaking. The crowd was so out of their minds that they started chanting 'palm, palm.' It was amazing—probably the most amazing thing I'd ever experienced."

Defending national champion Indiana was one of the season-opening victims, giving the Irish their first win over the Hoosiers in four years. But that win came at a price, as starting guard Ray "Dice" Martin broke his ankle and was lost for the rest of the season, leaving freshman Rich Branning to replace him in the starting lineup.

Bill Hanzlik: "I still remember that injury. It was a right ankle. And I remember Bobby Knight coming out to kind of console him a little bit and tell him what a great player he was. I thought that was a real class act. Because you knew he was done."

Danny Nee: "I can remember that vividly 'cause Digger and I were at the hospital. We knew what had happened. You could've dropped a pin in the building when that happened. A blind man could see how serious it was."

Duck Williams: "For me, it was a big adjustment. Ray and I were like brothers. We had played together for a couple of years and had worked out all summer preparing to be the starting backcourt. To see him go down was tough, because Ray was a tenacious defensive player and he really knew how to run the point guard position. It was a really tough experience for me.

"But Rich stepped in and played really well. He was very heady and steady as a freshman, and things worked out."

Bruce Flowers: "Dice's injury really changed our game. Dice's game was more related to speed, and when Rich Branning had to come in, we slowed down. But Rich was a steady player who wasn't going to turn the ball over often, so we became more of a half-court team."

Danny Nee: "Branning was a talent. He was smooth, confident. And he was one of the nicest people I've ever met. The kid was just a born winner and a born leader, and to come to Notre Dame and inherit that position the way he did was tough. I thought he did a pretty good job because he was totally unselfish."

The team wasn't able to adjust on a dime, though. After getting to No. 2 in the rankings following their season-starting surge, the Irish went into a five-losses-in-six-games free-fall, including a nine-point loss to a Marquette team on its way to the national title.

But the team gradually got used to its new style. Against Pittsburgh, the Irish got a much-needed win . . . along with some levity when Paterno heaved a full-court inbounds pass that somehow found its way into the basket.

Eight more wins in a row followed, and the record was 19-6 when undefeated and No. 1 San Francisco and its all-world center, Bill Cartwright, came into the ACC. The magic number for an NCAA Tournament bid was 20 wins, and Notre Dame's penchant for beating top-ranked opponents was at stake. A last-minute change in the schedule, requested by NBC, moved the game from March 1 to March 5. Given a week to prepare, Phelps would no doubt have plenty up his sleeves.

Jack Lorri: "Everybody knew Digger's record against No. 1 teams. Everybody knew Notre Dame could beat them. But Digger factored in that game maybe more than any game I've ever seen. Notre Dame played well, but Digger had them beautifully prepared. And he psyched the crowd up before the game—players walking down the aisle instead of out of the dressing room, and all of that. He was good at that.

"All of that hoopla is one thing. But the players played. He had a great game plan, and they executed. Digger could take a situation for a game coming up and he would say, 'All right, we are ahead by two with 10 seconds with the ball.' And he'd run that and run that and run that and run that on the night before the game. And you'd come up on the next day, and they are ahead by two with the ball with 10 seconds."

Wanting every possible advantage, Phelps turned to the sixth man. At a pep rally the night before the game, he told the students the time USF would be arriving at the A.C.C. for its shootaround, suggesting the Dons might want a little company. And company they got.

Duck Williams: "San Francisco got there a day ahead of time, and they were walking around campus. They were 29-0, and I'm sure their chests were sticking out. But you know how it is when you come in to Notre Dame undefeated—things happen."

Frank McLaughlin: "We had a rally the night before, and Digger told the students USF was going to be there at 11:30 or whatever, and we'd like all the students there early. I think it shocked USF. They came into the building, and there was the student section filled up already."

Ever the planner, Phelps had even provided the raucous students with an appropriate cheer.

Lou Somogyi: "I got in a half hour before the game. I got chills down my spine because you could hear the student body. It was just echoing throughout—TWENTY-NINE, clap, clap, AND ONE, clap, clap. Digger created that rhythm the night before. He said, 'Here is our cheer tomorrow.' It was so loud that it was just electrifying.

"And when the team came out on the court for the final time for warm-up, it got so loud you couldn't hear. You thought you had gone deaf.

It was just electrifying. I still get chills down my spine thinking about how raucous that place was."

Bill Hanzlik: "The students must have been there over an hour or an hour and a half before the game. The student section was over the top of their locker room. And the chant of '29 and 1' starting an hour and a half before the game—it was sort of like this taunting going on. It was great."

Jack Lorri: "The loudest crowd I've ever heard at Notre Dame. Even louder than the crowd for the game that stopped the 88-game winning streak, because that crowd really didn't believe it could happen for most of the game. And then at the end of the game, they were going crazy."

Bruce Flowers: "From the opening tip, you couldn't hear the referee's whistles because the fans were yelling so loud. Every time there was a turnover or a foul, they were blowing their whistles as loud as they could to make themselves heard. By the end of the game, I had a headache just from the sheer noise within the place. It just reverberated through you."

With the wall of sound roaring down from the stands, the Dons didn't have a chance. Duck Williams, in Adrian Dantley's isolation spot in the Four to Score, had a field day with 25 points. San Francisco could never get on track. After the Fighting Irish won 93-82, NBC recognized the efforts of the Irish sixth man and, for the first and only time in its history of broadcasting college basketball, gave the Notre Dame student body the MVP award for the game.

The win got the Irish their NCAA bid, and Paterno, Knight, Martin, and Kumicz became the first players in Notre Dame history to play on four NCAA teams. But Phil Ford and North Carolina knocked the Irish out in the second round of the tournament, 79-77.

Bill Hanzlik: "We had the ultimate upset going on. We were up 14, I think, in the second half, which, when there was no shot clock, was a huge lead. And Digger had devised this strategy of going with the inverted four-corner offense—sticking his point guard and two guard in the corner and bringing out his center and forwards because they handled the ball fairly well. Well, it backfired."

Bill Paterno: "Digger's four corners eventually lost us my only chance to go to the Final Four my senior year. We had a nine-point lead. Digger went to the four corners, and we ended up losing at the buzzer. It took the rhythm out of the team. Not being a great ball-handler, it scared me to death having to take the ball and dribble it instead of running the offense."

Six years into Phelps's tenure and with precious little NCAA Tournament success to show for it, the Irish faithful began to get restless. When, they wondered, would their flamboyant coach finally take the Irish to the Promised Land of the Final Four?

The answer would arrive soon enough.

22

Luck and Lore
(1978)

There's an old saying that luck is what happens when inspiration meets perspiration. By that measurement, the 1978 season was probably among the luckiest in the annals of Irish basketball history.

Rich Branning, Bill Hanzlik, Duck Williams, Dave Batton, Bill Laimbeer, and Bruce Flowers were returning, and Phelps brought in a recruiting class that on paper ranked with the 1971 Austin Carr group: Kelly Tripucka, Tracy Jackson, Orlando Woolridge, Gil Salinas, and Stan Wilcox.

Tripucka, son of 1940s Irish football great Frank Tripucka, was the key player in the class. His larger-than-life personality coupled with a fierce desire to win made him a team and fan favorite over the course of his career.

Duck Williams: "When I first saw Kelly Tripucka play, I said to myself, 'This kid has skills.' Kelly was a tough kid. A lot of people come in from high school with impressive credentials, but as I tell my son, everyone's an All-American when they go to college. When you get there, you have to separate your skills from everyone else's, and Kelly did."

Gil Salinas: "He was very intense. He was a little deceiving in that he didn't look as fast as he really was. He had a quick first step. I could never block a shot on him because he was just that quick. When he would grab the ball, it would be back up."

Tim Andree: "He was an incredible competitor at everything. We'd get together with Marc Kelly and Mike Mitchell and have backgammon tournaments, or he'd be out for a beer at Corby's and playing Pop-A-Shot. Whatever it was, Kelly wanted to win. It was obvious he'd grown up with older brothers in the house."

Phelps and the staff quickly set out to integrate the freshmen into an already imposing lineup.

Danny Nee: "On that team you had Laimbeer, you had Paterno, you had Duck Williams, you had Hanzlik, you had Flowers. . . . Count up the number of players who ended up in the NBA and had successful careers. It was scary.

"The young kids wanted to play. Tracy Jackson, Kelly, and Orlando were always just a little bit naïve, you know, but they were so talented. Digger did a masterful job, I thought, of balancing time."

Duck Williams: "Digger worked them in slowly. It wasn't a thing where these guys came in and took over positions. They competed in practice, but when it came to the games, they didn't play as much as the starters played. Kelly got to play more toward the end and he eventually started some games, but we had quality players and the freshmen accepted their role at the time."

Tracy Jackson: "We came in as freshmen and we were all helping each other and taking classes together. Having that as part of our learning experience made playing on the court so much easier. Obviously some of us matured earlier than others in a basketball sense, but we definitely helped each other out. There was a real unselfishness there that really fostered an environment of learning for all of us."

That "environment of learning" helped the Irish to wins in their first six games, and confidence was high as the team left for its first real road test of the season in Bloomington against the Indiana Hoosiers.

Bruce Flowers: "The South Bend airport was fogged in, so we bussed it, and the plane that was supposed to take us down to Bloomington turned around and went down to Evansville instead."

Ed O'Rourke: "I was originally supposed to travel on the charter with the team out of South Bend, and they called me first thing in the morning to tell me they weren't chartering because the weather was so bad. So I made arrangements with a couple of other people to take a private plane out of Lansing, which is the local little airport here.

"We flew down, and when I got down there the coaches and the kids told me the plane we would have been on had gone down."

Notre Dame's scheduled airplane had been rerouted to charter the Evansville Purple Aces to their game at Middle Tennessee State. Just after take-off, the plane crashed, killing all 29 people aboard. The last-minute change in plans hadn't been communicated to everyone, so there were some tense moments for the families and friends of Irish players, who were only told that a plane carrying a college basketball team in southern Indiana had crashed.

Kelly Tripucka: "Not too many people knew about that change. Everybody back at campus assumed we were flying, and then the way the news broke was there was a 'team from Indiana' flying down to that area. Everybody just assumed it was the Notre Dame team. So there were some anxious moments."

Duck Williams: "Normally when we would arrive at our destination, I'd call my parents' house or one of my brothers. When we got down there, I called my brother to let him know we had arrived, but I didn't have a chance to talk to my mom or dad. The next day when the media was reporting it in D.C., they thought the Notre Dame team had gone down. My mom was calling all around and everyone was calling her. Just the thought of it really made it hit home what had happened."

Tracy Jackson: "One thing that really stands out to me is when I got back to campus, the South Bend Tribune had pictures of all of the Evansville players and coaches who had perished on the plane. It was a very sad situation. Having lost my father earlier that year before I got to Notre Dame, it really put life into perspective for me."

Whether it was the reminder of their own mortality, the talent of the Hoosiers or the fact that wins in Bloomington have always been a scarce commodity for Irish teams, the undefeated season went by the boards with a 67-66 loss. But the team recovered. A five-point loss in Louisville to eventual national champion Kentucky notwithstanding, the Irish continued their winning ways. They swept UCLA for the first time since the series started. A 103-82 victory over West Virginia pushed their record to 13-3 going into a nationally televised matchup with the Maryland Terrapins and their colorful coach, Lefty Driesell.

But just as West Virginia left, the snow arrived.

Danny Nee: "Digger and I were talking and I said, 'Look at the size of these snowflakes.' They were coming down like half-dollars. We came out and we had inches of snow on our cars. We barely got home that night.

"By the next morning it still hadn't stopped snowing, so the whole town got shut down for a few days. We didn't have practice. I couldn't get in. The snow was so deep that you only could drive if you had a reason to drive. The neighbors had a snowmobile, and they took me over to the game."

Bill Hanzlik: "They couldn't plow the parking lot. They had half-tracks bringing in food to the dining halls. I remember students taking expeditions on sleds over to the liquor store and coming back with the goods."

Kelly Tripucka: "That was a shock. I just couldn't imagine it could snow that much in that short amount of time. They canceled everything, and looking outside, you just figured it never would stop. We knew we had a big game coming and we all wanted to play. We didn't know whether Maryland was going to be able to get in."

The Blizzard of 1978 was in full swing, and given the shutdown of just about everything else in South Bend, it was reasonable to believe the Maryland game would be a casualty. But as luck would have it, the South Bend airport opened long enough for the Maryland team to arrive. With NBC on the scene and ready to broadcast, it seemed the "Snow Bowl" would go on.

But how would they scare up a crowd?

Stan Wilcox: "The roads were so bad that nobody could drive. So they said anybody who could get to the game could get in free because they needed the stands filled for television."

Danny Nee: "We go out to warm up, and there were hundreds and hundreds of people coming across the snow—like ants just coming from all directions. The season ticket holders from Chicago and places couldn't get in. All the students had been locked in their dorms, and they wanted something to do.

"It was a whole different Notre Dame crowd. It was really wild. They were down behind Lefty's bench, they were down everywhere. It was a different, more blue-collar rooting crowd."

Bill Hanzlik: "It was a real fun time because it was a 'Notre Dame family' type thing. The students still got to the game. We still had a really nice crowd even though nobody could drive in."

With the A.C.C. rocking, the Irish and Terps battled in a close first half. Coming out of halftime, the university administration took a page from Phelps's book of psychological warfare to try and turn the tide in favor of the Irish.

Lou Somogyi: "I remember the teams coming out for the tip-off in the second half and the PA announcer, Jack Lloyd, saying, 'We have an announcement. Due to the weather conditions, classes at the university have been canceled for tomorrow.'

"The student body just went bonkers. They announced it just to get that momentum right away in the second half. The rest of the game was like a celebration because that's all they needed to hear. Notre Dame went on to win it by 69-54 and pretty much controlled the game from there on out."

Not to be outdone, Digger had some psychological tricks of his own up his sleeve. Butch Lee and top-ranked Marquette were in town a month later, and the coach wanted to be sure he had the team's attention after a bad first half against the Warriors. So he made a sartorial switch.

Stan Wilcox: "I remember going to the locker room and Digger doing the passionate speech. Then all of a sudden, he comes out with these green socks and tells us to put them on. I'm like, 'What the heck is this?' I guess our first response was thinking he was punishing us."

Danny Nee: "I thought they were the ugliest things in the nation. Digger loved them, and you know Digger would think that way. The shoes, the details of the socks, changes in uniform, change in the colors, wearing green or gold or blue—those were things that made Digger feel special. He respected tradition, and put the shamrock on it, wore the green."

Bill Hanzlik: "Digger always thought he was the greatest fashion consultant of all time. Like when he had the lime green uniforms. He always had a few gimmicks. And that was just him—to create some interest and show. It was good for Notre Dame basketball. Love it or hate it, it created some identity."

Tracy Jackson: "Some people took it very personally and thought, 'Oh gosh, I won't wear these on TV.' But I grew up looking at Notre Dame wearing green sneakers. I thought they were kind of cool.

"Digger knew when we were doing things like changing the jerseys and socks, it kept things in a lighter mood with these big games. It was a good move for us. It looked kind of funky at first, but it gave us an opportunity to have some fun."

With their feet clad in green and Bill Hanzlik turning up the defensive pressure, the Irish made the Warriors their latest top-ranked victim, 65-59. But the victory had a drawback. To the team's consternation, Phelps decided to stay with the lucky green socks for the rest of the season.

By tournament time, this Irish team was ready to achieve where prior versions had failed. Houston and Utah were dispatched in the first two rounds with neither fanfare nor problem, sending the Irish up against old rival DePaul, featuring Dave Corzine, Joe Ponsetto and, of course, Ray Meyer.

Meyer had won for the first time in the A.C.C. earlier that season by one point in overtime. This was DePaul's best chance at a Final Four since its 1943 team had gone, and his players really wanted to send Meyer back there. But on that cold day in Lawrence, Kansas, it was Phelps and Notre Dame who advanced with an 84-64 victory, giving Notre Dame its first Final Four berth.

Ray Meyer: "The trainer didn't show up to tape the kids, so they had to tape each other. You only had one hour to practice, and our kids came up to the floor one at a time because they were taping one another.

"We were playing three-on-three, and as the kids came up we'd add more. Randy Ramsey threw a low pass to Dave Corzine and dislocated Corzine's finger. They put a big splint on it. He still played, but he wasn't effective. It was like playing with one hand."

Kelly Tripucka: "We were in Kansas, in the middle of nowhere at Allen Fieldhouse, one game away from getting to the Final Four against our old rivals. I just never felt like we were going to lose that game.

"We played a very good ballgame. We figured out every defense they threw at us. We were able to rebound, we were able to score, we manhandled their guys, whether it was Corzine or Ponsetto or whoever."

Danny Nee: "It was a vicious, rough game. DePaul was hard-nosed, and we were inching along. No one wanted to talk about if we won the game, we were going to the Final Four. We just weren't talking about it. We would take the next game when it happened."

The team returned to South Bend to prepare for the trip to the Checkerdome in St. Louis and the attempt to become the first school to win the national championship in football and basketball in the same academic year.

Bill Hanzlik: "It was spring break, that was the unique thing about it. It was such a fun time because you were with your team and you didn't have to worry about books. You were jacked up about basketball, just going down and checking it out."

Tracy Jackson: "It was very exciting. Our fans, obviously, were very excited. The football team had won a national championship, so there was a lot of enthusiasm on campus. And it was really nice to be part of that as a freshman at Notre Dame."

Ed O'Rourke: "The University had X number of tickets—actually, it was more like the coaches having access to tickets. I can still see the assistant coaches working on who got what tickets in what place. Every so often the phone would ring, and it would be a new celebrity wanting tickets. So they'd have to move three people here and two people there."

Kelly Tripucka: "We were looking forward to playing Kentucky because we had played them in our typical battle at Freedom Hall, which was a lot of crap to begin with because that was not a neutral site. There were 15,000 people in Louisville and about 400 were for us. That's what they call neutral, at least in Kentucky. But everybody thought we were going to see them again in the Final Four.

"As it turned out, we both made it to the Final Four and we were in different brackets. We had to get through Duke and they had to get through Arkansas. But everybody was anticipating because of the big, big, team on Kentucky. It was almost two football teams going at it."

The dream matchup was not to be, however, as the Irish faltered in their Saturday semifinal against Duke.

Kelly Tripucka: "We breezed through, if you want to call it that, the first three games to get there. We didn't get much resistance. We felt in control. We played our best basketball leading up to the tournament and into the tournament. So there was no reason to think we weren't gong to defeat Duke as well. But it doesn't take much to get sidetracked, and we played a bad 20 minutes of basketball."

Duke, behind freshman Gene Banks and sophomore Mike Gminski, grabbed an early lead. But Notre Dame fought back, utilizing full-court pressure to force Blue Devil mistakes. With less than a minute left, the Irish had the ball down by only two and looking for the tie.

Duck Williams: "Our game plan early was to go inside. We tried it early in the first half, and the shots weren't falling for the big guys. I said to myself, 'Hey, this is my last shot at this.' The jump shots started going down, and next thing you know, we were back within two.

"On the last shot, I don't know if it was Tracy Jackson or Stan Wilcox who had the ball, but he passed it to me. I had all the confidence in the world that the shot was going to go down. I made the fake to get the defensive guy to move, and I took the shot. When it left my hand it felt good, but it went straight off the rim. But I always felt you have to have guts to take the shot."

Bill Hanzlik: "We were close. We were right there. That game with Duke was tight, and we had a chance to come back and tie it. Duck had an open 20-foot jump shot with Dave Batton wide open underneath the hoop for the lay-up, and he didn't see him and shot it. He missed. We had to foul and went from being down two to down four."

Two more Duke free throws sealed the victory, sending the Irish to the consolation game against Arkansas. They fared no better there, losing to

Sidney Moncrief and company on Ron Brewer's last-second shot. The two losses left a bad taste in the mouths of players who had been looking forward to making basketball history.

Danny Nee: "I hated playing in the consolation game. I knew we were in trouble because we were geared to win the national championship. And when we didn't do it, I thought the consolation was a waste of time. We played well and hard, but it was anticlimactic.

"I had never coached at a Final Four. Now when you lose, the coaches and players just hang out and enjoy the weekend. We had to try and avoid losing two, and then we lost at the final shot to Arkansas. We picked up two losses on what should have been the greatest weekend of our lives. It was like we were going through hell. I was humiliated, because we felt we had a great team. That hurt."

Bill Hanzlik: "I go back to one comment Digger made. Again, this isn't to blame him or anything. But Digger made a comment after the DePaul game like, 'You made the Final Four, and from here on out it's all gravy.' Meaning we've accomplished this great task, and anything else we do above it is great. But we were like, this is just the start. Forget that, we're focused on winning the whole thing. Not to say we weren't. But it sort of took the wind out of our sails a little bit on our effort and preparation."

Still, the team had achieved more than it dreamed possible at the season's start. The "Fab Five" recruiting class had three more bites at the apple. There was no reason to believe the Irish wouldn't be a Final Four fixture in seasons to come.

23

Magic
(1979)

Having tasted a Final Four, the new challenge for the Irish was to get back there and advance a little further than they had in 1978. Considering the feat had been achieved with a freshman-laden team, the chances of a repeat seemed good. Fan interest was at a peak, with Notre Dame freshmen forced to split season ticket packages to satisfy the student demand. With the talent the 1979 Irish featured, how could they not achieve at the highest level?

The question turned out to be more than rhetorical. Although they spent virtually the entire regular season ranked in the top three, the Irish didn't get out of their region in the tournament, falling in the Elite Eight to Michigan State and its renowned point guard, Magic Johnson.

Opinion differs on the reasons. One theory was Phelps had too much depth on the team, and trying to satisfy too many people with regard to playing time prevented the necessary chemistry from developing.

Bruce Flowers: "If you looked at our box scores from those days, you'd find everyone was playing 20 minutes a game. I'm sure Digger was getting phone calls from people asking why so-and-so wasn't playing, so he made substitutions based on even time for a 10-guy rotation. Unfortunately, that hurt our game, because it's hard to get into the flow when you're running back and forth to the bench so often.

"As a player, knowing you were only going to play 20 minutes a game, you went out there and played as hard as you could. That worked great defensively, and we were a good defensive team that year. Offensively, though, it was tougher, because with all the parts being plugged in and taken out, you really didn't know where the next guy was going and never got a feel for what the other players could do in a given situation."

Another theory was overconfidence. The players were discovering being the hunted was something very different from being the hunter.

Gil Salinas: "Some people thought we should have won championships for the next three years. Since we were the big team, other teams were coming for it, and emotionally we thought we were better than they were. And that's when people beat you: when you're overconfident."

The season's strong start belied its eventual finish. The first three opponents—Valparaiso, Rice, and Northwestern—were blown out in anticipation of No. 2 UCLA at Pauley Pavilion. The Irish were trying to become the first team to win there three years in a row, and they achieved that goal in dramatic fashion with an 81-78 win. That moved the Irish to No. 2, and when they subsequently traveled to Milwaukee to face Marquette, they had an opportunity to move up another notch. A fierce game against a strong rival took on even more importance.

Gil Salinas: "The whole team was excited. If it was a big game and a chance for us to shine, we were going to win. That's why these kids go to Notre Dame: those special moments you remember when you're watching television, whether it's football, basketball. . . . I mean, look what happened to UCLA with the winning streak. You just go into games like that knowing you're going to win."

Stan Wilcox: "I believe that was the game where I twisted my ankle. One of their players came down and stepped on my foot, which caused me to fall. So I went out of the game.

"We ended up winning, but what I remember is going off the court. I was either on crutches or somebody was helping me walk off after the game was over, and I was right behind Digger as we were going through the tunnel. All I can remember is how crazy their fans were. They were throwing things at us—popcorn, paper, whatever—as we were going through.

"And then I recall somebody running up to me as I'm hobbling off the court going through the tunnel, getting in my face and saying to me, 'I hope you die.' I'm thinking to myself, 'What?' All I got is a twisted ankle and they come running up to me and saying, 'I hope you die.' I recall all the things they were yelling at Digger and I'm thinking, 'Wow, these people are crazy, they really hate Digger,' and then all of a sudden someone runs up to me and says, 'I hope you die.' People are just crazy."

Crazy or not, Warriors fans went home disappointed after a 65-60 loss to the Irish, who regained the No. 1 ranking for the first time since 1974. This time, they managed to keep it for almost a month.

Kelly Tripucka: "I always thought it was fun. Obviously there's pressure with that, but that's what made competing so much fun. You didn't play top teams every single game, but it certainly made you prepared for those big games and the environment and the big crowds. You're playing in front of hostile crowds on the road and great crowds at home.

"There's nothing better than hearing the sound of silence when you go on the road. I always enjoyed that. That's part of competing. If you don't like playing against the best, then you're missing out on something. And for us, it was pretty much like that every single night. We prepared to play the best, and we knew we were considered one of the best. That's how we practiced and that's how we played the games."

One of those "best" games was against the North Carolina State Wolfpack. When the two teams met in Raleigh in February, the Irish were looking for the program's 1,100th victory while the Pack wanted to extend a nonconference winning streak that stretched back to 1968. The Irish prevailed, 53-52.

Tracy Jackson: "NC State and Maryland were very exciting games for me, having grown up on the East Coast and being surrounded by the ACC. So playing against those guys was just awesome for me. Some of the guys I played against in high school like Hawkeye Whitney and Derrick Wittenberg and Sidney Lowe. It was always exciting to play them.

"And it was interesting playing a conference school. You knew how much excitement they had in the A.C.C. But then again, we experienced that all over the country. We had UCLA, San Francisco. So that gave us the experience of playing against hostile crowds."

Kelly Tripucka: "That was a neat place to play—a fun old gym, a lot of history with their national championship, David Thompson, Jim Valvano, and people like that. We knew it was going to be a wild environment, and it was exactly what we pictured as far as the noise level and fans being right on top of you. But more than anything else, Digger won in that environment. It was another situation to be prepared for, and he said, 'I'll handle them, and you handle what's on the court.' He tried to take most of the so-called distractions away from us and put it on him. That's what he thrived on."

But all good things come to an end, and Notre Dame relinquished its hold on No. 1 four days after the triumph in Raleigh. Phelps wanted a fourth win in a row over UCLA and had the students chanting for a "Grand Slam." But in a sloppy game, the Irish fell to the Bruins 56-52.

Gil Salinas: "I remember being disappointed. Here we are at home, and somebody's coming into our yard and then has taken away our ball. It was very puzzling. It was not a good feeling. People were very quiet. In the dining halls, in the dorms, even walking home, the whole campus was quiet."

The team shrugged off the misfortune, winning its next five games. But something seemed different. The Irish didn't finish well, suffering consecutive four-point defeats at Final Four-bound DePaul and in the Pontiac Silverdome against old nemesis Michigan to close out the season.

Kelly Tripucka: "I don't think I'd ever use the phrase 'run out of gas' because we didn't play enough to ever run out of gas. I mean, it's not like a pro's schedule. DePaul was solid, and at Michigan we didn't play well. That might have been a different environment, playing at the Silverdome. We just didn't play well for whatever reason. No disrespect to Michigan, they had some solid players—Phil Hubbard, and people like that. But we were clearly a better team. We just didn't play well.

"Losing that many times is a little bit of a cause for panic if you're hot, and you've got to figure a way to get it back. You know you've got to practice a little harder and play a little better. You've got to get your confidence back."

The start of the tournament, however, gave the Irish little wiggle room for a confidence search. Even with a No. 1 seed in their region, the shakiness continued. They survived their opening-round game against Tennessee by six, and unheralded Toledo gave them a scare before succumbing by six in Indianapolis.

In the meantime, a bizarre situation was unfolding with the NCAA. Marc Kelly, a freshman walk-on for the Irish, had been an extra in the movie *Fast Break* during the summer before the season. Because he had been compensated for portraying a basketball player in the movie, the NCAA was considering whether Kelly was a professional and, as such, ineligible.

Marc Kelly: "There were a couple of media articles that went national on how a Notre Dame walk-on player was in this movie. I think an anti-Notre Dame fan read the article and turned it in to the NCAA. And the NCAA deemed it a rules violation.

"I was completely shocked when Digger told me after practice. I didn't make the travel squad that year, so the NCAA trip was going to be my reward for the whole year. He told me they had put me on probation and I couldn't dress with the team. And that kind of broke my heart.

"It was a pretty quick resolution. The NCAA had a conference call and I agreed to pay the money back I had earned. I can't remember how much it was—$500 or something. Once I paid it back to the movie company, they reinstated my eligibility. But it was too little, too late, because I missed the NCAA tournament."

Roger Valdiserri: "We had to abide by NCAA rules, but we thought it was really stupid. The fact they would prohibit him from doing that when he wasn't on scholarship seemed ridiculous. I mean, would they let an accounting major work in an accounting firm? It was directly related to his studies. It was like an internship."

Amid the confidence crisis and NCAA circus, Notre Dame and Michigan State took the floor in Market Square Arena in Indianapolis with a trip to the

Final Four at stake. Perhaps feeling snubbed by the selection committee that gave the Irish the top regional seed in their stead, the Spartans took the floor with a special sense of purpose and blitzed Notre Dame from the opening tip.

Danny Nee: "I felt that was really the game for the national championship, because we felt we were better than Indiana State or whoever else got in there. We felt if we could get by Michigan State, we were the big dog rolling back in.

"But I don't remember the game being close. They jumped over us. Jud Heathcote was a hard, crusty old coach, and these guys were playing their asses off. They knew what was at stake."

Gil Salinas: "They were on fire. They just knew they were going to beat us, and they did. I don't know if we were intimidated with how they played, how their attitudes were, but they had the same feelings we had with DePaul—knowing they were not going to lose."

Stan Wilcox: "I recall that being the game that made the alley-oop dunk kind of famous, because they must have had about three or four of those on us. Those were being used as an advertisement following each game, because when I came home that summer I recall my friends saying, 'Hey I saw you on a commercial being dunked on.'

"I remember Magic Johnson on a fast break. I'm the only guard back, and here's this 6-foot 9-inch guy dribbling down. I'm thinking I'm going to fake him and steal this ball, so I give a jab fake and go for the ball. Next thing I know, he's done some kind of move and flipped the ball, and I'm like, 'Where in the world is he flipping this ball to?' I turn around, and I see Greg Kelser's shorts going past my face, and he grabs the ball and dunks it."

Kelly Tripucka: "It hurt even the way we started because they got the tip and Kelser got a dunk and everybody thought we were done then. But we fought our way back into it. I don't think we shot the ball real well, and Michigan State was playing as well as they could. Maybe if they weren't as hot as they were, we might have had a chance to beat them, and we certainly weren't intimidated by them or thought they were better than us. They were just playing a little bit better than we were at the time, and we didn't play a great game, but they had something to do with that.

"When you look at it, they ended up beating Indiana State, and we would have probably done the same thing. Man, we would have changed history, because it wouldn't have been any Larry Bird and Magic. It would have been Larry Bird and us. It's a stupid comment in a way, but as far as I'm concerned there's no way we wouldn't have handled Larry Bird and his team. We were just too strong. We would have won it."

Games aren't won on thoughts, though, and the Irish were left to contemplate what might have been during the off-season as the Spartans went on to win the national championship. With only Flowers and Laimbeer to replace on the roster, continued success was not out of the question. Perhaps the team could regain the confidence and swagger from the start of that season. Perhaps the Irish could catch lightning in a bottle come tournament time.

Perhaps.

24

94 Feet from Glory
(1980–1981)

Tripucka and his cohorts were seasoned juniors in 1980, and the senior leadership of the team was strong with Bill Hanzlik and Rich Branning. But it would be the play of freshman John Paxson that would attract the early-season headlines for the Irish.

Gary Brokaw: "Pax was one of my favorites. I think I gave Dwight Clay the name 'Iceman,' but I know I gave John Paxson the name 'The General' just because he was in charge. My wife, who was in graduate school at the time, did a documentary on basketball, and Pax did a nice video shoot for her. And I talked to my wife and I said, 'You know what? He's The General.' Even now if I see him I call him The General. That's how special he was. He was a great college player. Mr. Clutch."

Kelly Tripucka: "John ended up finding his niche in the pros, but he was a better player and had more responsibility at the college level. John was just a solid, fundamental ballplayer, much like his brother Jimmy. Jimmy may have been a little bit more of a scorer, but John came in with a scorer's mentality from high school and he was asked to do a little bit more.

"John played his role very well. He was a heck of a nice guy. He's very fundamentally sound. John knew the game of basketball and loved to play. He got to know us on offense, knew who could score, who needed the ball in certain spots."

Tim Andree: "John came to Notre Dame as an 18-year-old, but he had a 35- or 45-year-old's mentality. He was very mature. He knew who he was, shunned the spotlight. As he became more successful, he became more retiring—he didn't want to bask in the attention he could have had. People who knew him in high school as I did say he hasn't changed one bit throughout all of it. Even now after three world championships and winning one of them with a last-second shot, he's still the same guy."

It didn't take long for Paxson's feet to be held to the fire. Bill Hanzlik missed the early part of the season with a dislocated finger, and Paxson was called on to help fill the void. So in the fifth game of the season, it was a freshman instead of a senior at the line against UCLA sealing a victory with clutch free throws.

John Paxson: "The one thing I remember is Orlando Woolridge coming up to me and starting to say something. And I just said, 'Get away. I don't want you to say anything. Just get away.' I didn't need somebody in my ear. So he left, and that was fine. Nobody else came out. Those are the types of moments where you just concentrate on what you are doing.

"I don't remember being nervous. I just remember getting up there to knock them in. But the greatest thing about that is it was so early in my time there, and all of a sudden I'm in this big game.

"I have a friend who still works for the university and is the godfather of my two kids. I didn't know him at the time, but he says he remembers sitting up in the stands and there was a woman right next to him who said, 'If he makes these free throws, he can be a great player. But if he misses these, he will probably never play here again.' So that's kind of the impact it had."

Paxson wasn't the only player coming through in the clutch that season. Tracy Jackson filled that role against Maryland and Villanova, rescuing the team with last-second shots after the Irish had blown big leads. Orlando Woolridge scored 13 points in two minutes to hold off an upset bid by

Fordham in Madison Square Garden. And then against undefeated and top-ranked DePaul in the A.C.C. in late February, it all came together.

Tim Andree: "The crowd showed up about a half-hour before we even started warming up. I remember coming out to warm up and the place was nearly full with the crowd chanting '25 and 1.' For a freshman on that team, it was the most exciting thing to see—how the Notre Dame sixth man could come in and be part of a storied game like that. Digger walked out before-hand and he wouldn't let the team come out. He kept whipping the crowd up. When we ran out, the wall of noise was like nothing I had ever experienced in my life.

"The thing that was great about Notre Dame was you were going to school with such great people. The guys on the team were just tremendous men. I remember being upset before that game because I was playing on the blue squad in practice and I knew I wasn't going to get much playing time. I had said to Gil Salinas before that game that maybe coming to Notre Dame was a mistake and that I couldn't remember why I'd come there. In the warm-up, with the place going crazy and things very exciting, Gil ran by me and yelled in my ear, 'This is why you're here.'"

Gary Grassey: "It was just one of those moments in that time frame that Digger pointed to. The hype was there, along with the national media. DePaul was undefeated and No. 1. They had Mark Aguirre, Terry Cummings, Skip Dillard, Clyde Bradshaw—an unbelievable team. And we had a fantastic team.

"I've never been to a louder game in the A.C.C. The place was full, and it was rocking. I seem to remember it was a weeknight. And I remember that the students never sat down. We were as hostile as any crowd I ever saw at a Notre Dame basketball game. Everybody emptied out the rolls of toilet paper from the bathrooms of the dorms, and it was raining down from the stands."

Bill Hanzlik: "Rich and Tracy had big shots in that game. It was nip and tuck the whole way. That was probably the highlight of our year, because they had some horses. Big-booty Mark Aguirre was waddling down to that post, and he was tough."

With the crowd going crazy, Jackson and Woolridge reprised their clutch-player roles with free throws—the former's two sending the game into its first overtime and the latter's two with 19 seconds left in the second overtime providing the winning margin. The Blue Demons left with their first defeat, and the Irish had another No. 1 notch on the belt.

It's possible, however, that the team peaked with that win, because everything fell apart against Missouri in the NCAA Tournament.

Danny Nee: "Missouri had to play a play-in game to get in. So they came on Thursday and played, and we had to play them on Saturday. I coached against Norm Stewart some 14 years in the Big Eight conference. He had a bull's eye for us. Our kids didn't think anything special of them. And we were just flat as a pancake."

Kelly Tripucka: "That was kind of depressing, because we were not supposed to lose in that round. We certainly had expectations, particularly after going to the Final Four and then losing in the regional final. We were expecting to get right back and at least have an opportunity to go back to the Final Four. We certainly thought we had enough talent to get back to where we should be."

John Paxson: "They had a talented team. They had guys who would go on to play significant time in the NBA, like Steve Stipanovich and Larry Drew, and they also had Ricky Frazier. But the guy who killed us was a guy named Mark Dressler, who was really not a known guy and not an athlete, and he had 32.

"I remember going in the locker room after that game in Lincoln, Nebraska, and looking at Hanzlik and Rich Branning and knowing that their careers and their days at Notre Dame were over. I remember feeling real bad for them because none of us wanted them to go out that way. Especially the way they played the two years before. And that was really a disappointment."

Stung by their early exit in 1980, the Fighting Irish went into 1981 determined not to relive that disappointment. The coaching staff had added McDonald's All-American Joe Kleine to an already potent lineup. Members of the great recruiting class of 1978 were now seniors at the top of their game, and this would be their last chance for postseason glory.

After a season-opening loss to UCLA at Pauley Pavilion—Notre Dame's first loss there since the 1976 season—the Irish roared into a nine-game winning streak that included a win at home against an Indiana team that would go on to win the national title.

Tracy Jackson: "That game really solidified just how good John Paxson was, because he did an excellent defensive job on Isiah Thomas. It was a great victory because they went on to win the national championship. Indiana always had tough players, and they were going to come ready to play."

Gary Grassey: "I remember that being John Paxson's breakout game. He'd come on to the scene the year before, early in the season when we beat UCLA. But he went toe-to-toe with Isiah Thomas and just played a tremendous game.

"That was a real early indicator that the team could be special, because he was filling the role that Branning and Hanzlik had the year before. Pax really stepped in early on and made a statement the way he played against Indiana. He had 18 points that night and was all over the floor."

Two weeks later, Notre Dame found itself in Louisville for the annual "neutral-court" game with Kentucky, then ranked No. 1 in the polls and featuring Mel Turpin and Sam Bowie. Thirty points from Tripucka meant his class wouldn't leave Notre Dame without a win over the Wildcats.

Kelly Tripucka: "The Kentucky game was the biggest win. Playing at that stupid neutral site and going down there and losing close games every year. . . . I just hated Kentucky. And I said, 'We've got to win. We can't go 0-for-4 against this team. I'm just sick of it.' Having lost down there three times, there was no way we were losing again. It was certainly one of the more gratifying, satisfying wins of my Notre Dame career just because we beat Kentucky and we were able to shut up all of those Wildcat bluegrass fans."

Tracy Jackson: "Kentucky was always a big nemesis of ours. We would go down there and play them on a neutral court in Lexington. After we got to be seniors, I remember talking with Orlando Woolridge and saying, 'We've got to beat these guys this year. We lost to them three years previously.'

"And we were just ready for them. The crowd was very hostile; it's one of the toughest places to play in. But it was probably one of the most gratifying victories I experienced at Notre Dame to beat them."

Having weathered a sweep by UCLA and an upset loss at San Francisco, the Irish got their second shot of the season at a top-ranked team when they traveled to the Rosemont Horizon in the northwest suburbs of Chicago to take on Ralph Sampson and Virginia.

Gil Salinas: "I was Ralph Sampson all week long. I was taking a lot of shots in practice like the jumpers Ralph did. As a matter of fact, one of the assistants got hold of a broomstick so I could be as tall as he was and have the same reach."

Kelly Tripucka: "With Ralph Sampson, Jeff Lamp, and Lee Raker, they were a great team. But we had a week to prepare. Digger devised a couple of junk defenses. We had every door covered. There wasn't anything they could do that we didn't know what we were going to do right back."

Tim Andree: "The Ralph Sampson game was one of the best games Digger ever coached. The game plan came together. We were having Orlando front Ralph Sampson and I was guarding Craig Robinson, their power forward. Digger told me to completely ignore him and play behind Sampson. We left Robinson open for 10-footers the entire day, and the guy couldn't knock it down. We held Ralph to 10 points."

John Paxson: "It was tied at every two-point interval up until around 32. There was never a swing of more than two points probably the whole first half.

"Again, the great thing about being at Notre Dame was playing those types of games. And the Virginia game was really memorable from how tight it was. And then Orlando made that shot to end the game."

Tim Andree: "At the end of the game, Tripucka took the ball out of bounds, and it was a broken play. We were trying to set a screen to get the ball to Paxson or Tracy Jackson for an open 15-footer, and the ball was deflected underneath. It rolled out to the right, and Orlando got to the ball. It was an off-balance, ugly shot that went off the board and in.

"The place just went crazy. It was such a mob scene. The crowd had rushed the floor, and we had to get all the way in to where the locker rooms were upstairs. There was a little balcony where you could see back over the floor. I remember getting to the top of that and seeing a wave of people partying and going crazy.

"We all got in the locker room, and the door closed, and everybody was just in there panting. It was a silent locker room for about two minutes.

Everybody was just kind of stunned. Digger was always good after the games and had the right words for stuff, and it became more celebratory, but I'll never forget the two minutes of everyone just sitting there smiling and staring at one another completely out of breath."

That win sent the Irish into the postseason riding high. Their first-round NCAA opponent, James Madison, was dispatched 54-45. A third chance against UCLA loomed in the next round, with Irish victim Virginia the likely final obstacle to the Final Four. And when Brigham Young upset UCLA, Notre Dame seemed to have a clear path.

The BYU game started well for the Irish. They had a 10-point lead at the half and added to it early in the second half. But with 11 minutes left, Phelps made a decision he would come to regret.

Kelly Tripucka: "Danny Ainge was the only guy on that team. We should have blown out BYU by 20 to begin with. In fact, we had them in that situation. They were slow, and we were just burying them.

"But we changed from pouring it on. We decided to go slow-down. We buried our guards, Paxson and Tracy Jackson, and we had our big guys handling the ball outside. For whatever reason, Digger thought we'd control the game.

"But then we started to turn the ball over, and that's what let them back into the game. We could have run up and down and attacked them and put the game out of reach. But slowly they got back in and we got behind."

John Paxson: "We were up by 12 or 14 with about 10 minutes to go. And I still to this day feel that had there been a shot clock, we never would have lost that game. But Digger decided to hold the ball and we didn't take care of it. All of a sudden we went from being an attacking, aggressive team to one playing defensive on the offensive end of the court. That really hurt us. We lost our lead and our composure."

Over the final 10 minutes, the Cougars whittled away at the Irish advantage, finally overcoming it and taking the lead in the waning moments. But Tripucka drained a jumper while falling out of bounds to give the Irish a one-point lead with eight seconds left. As BYU called timeout, all the Irish had to do now was play solid defense for those eight seconds against BYU's one-man team.

Kelly Tripucka: "We were up one, and they had to go the length of the court. Digger was trying to set something up as the buzzer rang for us to come back on the court. And all I remember is everybody looking at each other. Nobody knew what we were supposed to be doing, and that was a scary thought. I think he was trying to set up a press, but it was kind of a fake press. And that's what confused everybody."

Tim Andree: "Nobody knew what Digger had said in the huddle coming out of the timeout, but I heard him call a 2-2-1 zone press. We hadn't practiced it. We were all saying, 'What the hell are we in?' because none of us knew what Digger had called."

John Paxson: "I was the first line of defense, and I was trying to make him (Ainge) catch the ball going toward our basket. I accomplished that to some degree. But I let him get an angle where he caught it on a running start instead of having to stop, catch, and turn. I was the first guy he got by."

Tom Sluby: "We were trying to deny him the ball, but he got the ball inbounds and he went over to the right sideline. I was able to get over there and cut him off. John was trying to catch up so we could trap him in there, and he spun back around that, got across halfcourt, and went over to the other sideline. I happened to make it over to that sideline, too. Digger's thing back then was to make sure I had my foot on the sideline, so I had my foot there and we tried to get a trap on over there again. But he did the same thing where he spun back into the middle of the court."

Kelly Tripucka: "Now he's heading up the floor. He's behind two guys, and he crosses over in front. You can't foul him because he's a good free-throw shooter and you don't want to put him on the line.

"As he crossed halfcourt, he had beaten four of us. Our last line of defense was Orlando. Not to put it on O—certainly he'd gone by all the rest of us. But Orlando waited for him. Instead of coming out to meet him, he stood underneath the basket, figuring he was going to block his shot. And Orlando was too far under when Ainge laid it up. It looked like Orlando got his hand caught in the net."

Pete Gillen: "Orlando, if he was healthy, could have blocked it. But he had a deep thigh bruise, so he couldn't really explode like he usually could."

Stan Wilcox: "I remember seeing Orlando waiting under the basket as Ainge was coming at him. Orlando was going to do his powerful leap and try to swat it, which he would normally do. But Ainge got the ball up just beyond Orlando's fingertips, and the ball went straight through."

Just like that, Notre Dame's season was over.

Tom Sluby: "What really ticked me off was that Paxson had pretty much shut Ainge down the whole game. John had such a tremendous defensive game. I remember being so upset for him at the end—he had shut him out, but Ainge still had the big moment."

Kelly Tripucka: "It's pretty silly to think, but it never should have happened. We certainly should have been better prepared. If we didn't know, we should have taken a timeout. It seemed like everybody was so excited after my shot that we didn't get ourselves prepared to play. And what you don't think should have happened or could have happened, happened. It was the worst feeling in the world. That's how my college career ended."

The team that was supposed to win it all had not. And whether people realized it at that time, a corner had been turned in Irish basketball fortunes.

Gary Grassey: "When you think about what happened to the program after that—the back half of Digger's career—that game was the last real high point for a very long time. The Virginia game marked the last truly great team of the program, where we were playing with the best and when we had a collection of talent that could beat the best team in the country.

"In retrospect, I look at that as a marker. ND basketball had been beating No. 1 teams and cranking out NCAA tournament teams for eight or nine years. You didn't think it was going to stop."

Lou Somogyi: "I've always divided the Digger Phelps era into two 10-year increments: the first 10, which ended with that Danny Ainge game, where this was one of the top-10 programs in the country, and then the next 10 where the slide began. Digger had created the monster, but it had to be fed now. And from there on it was difficult."

The
Digger Phelps
Years

Part II—
The Second 10

(1982–1991)

25

There and Back Again
(1982–1984)

The Irish had finished the 1970s on a roll. Seven of the eight seasons between 1973 and 1981 ended with 20 wins or more, and the eighth just missed at 19. The Irish made the NCAA Tournament in all eight seasons and won at least one tournament game seven times. Seven players received some kind of All-America mention, six were first-found NBA draft choices, and 16 played professional basketball.

But those stats quickly became a distant memory. Over the next three seasons the Irish would not reach 20 regular-season wins or make the NCAA Tournament.

What caused things to go south so quickly? According to observers, the answer was recruiting and injuries.

Lou Somogyi: "The class that really did Digger in more than any was the 1980 recruiting haul. That was such a pivotal year for recruiting because Tripucka, Woolridge, and Jackson were entering their senior year and you had to get the heirs apparent ready. And Digger did a fantastic job. He got his three McDonald's All-Americans: Joe Kleine from Missouri, Tom Sluby from the Washington, D.C., area, and Barry Spencer, from Detroit. But Joe Kleine transferred after his freshman year. Tom Sluby and Barry Spencer both became academically ineligible and had other issues during their careers. Sluby didn't really come to the forefront until his senior year."

Gary Grassey covered the Irish for the student newspaper *The Observer* and walked on to the team for the 1982 season.

Gary Grassey: "Mike Mitchell was the only scholarship player in my class. Mike had three major knee surgeries that combined to dramatically limit his career on the court. He was a fantastic high school player. Ultimately, he captained the 1981–1982 team and despite constant pain and limited mobility, played every game. Given his physical limitations, Mitch's performance that season was remarkable. But the fact that much of his talent was adversely affected by the injuries certainly influenced the 1981–1982 results and perceptions about recruiting."

The 1982 season wasn't supposed to be a bad one. Even with the departure of Tripucka and his class, the Irish had the talent to be competitive, at least on paper. But the quality diminished a bit when Joe Kleine announced he was going to transfer to Arkansas.

Gary Grassey: "Joe Kleine was from the smallest town on the planet in Missouri. And in some ways, I don't know if he ever really felt comfortable at Notre Dame. That was more suspicion on my side—I'd interviewed him a bunch of times and written a couple of features about him. Nice kid, but he just seemed to be a fish out of water. It was more than just the prospect of sharing time with Tim Andree or playing for Digger—who, right or wrong, had acquired a rep for not having a system that would effectively enable post players to develop and grow."

John Paxson: "Joe and I were friends. I like to think I had a part in him wanting to come there. But as the year went on and the more we talked, I could tell he wasn't real happy. I knew his dad wasn't crazy about Digger. It just kept going on and on, and he didn't feel he was going to develop as a center the way he wanted to. And you can't knock somebody for that. If I didn't feel like I would have played, I wouldn't want somebody to try to make me stay.

"But that as much as anything killed our program. That was the beginning of the end. When you look at it, we had Tripucka, Woolridge, Tracy

Jackson, Salinas, and Wilcox, who were just good solid guys. We lost them, and then we lost Joe Kleine at the same time, and we brought in two guards, Dan Duff and Ron Rowan to replace those players. It was brutal."

"Brutal" describes the situation nicely. The Irish, who started the season ranked in the top 20, started off 2-9 with losses at home to Murray State and Northern Illinois. The already shaky personnel situation got worse when Tom Sluby became an academic casualty in the second semester.

Tom Sluby: "I was dealing with some personal problems. I was eligible by NCAA standards, but I wasn't eligible by Notre Dame's standards. That was a very important stage in my life at least because it taught me a few lessons. I had to make sure I was taking care of what I was supposed to be taking care of, even though I had some difficulties and some challenges. At the same time I had the support of Digger to try to turn myself around and get back where I could be productive both in the classroom and on the court."

The coaching staff tried to make the best of what was becoming a bad situation.

Gary Brokaw: "We had gone through some tough times when I was playing. As coaches, we felt the only way to get out of this tough time was to out-work people. So we wanted to out-work people in recruiting, in game preparation and in developing the skills of our players."

Tim Andree: "Digger started trying everything. He had all sorts of gimmicks. We were in New York, and he had us go see *Chariots of Fire*. There was a line in the movie that said, 'if you don't run, you can't win,' so Digger's big message was 'if you don't play, you can't win.' Nobody knew what the hell he was trying to tell us.

"Then he played the movie *Ocean's 11* in one of the team meetings, and he started calling us the 'Rat Pack.' I guess his message was we were all a bunch of misfits and we weren't all that good, but if we banded together with John Paxson as our Frank Sinatra, somehow we could turn it around."

No game better illustrates the frustrations of that season than the one against Kentucky. Knowing his team was overmatched against the third-ranked Wildcats, Phelps decided on a strategy to level the playing field.

Tom Sluby: "We didn't think we could match up with them man-to-man. They were a very deep team, and Digger thought the best way for us to be competitive and pull that game out was to stall."

Gary Grassey: "The whole deal was to freeze the ball. There was no shot clock. It was just Rowan and Mitchell and Paxson tossing the ball around the outside and playing keep-away. Every once in a while, Pax would get a clear shot or Rowan would get a clear shot and score. And they played great team defense. Kentucky was very frustrated by the zone, and they didn't get second shots when they missed. We just hung in the game.

"Kentucky fans were coming down behind the bench and screaming at Phelps—I mean, the worst stuff you could possibly scream at a human being. The cops and the security were not dragging these people away. And they were just spewing this garbage at Phelps—way over the top for guys used to listening to some pretty nasty stuff. But Phelps was immune to it."

Marc Kelly: "I thought it was a brilliant game plan because they had so much more personnel than we did. We didn't match up with them at all. So Digger devised a way he thought we could win, and he almost pulled it off. But it was interesting. Those Kentucky fans were yelling and screaming every curse word they could at Notre Dame. They weren't happy with the Irish."

John Paxson: "That was one of the most embarrassing games we played. It was one of those games where you were playing and you were thinking, 'It shouldn't be like this.' Digger's perspective was probably right, because we took it into overtime. But I remember thinking to myself, 'This is not why I came to Notre Dame, to play this type of game.' It was not a real pleasant experience."

Even the 10-17 record—Phelps's second sub-.500 season at Notre Dame—didn't dampen the enthusiasm or camaraderie of the team.

Gary Grassey: "Preparing for UCLA, we were down to six scholarship players and three walk-ons who were healthy enough to travel and dress for the game. UCLA had already pounded us by 26 points on national TV at the A.C.C. a few weeks earlier.

"Digger invited Keith Penrod, a long-time friend of ND's athletic programs, to speak to the team in the locker room before tip-off. Keith has cerebral palsy, and he was a familiar face near the bench where he usually sat in his wheelchair. I don't know whether Keith had ever been to an ND road game before or since, but Digger wanted him at UCLA to offer a few words.

"Keith got up in front of the team and offered a motivational pitch about overcoming adversity and what ND meant to him that could just as easily have come from the mouths of Ara or Lou Holtz. Keith promised if we beat UCLA, at our next practice, he would walk from one end of the court to the other without using his wheelchair for support.

"The outcome was in doubt until the final seconds, but we lost by a point or two. We had clearly made some dramatic improvements after the 2-9 start. And the next day Keith walked the length of the court."

Having been caught short in 1982, Phelps vowed it wouldn't happen again. So for 1983, he brought in a strong class of five freshmen he hoped would be able to step up quickly: Ken Barlow, Tim Kempton, Jim Dolan, Joseph Price, and Jo-Jo Buchanan.

Pete Gillen: "We liked Kenny Barlow for his size. Indianapolis Cathedral, his high school, had some Notre Dame roots. So we thought we had a shot with him. Kempton and Dolan, we had seen the previous years. We wanted to get some big guys. Jo-Jo Buchanan was a good solid player from Seattle. And then we had Joe Price, from Marion, who was a good player, too."

John Paxson: "They were competitive kids, and you could tell they wanted to be good. Jim Dolan became my roommate on the road, and he and I became good friends. I enjoyed being around that class. They were a lot of fun. I never really established much of a relationship with the two guys who came in my junior year, and Ron Rowan ended up leaving anyway. So this class made it fun for me."

Phelps wasted no time getting the freshmen involved. Kempton, Price, and Barlow were in the starting lineup in their first game against Stonehill. The results were predictable for a lineup of inexperienced players, but the learning experience was to pay dividends later.

Ken Barlow: "We all came in under the impression we were going to be able to contribute right away. We developed a bond and we kind of understood this could be a big class and we were there to make an impact. Digger told us that when he was recruiting all of us individually—we'd come in and play right away. So we felt if we could get in and get the experience early it would carry over in the next few years."

Tim Kempton: "The first week we played Indiana, Kentucky and UCLA. UCLA had Rod Foster and that crew, Kentucky had Mel Turpin and Charles Hurt, and Indiana had Ted Kitchell and Randy Wittman. We went right into the fire and got thumped in all three games, but that's why you go to Notre Dame—you want to play that kind of schedule."

Thanks to the freshmen and a schedule that could generously be described as less arduous than the norm, the Irish finished the season 19-9 and picked up a 43-42 win against eventual national champion North Carolina State in Raleigh.

Ken Barlow: "We were playing at NC State in my freshman year, and the score was tied or they were up one or something. It was one of those games where we had run over these situations a thousand times. Out of my four years at Notre Dame, the fans at NC State in that fieldhouse they played in were as loud as I had ever heard. That's the only time I've ever been in an arena where I really couldn't hear.

"We were going back on the court, and I walked up to John and I said, 'Pax, I didn't hear anything Digger said. What am I supposed to do?' And he was like, 'Get out of the way, I'm shooting.' I don't know if he remembers that, but he got the ball, he shot it, he made it. That same year, NC State won the national championship."

But all that wasn't enough for the NCAA selection committee.

Tim Andree: "We were ripped off. I was so disappointed. They took Marquette, which had the same or a similar record, and we had beaten Marquette at Marquette. I was very upset when I found out we didn't get it. I never understood that decision."

John Paxson: "This still gets me to this day: My last year was when the conferences were experimenting with a three-point line and a shot clock. Every time we would play, we would have the option of using them or not. Digger always chose not to play with it because his logic was, come NCAA tournament time, there would be no three-point and shot clock, so we would be more prepared than anybody else.

"Well, we didn't get into the NCAA tournament. We got into the NIT with a 30-second shot clock and a red, white, and blue ball. I tried to tell myself this was OK—we got the NIT, and that was cool. But we hadn't approached it the right way. It was a little anticlimactic."

The NIT invitation wasn't quite what the players expected, but they tried to make the most of it. One problem, however, was they wouldn't be playing their opening game at home.

Pete Gillen: "I don't really remember what happened on that one. I know they told us we would only be able to play two home games. But that was not true: some teams played three home games. I think Digger decided to play the first one away, and then hopefully get the next two at home. So it was just Digger looking ahead and saying, 'Hey, let's play the first one away. We can beat Northwestern.'"

Unfortunately, no one told the Wildcats.

Joseph Price: "It was St. Patrick's Day, and we were in Chicago. It was kind of bizarre. We obviously wanted to win, but I guess I could say we just weren't focused like we should have been. It was pretty difficult—with 'lucky charms' and St. Patrick's Day and the color green, you are supposed to be winners."

Tim Andree: "They were fired up to be playing against Notre Dame. They certainly weren't the powerhouse of the Big Ten, but they came out incredibly fired up to play us, while we were thinking we were going to take care of Northwestern and move on. It was during spring break, so there were few students and fans there."

John Paxson: "We played a good first half, but in the second half I played bad. I shot really poorly. I remember looking at that red, white, and blue ball as it left my hands and watching the ball rather than watching and concentrating on the rim. But again, we weren't a real up-and-down team. We were always a ball control team under Digger. So a 30-second shot clock was not what we had prepared for."

The 71-57 loss sent the Irish home disappointed but hopeful that they had something to build on in 1984, provided the loss of Paxson could be overcome.

The team struggled to find a rhythm as it opened 7-5, including an overtime loss at Northwestern. Phelps juggled a number of starting lineups trying to find the right combination. But over the Christmas break, two things happened to reverse the team's fortunes. The first was a renewed effort at leadership by Irish captain Tom Sluby.

Tom Sluby: "I was at home for Christmas break and I got a couple of phone calls from Gary Brokaw and Digger, and we discussed my role. They both were very clear that I needed to be a little more assertive and they needed more leadership from me. So I tried to get myself prepared in the short time before I got back to do those things. And when I came back, I felt like I had even more support to be aggressive out on the court. I had become more comfortable in my role as a captain, and those things helped us push forward."

The other was the availability of guard Joe Howard, newly available from his football duties. Howard arrived just in time to help the Irish to a season-saving win at Oregon.

Ken Barlow: "Joe Howard was coming straight from the Liberty Bowl to play Oregon. He showed up and he never missed a beat. He came in and was a leader and probably did more than anyone really expected of him to do. He came out at the Oregon game and solidified our backcourt. He carried us through the rest of the season."

Pete Gillen: "He was a gutsy little guy. He was quick, had no fear, played good defense, and helped us win some games. He could score a little bit. He gave us some toughness. He was a big plus for us. He really helped us have a jolt."

The 66-54 victory over Oregon sparked a seven-game winning streak, and after a 52-47 win over No. 5 Maryland, the Irish sat at 14-5 and seemed positioned for the NCAA bid that had eluded them the previous season.

But it wasn't to be. Although he was willing to muscle through the pain, Tim Kempton was suffering from stress fractures in his lower legs and missed the remainder of the regular season. Without their starting big man, the Irish lost six of their last nine to finish out of the running for the NCAA.

Once again the NIT came calling. And with Kempton back in the lineup, the Irish put a postseason run together that got them to the championship game, where they fell to Michigan and Antoine Joubert by 20.

Tom Sluby: "We didn't appreciate getting snubbed two years in a row. But we had freshmen who matured a lot because they had a lot of playing time. We didn't do poorly that year. We thought we just played well enough to be there, and we were disappointed in not making it. And we wanted to go, as any team does, into the NIT and show the selection group they made the wrong choice."

Ken Barlow: "Michael Adams was the point guard at Boston College. Digger came in the locker room and said some stuff that Michael Adams was saying. I can't remember any direct quotes, but he was saying things—stuff you really shouldn't say to give the other team fuel to come out and play. He had probably 20 quotes from Michael Adams. And we ran Boston College right into the ground up in Massachusetts."

Tim Kempton: "We played very well. We had improved on our freshman year and had beaten some quality people. We definitely deserved the NCAA bid. I guess going to the NIT finals was an example of that. Michigan thought the same thing—they had Antoine Joubert and Tim McCormick, and had a very good team also. They could have been in the NCAAs, too. We thought we represented ourselves well going to the Finals."

But the NIT wouldn't do the next season. Having pulled out of the post-1981 dive, the Irish were itching to prove they could achieve NCAA success once again. All they needed was one special player to help get them there.

26

King David
(1985–1986)

Regardless of how people felt about Phelps's recruiting in the years following Kelly Tripucka's class, the success of his campaign in 1984 was undeniable. He landed Parade All-American Matt Beeuwsaert. Yugoslavian star Drazen Petrovic signed a letter of intent to play at Notre Dame before deciding to remain in Europe. And to complete the trifecta, he brought in a point guard from Jersey City who he believed could lead the Irish back to the Final Four.

Gary Brokaw: "David Rivers was dominant, amazing. He was the best ballhandler I ever saw. The gym they practiced at in Jersey City was such a small place, and he was still dominant there. He had the ability to make others better. And he was ahead of his time with some of the ballhandling things he was capable of doing at the speed he could do it."

Pete Gillen: "I knew Bob Hurley, his coach at St. Anthony's in Jersey, and he told me about him. I went to see him as a junior and we followed him through the summer.

"It was a war to get him. NC State, who was the defending national champ, was after him. Boston College, Villanova, Seton Hall, a couple of others—it was a recruiting war. And Bob Hurley was great in being fair with us. He didn't push him anywhere. But he gave us a chance."

Ken Barlow: "If you are already playing, you have the young guys coming in and you're hearing the hype from the coaches or from the media or whatever, you're thinking, 'He has to show me.' But when Dave came in, he was impressive right off. We used to play pickup games up at the Rock before the season started. His talent was his ability to control the ball. We knew right away when we saw him play live, he was real good."

Lou Somogyi: "Notre Dame hadn't seen anyone like this. Most of the point guards were efficient, consistent, methodical type guys, more efficient than spectacular. Even John Paxson wasn't going to overwhelm you with incredible quickness. Then you had David Rivers coming in . . . a different caliber of point guard."

The hype surrounding Rivers's arrival was intense. Jo-Jo Buchanan, perhaps seeing the writing on the wall, decided to transfer to the University of California at Irvine.

Ken Barlow: "My whole sophomore year, we probably heard more about David Rivers than we heard about anybody on the current roster. I remember Scotty Hicks making a move in the open court—he went between his legs and behind his back around a guy, then made a no-look pass to Donald Royal for a really nice dunk. We were watching game films, and Digger was saying, 'David Rivers does this every play.' I don't think it was anything to take away from Scotty's play, but it would let you know how really high he was on David.

"Jo-Jo was my roommate my freshman year. He and John Paxson were sharing the backcourt, so he was playing a lot. But Digger had recruited Dave and was really, really high on him."

Tim Kempton: "It was one of those personality things. Digger is a very rough, aggressive, caustic kind of coach. He never really coddled anybody; he laid it on the line. That didn't sit well with Jo-Jo. He needed more of a pat-on-the-back-hey-you're-doing-great-we-need-you kind of guy. And Digger wasn't going to change for anybody."

Rivers wasted no time getting started in 1985. He scored 23 points against 11th-ranked Indiana and outplayed Hoosiers star guard Steve Alford. At Marquette, he went the length of the court in the closing seconds and hit a buzzer-beater to give the Irish a victory. And in Los Angeles against UCLA, he called a time-out while going out of bounds, prompting sportscaster Al McGuire to gush, "He's an Einstein! He's a Michelangelo!"—effusive praise that earned Rivers some ribbing from his teammates and other high-profile campus personalities.

David Rivers: "I always thought the way I played the game was artistic and entertaining. It wasn't the first time I'd heard something like that, so I didn't think a whole lot of it, even though it was coming from someone I thought was an icon in the world of collegiate sports. I considered it a great compliment, and I took it in stride because I wasn't about to lose my focus.

"But later, I got challenged by [popular Notre Dame chemistry professor] Emil T. Hoffman. He came to my dorm and posted a challenge for me to take one of his quizzes, since I was being called an Einstein."

The Irish were swept by DePaul, had horrid performances at Maryland and against Duke and were upset at Butler in overtime, but won six of their last seven games to get to the 20-win level. They received their first NCAA Tournament bid since 1981 and were given the opportunity to play the first two rounds in the Athletic and Convocation Center.

Tim Kempton: "As a junior class, we felt very good for ourselves, because everything was going according to Digger's plan when we came in. We could have very easily gone to the NCAA the year before, but every year was a steppingstone. We were improving as a class, providing leadership, and we were the mainstays of the team."

Pete Gillen: "It was odd. We didn't have the great home-court advantage even though it was certainly home-court advantage. But it wasn't the same because the tickets were distributed between eight teams."

Even though Barlow was out with the flu, the Irish had little trouble with Oregon State, dispatching the Beavers by nine points. Two days later, they had North Carolina in a tie game with David Rivers dribbling the ball as the clock wound down. But the freshman made a freshman mistake, dribbling the ball off his leg and into the hands of Tar Heel guard Kenny Smith, who drove the length of the court for the game-winning basket.

Ken Barlow: "I thought we had them beat. Probably at the worst, I thought we were going into overtime. And we had the ball where we wanted to have it. Somehow between Kenny Smith and Joe Wolff, Dave lost the ball off his leg trying to do an in-and-out move and Kenny Smith picked it up and took it in at the end of the game. But I don't think there were any regrets on losing that game because that's exactly where we wanted the ball to be: right in Dave's hands."

David Rivers: "I was excruciatingly tense after that game. I grew up playing the game and knowing from Day One that I was the best because I was putting in the time and I had a gift. So I couldn't have been angrier with myself. It was a disappointing moment.

"But it was just a moment, and I understood there would be many more moments to come in my playing career. Walking down the hall with Digger, he said, 'That's OK, baby, we'll get them next time,' and patted me on the back."

Being a freshman, Rivers would certainly have plenty of opportunities to have better moments. But that final play against North Carolina prompted some to wonder if Rivers was trying to do too much on his own.

The team certainly seemed to go as Rivers went in 1986. If Rivers was on, the team did well. But when he was not, the team did poorly, and that's when the question of teammate involvement popped up. At Indiana, Winston Morgan shut Rivers down and the Hoosiers routed the Irish by 15. At BYU, Rivers scored 28 points but shot poorly and the team lost by four in overtime. And in a one-point loss at second-ranked Duke, Johnny Dawkins stuffed a last-minute attempt by Rivers and sealed the Blue Devils' victory.

David Rivers: "Did I keep my teammates involved enough? I would say yes, because I've always played the game with the intention of making other people better. Being that kind of creative player, I was always looking for that opportunity for my teammates. But I never lost sight of the ultimate goal, which was winning, and when it came to that, I did whatever it took. Taking shots when a teammate may be open is a tough decision to make, and only leaders can make those kinds of decisions. That's what I was able to do."

The coaching staff, including new assistant Matt Kilcullen didn't see that problem in Rivers's game.

Gary Brokaw: "He tried to get them involved. But there were many times in practice when he'd come down and try to get them involved and the ball would end up hitting guys in the hand or the head or the stomach. The style of play had changed so much once he got there that people had to catch up with what he was doing. And they did eventually."

Matt Kilcullen: "If you have a scoring point guard, there are going to be times where people said he should have passed instead of shot. But yet when he makes the shot, they say, 'Good shot.' David Rivers was never a selfish player. When he penetrated, did he look for his shot? Yes, because that's what he was taught to do in high school and that was his mentality. And were there times maybe when he should have passed? Well, you can say that about any point guard who penetrates into the lane and decides to shoot."

But among the players, there was a doubt or two.

Tim Kempton: "I don't think David made that team better. John Paxson made us much better when we were freshman. David was a very good college player, but he didn't make us a better team.

"Did David and I have a great relationship? No. Do I dislike David? No, I don't dislike David. David and I lived together in Orlando. I played against David numerous times over in Europe. I don't fault David. I fault Digger for making him bigger than the team was at the time—molding the team around David instead of molding David into the team."

Joseph Price: "Coach Phelps was the boss. We always had confidence that he was doing the right thing, and we respected him and respected David. If you were in David's situation, what were you going to say? David did a tremendous job for us. He took a lot of pressure off of a lot of us, and he accepted that pressure.

"With the confidence that Coach had in him and the type of role that Coach gave him, that's just what fell in place. Maybe if he would have made a few extra passes, we could have won a couple of more games. But that's hard to say because he was just doing what Coach wanted him to do. If Coach didn't want it, I'm sure he wouldn't have done something like that."

But there was more to this team than Rivers. And going into the tournament, the Irish had every reason to expect success.

Ken Barlow: "That was probably the most complete team we had in the four years I was there. The four seniors were leaders and experienced. Scotty Hicks and Donald Royal were big parts of that team as juniors—they played a lot of minutes, they had been to the NIT their freshman year, and they had tasted the NCAA second round the year before. Dave was fantastic as a sophomore. Mark Stevenson was a whole lot better than people realized and was playing a lot of minutes as a freshman. That team from the freshman class to the senior class was like a little typhoon."

The 23-5 record was good enough for a No. 3 seed in the NCAA Tournament, and odds makers had the Irish at 10-1 to get to the Final Four. Their bracket at the Metrodome in Minneapolis was relatively favorable, including a first-round game against Arkansas-Little Rock, a school playing in its first ever NCAA Tournament.

But strange things happen in the NCAA Tournament, and strange was the rule that weekend in 1986. The Irish didn't receive any videotape of UALR until three days before the game. Weather delays made the trip to Minneapolis a six-hour odyssey. A number of double-digit seeds advanced to the second round, including Cleveland State, which upset Indiana on the morning of Notre Dame's game. Still, no one thought for a moment that a 5,000 to 1 shot could knock off the heavily favored Irish.

At least not until the game was over.

Matt Kilcullen: "That was the beginning of parity in college basketball. These other schools had good basketball players. Just because you didn't hear about them or you didn't know a lot about them didn't mean they weren't good basketball players and, on any given night, capable of beating somebody.

"In that game, Arkansas-Little Rock did a tremendous job in their half court zone. It caused us some problems. We definitely had an opportunity to win the game. We just didn't make the shots."

Ken Barlow: "Arkansas-Little Rock was a lot better than we really thought they were. They had Pete Meyers and Myron Jackson, a real big guy, who were pretty good college players. Maybe we took them a little lightly until it was late in the game."

Joseph Price: "I was ready to play, because as a senior I wanted to go out with a big bang. I had hopes of getting drafted and playing in the NBA, and so I knew the further we went, the more I would be able to show what I could do and maybe get picked or get drafted higher.

"But I'll never forget it because that was the day Cleveland State beat IU. There were a lot of upsets that weekend. And we were back in the hotel going, 'That isn't going to be us.' But we went out there and they just wouldn't fall for us."

Tim Kempton: "It was very, very disappointing. We had gotten to the point where we were a good team, and we should have done a lot better in the tournament. Once you get one or two games under your belt, the tournament becomes all about who is hot at the time. You get past that first-round game and you get that confidence everything can go right."

But nothing seemed to be going right at that point. Barlow, Dolan, Kempton, and Price were left with a shocking defeat to close out their college careers. Matt Beeuwsaert decided to take his game west, transferring to Cal-Berkeley. Assistant coach Gary Brokaw left for the head-coaching job at Iona, replaced by another former Irish All-American, John Shumate.

And early in the morning on August 24, 1986, the life of the team's most high-profile player would be hanging by a thread on the side of an Indiana country road.

27

"Basketball Has a Place at this University"
(1987)

David Rivers: "Lying in the ditch in the middle of the night looking at the full moon, I learned what true value is when it comes to life and how you want to be remembered before you leave this earth. I still wake up every morning to the scars I got that night, so there isn't a day that goes by when I don't think about it. It was a very, very spiritual experience."

"Spiritual" would be one way to describe it. But other people involved in the immediate aftermath of the car accident that almost took David Rivers's life, such as trainer Skip Meyer, remember it in a way a little less ethereal.

Skip Meyer: "I remember lying in bed and getting a call from Donald Royal at 2:00 in the morning saying they'd been in an accident and David had cut his stomach. Not knowing what was going on, I got over to the hospital in Elkhart and found out he had been thrown through the windshield and opened his whole self up. His intestines were basically lying on the ground. Kenny Barlow, who was in the accident also, covered up

David's intestines with his shirt. It was thanks to his quick thinking that things turned out well.

"It was lucky for David that the emergency room physician was trained and had worked in Vietnam. He said it was just like some of the shrapnel wounds he had seen over there, and because of his expertise, he was able to save David."

Rivers was fortunate to be alive. The 15-inch slash in his abdomen required immediate surgery, and the junior guard was in for a long season of rehabilitation and more surgery after the season. Most players would be distracted by such a life-altering experience. But Rivers didn't consider himself to be like most players, and quickly set himself the goal to play during that 1987 season.

Matt Kilcullen: "The main thing we were concerned about was whether he was going to live because they said he was cut open from his stomach up to close to his heart. And the doctors did what they needed to do. The next prognosis was he wouldn't be able to play basketball this year. But they didn't know David Rivers, because he rebounded quickly and was back up and playing before you knew it."

Skip Meyer: "I remember when David finally came back, his first workout was to just walk around the building. It took him five minutes. I spent hours and hours in the swimming pool with him, jogging in the pool, listening to 'Rocky.' He's a competitor, and it was up to me to slow him down. He wanted to go 100 miles an hour when he really should have only been doing 10.

"The biggest problem was his strength and the weight loss, because he couldn't eat for a while. But he'd been hurt over the summer, so we had three months to help him get back. And it took every day of that."

For the freshmen arriving on campus, Rivers's injury was a shock.

Scott Paddock: "The thing I remember most about him was his determination to come back and how hard he worked to get back. Despite what the doctors said, he was determined he was going to play on opening night in the preseason NIT in November, which was just a couple of months of recovery time."

Rivers worked diligently to fulfill that promise he'd made to himself and his teammates. And it was a promise he would keep, coming off the bench to play against Western Kentucky and returning to the starting lineup when the team faced third-ranked Indiana.

But the coaching staff had issues beyond Rivers's recovery. Heralded freshman Keith Robinson had not met the standards of the newly introduced NCAA Bylaw 5-1-j, better known as Proposition 48, which established minimum standardized test scores to go along with a minimum GPA in 11 core courses. Robinson's GPA was well above minimum, but his SAT score was insufficient to meet the new requirements.

All in all, it was a disastrous way to start a season. The Irish lost their first two games at home to Western Kentucky by 17 and to Indiana by five. When Ivy League member Cornell was only dispatched by four points two days later, the Irish faithful figured they were in for a down year.

But it didn't turn out that way, primarily because the coaches and players wouldn't allow it to.

Matt Kilcullen: "I thought they did an absolutely tremendous job that year as a team. They played together. Their chemistry was terrific. And I give credit to the senior class for that happening."

Scott Paddock: "I think Digger was more motivated going into that year because he had a Final Four team the year before that had lost in the first round of the tournament to Arkansas-Little Rock. He was absolutely devastated, and some of that heartache carried over to the next season. He was getting a lot of heat and pressure about that, so the next year was about proving Digger was still Digger. I recall him at practices freshman year saying that the game coming up was not going to be another Arkansas-Little Rock. He was more prepared and they watched more game film than ever before."

After the 0-2 start, the team put together an eight-game winning streak, and was 11-5 on February 1 when top-ranked North Carolina came to town. Seeing a chance to extend the Irish home hex against top-ranked opponents and really grab the momentum for the season, Phelps, as was his wont, pulled out all the psychology stops.

Scott Paddock: "It was my first real insight into how intuitive Digger was. That's why he has such a track record of beating No. 1 teams. He was so good at the psychology of the game. He understood what motivated players. He had us come down through the student section before that game to get the students into the game. He was big on the psychology and the myth of preparation."

Joe Fredrick: "I remember Donald Royal and Scott Hicks cutting down the last threads on the net in practice, and how odd that was. Coach made us do it. He said we were going to win, and he wanted us to practice cutting down the nets. He had total confidence we were going to win. He got us to buy into it. I don't think a lot of us believed we were really going to beat North Carolina. But I'll tell you what, after that practice, we believed it."

One of Phelps's preparations was a matchup zone defense that he believed would take the Tar Heels by surprise. Not wanting to give Dean Smith the opportunity to adjust to it, he held off on using it until the second half. The strategy almost backfired as the Tar Heels went up big in the first half, and Rivers was held scoreless.

David Rivers: "I was frustrated like you wouldn't believe in the first half. It was the first ND game my father attended, so I wanted to play well, but I finished the first half with zero points. Walking off the court, Digger said to me, 'Don't worry about it, you'll get 'em in the second half.' "

Matt Kilcullen: "We were down nine at halftime, and they had been up big in the first half. And then we made an adjustment with a matchup zone in the second half, and Digger caught them off guard. They didn't have time to make an adjustment. They certainly had their chance to win it, but give credit to Coach Phelps in not showing this particular defense until the second half."

Joe Fredrick: "Coach Phelps won that game. That's one game I can say there is no doubt he won. He was so much better at big games than he was at games we were supposed to win. The confidence he had in you in an upset-type game was greater than a game we shouldn't lose."

With the matchup zone, the second half was as great for Irish partisans as the first had been doleful. Rivers scored all 14 of his points. Gary Voce, blossoming into an effective low-post player under the tutelage of John Shumate, got 10 rebounds and had six of his 15 points in the final three minutes. Yellow placards distributed before the game came raining down out of the stands as the clocked ticked off Notre Dame's sixth victory over a No. 1 ranked team at the Athletic and Convocation Center.

Scott Paddock: "I remember the euphoria and the exuberance and getting mobbed by the students after the game and knowing basketball did have a place at this school. During the recruiting process, that was one of the recruiting ploys other coaches used—you don't want to play second fiddle at a football school. So more than anything, it was the recognition that basketball has a place at this university and the students are passionate about it."

With the players now believing in themselves, more good games followed. The Irish played host to No. 15 Duke and came away a four-point winner. Ten days later, they avenged a five-point loss to No. 4 DePaul in Chicago with an 11-point victory at home. By season's end the Irish had cracked the top 20 and then won their first two games in the NCAA Tournament, earning a Sweet 16 rematch against North Carolina at the Meadowlands in East Rutherford, N.J.

But that's where the Cinderella story ended. Tar Heel guard Kenny Smith, who had missed the first game with an injury, scored only four points but played excellent defense. Freshmen J. R. Reid, who had scored 12 in the February game, throttled Notre Dame with 31 points, scoring 16 of UNC's last 17.

Scott Paddock: "A team like North Carolina is tough to knock off twice in one season. We gave them their wake-up call early on that we were for real. That game at the Meadowlands went back and forth, and their guards got hot at the right time."

David Rivers: "J.R. Reid killed us. We couldn't stop him even with our team effort. We could score points but couldn't slow him down. We controlled Kenny pretty well, but J.R. was unstoppable."

Still, given the abysmal start to the season, a 24-8 record and a Sweet 16 appearance certainly exceeded expectations. Phelps and his staff seemed to get the most out of a talented team, and there was no reason to believe they couldn't continue to achieve at a high level.

But 1987 would represent a high-water mark for the Irish program of the 1980s and 1990s. And before it would return to those heights, the program would endure some soul-shaking depths.

Signs of Decline
(1988–1990)

Irish basketball was in a strong position going into the 1988 season. Keith Robinson was newly eligible after sitting out a season because of Proposition 48. David Rivers was up to 183 pounds and was getting preseason All-America mention. The team had a Sweet 16 berth from the previous season on which to build. And in November 1987, Phelps and his staff, including new assistant Fran McCaffery, signed what some called the best Irish recruiting class since Tripucka and his group, highlighted by McDonald's All-American LaPhonso Ellis.

But that position would gradually erode as the 1980s ended on a mixed note for the Irish. They had two 20-win seasons in three years and made three straight NCAA Tournament appearances, but the overall atmosphere was one of trepidation and uncertainty.

The arrival of Ellis and company for the 1989 season bolstered the spirits of Irish fans who had been through an up-and-down 1988 campaign. The high expectations for Rivers's senior season were never really met as the team mixed high-profile wins over ranked teams like Louisville and eventual national champion Kansas at the newly renamed Edmund P. Joyce

Center with a season sweep by DePaul and a stunning defeat by Lafayette in Philadelphia.

David Rivers: "I remember being very upset and angry about the Lafayette loss, especially considering we were more talented than they were. It came down to playing hard and getting the job done, and we didn't. People were really upset, because our expectations were high and we had disappointed."

Scott Paddock: "You go into the locker room and sit in stunned silence for an hour, listening to the exuberance in the next locker room. That's when you recognized Notre Dame was every team's Super Bowl. I remember doing a lot of soul-searching at Lafayette. Games like that give you the wake-up call, and how you respond to those games makes or breaks your season."

Compounding the difficulties was the loss of Mark Stevenson. Two months after being caught shoplifting at a local mall, he was charged with possession of alcohol by a minor after the big win against Kansas. Suspended for four games—during which the Irish went 1-3—he ended up leaving the team.

Scott Paddock: "It kind of reinforced what we all believed: Notre Dame is different, and you have to conduct yourself with a lot of integrity and honesty and be concerned with how you carry yourself because they're not going to tolerate it. Maybe some other programs would have given Mark another chance.

"It was the best thing that could have happened to Joe Fredrick's career, because it gave him an opportunity for playing time and minutes. He almost transferred after our freshman year, but he chose to come back. The situation with Mark gave him an opportunity to make a name for himself. I don't think he would have gotten that opportunity if Mark had stayed around."

Joe Fredrick: "During Christmas break of that year I went in to tell Coach I was leaving. I was packed up and ready to go. I was tired of not playing. He said Joe Montana wanted to transfer one time, and he had told Joe he wasn't going to let him. I guess they were buddies somehow from football. And then he told me he wasn't going to release me until the end of the season.

Mark got thrown off no later than a week to 10 days after that, and I started from that point on."

A 20-8 record was sufficient for a fourth straight NCAA bid. But David Rivers's college career ended at the hands of Southern Methodist University and their star guard, Kato Armstrong.

Matt Kilcullen: "Kato knew how to read all nine guys on the floor, specifically in transition. When he was coming down the floor, he would run our guys into our own guys. He would run our guys into his guys. He was just a master of getting himself an open shot in transition."

Scott Paddock: "We got embarrassed by Kato Armstrong. Just like teams got up to play Notre Dame, point guards got up to play David Rivers. He was the All-American. He was the standard for point guards in college basketball at that time. Kato Armstrong was fired up to play him, and they literally went after him."

But all that disappointment would be a forgotten memory once Ellis, Keith Tower, Daimon Sweet, Elmer Bennett, and Keith Adkins came to town—or so said the conventional wisdom. Irish assistant coach Fran McCaffery, who took John Shumate's spot on the staff when Shumate left to take over Southern Methodist at the end of 1988, was impressed by the new arrival.

Fran McCaffery: "Phonz was without a doubt the most impressive freshman I've been around in my 20 years of coaching. He was a little heavier than he is now, so he reminded me of a bigger Charles Barkley. He was just a phenomenal rebounder.

"The thing that impressed me was how pleasant and mild he was off the floor, while on the court he was a ferocious competitor. That's what really made him special. He was able to keep his emotions under control, yet still dominate a game."

Scott Paddock: "When he announced he was coming to Notre Dame, Digger and Shumate came back to South Bend [after the press conference]. They were overcome. We all thought this guy was our marquee player we had been missing for a few years. Digger came to that practice with intensity.

He gathered us all together and told us, 'It starts right now,' because this was the guy who was going to take us back to the Final Four."

Lou Somogyi: "When LaPhonso sent in his Letter of Intent, there was incredible elation. I think Digger was even quoted somewhere saying, 'Now we can win the national championship.' He already had Elmer Bennett, who was a Parade All-American, and Keith Tower, who was considered one of the best big men in the country."

Joe Fredrick: "LaPhonso had all the publicity and reputation, but he was really unselfish. Phonz was all about the team. Even to this day, you wish for Phonz to get a trillion-billion-dollar contract, because he's such a great guy it just warms your heart."

But as it turned out, 1989 had a lot more of 1988 in it than 1978. A four-game win streak to start the season came crashing down when the team traveled to Valparaiso and was upset, 71-68.

LaPhonso Ellis: "Digger always cautioned us about those in-state rivalries, especially when we would go in their backyard. Notre Dame was probably the biggest game they were going to play all year long. He warned us to be sensitive to that and have our antennas raised and to be ready and to make sure we not allow their energy to exceed our energy."

Joe Fredrick: "The Valpo game was just before Christmas. We were undefeated going into that game, and we were starting to climb a little bit. We obviously took them for granted. It was one of those things where you could just feel the momentum going their way. A guy threw in a running bank shot. LaPhonso had some foul trouble. And I missed a big one-and-one down the stretch.

"You hate to say it, but when you play 100 games in your college career, there are going to be games where you just say man, how did that happen? Unfortunately, we had too many of them—six or seven or eight. I said Lafayette was one of the two worst losses of my career. Well, Valparaiso was the other one."

Two games later, though, the Irish traveled to San Francisco. The opponent of "29-and-1" fame had fallen on hard times, and was in its third year of a restored program after three years of not having a team. But a packed gym and unfavorable officiating calls were not conducive to an Irish victory.

Fran McCaffery: "We noticed that every game USF played—and that was the fifth or sixth game of the season—had at least one official from our game. So there were red flags right from the beginning with the officiating. It was the same folks we were seeing come up every time we looked at a box score or looked at a game tape.

"LaPhonso was wearing them out, and we were doing quite well. And then all of a sudden, boom, Phonz got three fouls and he was on the bench. And the rest of the game was a struggle."

Joe Fredrick: "We never got into the flow the whole game. I remember I got in some foul trouble. LaPhonso got in some foul trouble early. They packed that zone in. And with Phonz and myself out, we couldn't score points. That hurt us. And they had a big guy who went off that game."

The big guy was forward Mark McCathrion, whose 26 points led the Dons to their 79-75 upset win. Irish fans began to wonder whether these losses to the lesser lights of the schedule were signaling a trend. The players noticed a difference in philosophy when those teams came up.

Scott Paddock: "There were times where, looking back, I think we should have done things differently against teams like that. There was a lot of pressure not to lose, versus 'hey, this team is not any good, let's just go out here and kick their ass.' That's the mind-set I would have taken instead of playing not to lose. We always played to win in the bigger games and almost not to lose in the games we were supposed to win."

There were other games the Irish were supposed to win left on the schedule, and a few more came up as losses as the season progressed. Eleventh-ranked Syracuse defeated Notre Dame 99-87, scoring the most points in the Joyce Center since Phelps's first game there. For the first time since 1983 and for only the third time in Phelps's Notre Dame career, the team finished the season without a win over a ranked opponent.

Still, the Irish tried to make some noise in the NCAA Tournament. They dispatched Vanderbilt in the first round, and faced a second-round test in No. 2 seed Georgetown and Alonzo Mourning. They led at halftime, but a second-half surge by Mourning and Big East Player of the Year Charles Smith led the Hoyas to an 81-74 win and sent the Irish back to South Bend looking forward to the next season and the success they expected from a more mature Ellis.

That success would prove frustratingly elusive in 1990, a season best characterized by the phrase "but it didn't happen."

Everyone had returned from the 21-9 team of 1989, and the arrival of future NBA star Monty Williams strengthened the roster. The Irish started the season ranked in the top 25, but lost Ellis to academic difficulty in the first semester and came out of the gate 1-4.

LaPhonso Ellis: "I hit a crossroad. I got off to a pretty good start, but a couple of classes didn't go well for me and I ended up being academically ineligible."

Matt Kilcullen: "Whenever you take a player like LaPhonso who can terrorize a team inside and outside on both ends of the floor, it takes a big cog out of your offense and defense. So we just had to adjust. He was a tough loss that first semester."

With the Irish in a tailspin, undefeated UCLA came to the Joyce Center looking for a big win. But it didn't happen, and the Irish used a 30-5 run to pull off an 88-86 upset. The schedule featured some easier competition over the holidays, giving the Irish a chance to use the UCLA victory as a springboard to salvage the season.

But it didn't happen. After winning four games in a row, the Irish went to Omaha, Neb., to face Creighton, and the Jays erased a nine-point deficit in 80 seconds and upset Notre Dame by two. A week later they went to Philadelphia to play LaSalle, and Lionel Simmons dropped 27 points on them as the Explorers won 86-78.

After getting blown out by LSU and losing decisively to Duke and Houston, the Irish traveled to the Carrier Dome to play No. 4 Syracuse, staring another defeat in the face. But it didn't happen. Elmer Bennett's last-second jumper gave the Irish a much-needed 66-65 victory and sent Phelps dancing across the court to shake the hand of Orangemen coach Jim Boeheim.

Keith Tower: "The ball was thrown to Keith Robinson and he flipped it to Elmer on the wing. As soon as it left his hands, you knew it was good.

It was like it was in slow motion—just a matter of 'will the ball finally get there and drop'?

"And I remember Digger's dance. That was a point of desperation for us. We really needed a big win to get to the tournament, and he had a lot of emotion. He ran over and wanted to give a big hug to Jim Boeheim. He was dancing and he was running and he skipped over ready to hug their coach. Boeheim looked like he wanted to knock him out."

A big win might ignite a late-season charge toward a tournament berth. But it didn't happen. Three days later, DePaul overcame an 18-point deficit and beat the Irish by one at home when Stephen Howard stuffed in a Chuckie Murphy air ball. Two more losses followed, including an 18-point blowout by Dayton. With No. 2 Missouri coming to South Bend, Notre Dame's postseason hopes were headed for extinction.

But it didn't happen. The Irish rose up and sent Norm Stewart's Tigers home on the wrong end of a 31-point pasting that was sure to get the attention of the NCAA selection committee. All Phelps and his crew had to do was salvage a split with DePaul in Chicago to lock up the berth.

But it didn't happen. The Blue Demons' 64-59 win gave them a sweep, and with only 16 wins, the Irish had no reason to expect the NCAA to come calling.

But . . .

Matt Kilcullen: "I didn't think one or two games would ever make a difference when you look at all the teams we played that year: Louisville, Indiana, Marquette, UCLA, USC, Boston College. I don't think Digger ever ducked anybody. I don't think whether you won or lost to them was going to make a difference if you look at the schedule that year."

Fran McCaffery: "I probably was not as tuned in to the RPI at that time as we all are now. Digger was on top of that kind of stuff. And he kept saying we are 38 or we are 39 and they are 68 or 69 in the RPI. So that is one advantage of playing the more difficult schedule."

Scott Paddock: "I know Joey Meyer was livid. It probably made the anti-Notre Dame fans more anti-Notre Dame because Notre Dame got in when probably there were a lot more deserving teams that should have gotten in."

The Irish seemed to have been given a bid most thought they didn't deserve. They went to Richmond and played like it, and were sent home 75-67 by Virginia.

Joe Fredrick: "I think what got Coach in the most trouble was that 1989 team. That 21-9 [from 1988] should have easily been 23-6. We had Georgetown pretty well beat, and we led in most of that game. We had every single player returning. There are a lot of people even to this day who talk about how much talent that team had. Then we went 16-13. And that's when the administration got really upset."

How upset would be determined quickly. The period had started off with plenty of promise and talent, but success had proved elusive. And Digger Phelps would end up paying the price for that lack of success.

29

Snakebit and Sayonara
(1991)

In the late 1980s, Notre Dame underwent a regime change. Longtime university president Fr. Ted Hesburgh and executive vice-president Fr. Ned Joyce retired, replaced by former Irish hoopster Fr. Edward "Monk" Malloy and Fr. E. William Beauchamp. Gene Corrigan, who had succeeded Moose Krause as athletic director in the early 1980s, took a job with the Atlantic Coast Conference and was replaced by another Irish basketball great, Dick Rosenthal.

The three men began their jobs intent on evaluating the various athletic programs and making changes they felt appropriate. Digger Phelps's future was suddenly called into question.

In her 1994 book *A Coach's Wife*, Phelps's then wife, Terry, accused the administration of conspiring against her husband because they wanted him out. She alleged that Rosenthal—who, in an unusual move, had taken over the responsibility of scheduling from Phelps—had put together killer schedules to undermine Phelps's chances for success, with the blessing of Frs. Malloy and Beauchamp.

How valid are those accusations? It depends on whom you ask.

Dick Rosenthal: "I wanted us to play a great basketball schedule. I wanted us to play a great football schedule, too. I thought it was a good thing for the university and the kids to appear on national television for basketball, so we wanted to get the kind of games that could merit playing on TV."

Fran McCaffery: "I would say there were definitely disagreements within the basketball office and the athletic administration as to how scheduling should be handled. We were in the Midwest Collegiate Conference in everything but football and men's basketball, so we made an agreement to play all of those teams. So now you are playing teams like Detroit and Evansville on the road, who were very good teams. And at the same time we were still playing Duke, Kentucky, Indiana, UCLA, USC, Missouri, DePaul, and Marquette. There was really no balance on our schedule to assure that we would get the proper number of wins to get in the NCAA tournament because we had no conference tournament as sort of a 'second season' to propel us into the NCAA tournament."

Fr. Bill Beauchamp: "My response to that would be it isn't true. The University of Notre Dame has never shied away from tough schedules. I don't think their schedule was any tougher than it is now. You also deal with the RPI rankings and things like that. It has changed somewhat. It used to be important to get 20 wins, so you'd play the Little Sisters of the Poor. It wasn't like we were only losing the games against the tough opponents."

Joe Fredrick: "Dick Rosenthal was at practice one time, and Jamere Jackson and I told him we wanted to play tough teams. We thrived on playing Indiana, Duke, Carolina, Syracuse, UCLA, Louisville, and Kentucky. Back then, we were on national TV every Saturday."

Scott Paddock: "I think there was a message being sent, because Digger had a lot of control over scheduling taken away from him. You could tell there was an underlying tension between Digger and Dick Rosenthal."

Lou Somogyi: "Look at John MacLeod's first season. That schedule was intended for Digger. Where in history have you ever seen a schedule where you play nine straight road games against the likes of USC—which had

Harold Minor and was in the top 25 at the time—North Carolina at Madison Square Garden, Marquette, West Virginia, Virginia, and LaSalle?"

Regardless of the schedule or the motivation behind it, the Irish weren't going into 1991 as confident as they had been the previous seasons. Primary among their concerns was the health of sophomore Monty Williams.

Skip Meyer: "We did the routine physicals his sophomore year, and we had a brand new physician who had been on the job for about three weeks. During Monty's physical, he heard something a little funny—a murmur type of a sound—and he was sharp enough to say we should get it checked out.

"The next step was to go down for an echocardiogram. No big deal, we're not looking for anything, just want to make sure everything is fine. We'll pick the results up tomorrow, go back to practice, and go on with our lives.

"Well, the test came back showing he had a significant problem. We were in the doctor's office totally shocked that someone as healthy as he was who felt fine would be told he could never play basketball again. We sat in the office in complete shock, because it was the last thing we expected to hear."

Fran McCaffery: "Digger had taken the staff up to Chicago to a Cubs game and we were having dinner. They tracked him down there and Skip gave Digger the word it was a lot worse than we thought—he had hypertrophic cardiomyopathy, and he wouldn't be able to play again.

"That was probably as low as I've been in coaching. When you set aside the impact that had on our team, knowing Monty Williams and knowing his family and knowing what a bright future he had and how that was going to affect him was one of the saddest things I ever had to deal with."

Williams's departure was the first setback in what analyst Al McGuire would describe as a "snakebit" season for the Irish. LaPhonso Ellis once again was academically ineligible, missing the second semester and rendering a weakened Irish offense more ineffective. Freshmen Brooks Boyer, Carl Cozen, and Joe and Jon Ross were pressed into service as the injuries—and losses—mounted.

LaPhonso Ellis: "My academic ineligibility was a huge part of that. Any time a guy who you brought in to be the anchor of your program goes out, that puts a great deal of strain on your offense and your defense. I don't know if snakebit is necessarily the word, but we were definitely unfortunate."

Matt Kilcullen: "We lost a bunch of close games. It's like Murphy's Law: whatever could go wrong would go wrong. If you look at all the success Coach Phelps had in his coaching career, there were also going to be times when the ball doesn't bounce the way you want it. We just didn't get a lot of breaks going our way."

Brooks Boyer: "We had the pieces to a really good team. And then Monty went down. We were playing Kentucky and Tim Singleton went down. LaPhonso became ineligible. Freshmen were forced to play a lot, myself included. When you have a bunch of 18-year-olds playing against 22-year-olds, usually you have some challenges. Well, we just lost it."

As he had so many times before, Phelps tried psychological ploys to inspire the team, including neon green uniforms for the home game against Syracuse.

Keith Tower: "They were introducing the starting lineups and here we are in our neon green and Syracuse is there in their bright orange. I thought of my poor sister sitting there trying to adjust the tint or the color to figure out what's wrong with her television."

Fran McCaffery: "That was a test product. We were still wearing Champion uniforms at the time, and they wanted to test market that color. So we broke them out and people were adjusting their television sets. I don't think the fans liked them all that much. I don't think we ever wore them again."

As the curtain came down on a 12-20 season—only the third losing season in Phelps's 20 years at Notre Dame—fans were questioning whether Phelps would be on the sidelines in 1992. Some believed the team had been a victim of bad luck. Some believed Phelps had lost interest in coaching, as evidenced by the team's meltdown and a downturn in recruiting. And some had just tired of Phelps's arrogant style.

The answer came down soon after season's end . . . with a twist.

Fran McCaffery: "I was on the road recruiting. I landed in South Bend and [assistant coach] Jimmy Dolan was waiting for me at the airport, which I thought was kind of strange. He came up to me and said, 'I was instructed to come and get you. We're going over to Digger's house.' And I said, 'What's going on?' And he said, 'Well, I think he resigned.'"

Brooks Boyer: "We went the next morning and Digger walked in and said, 'Boys, it's time for me to go.' He didn't blame anybody, and he didn't point fingers. He said, 'I didn't get it done this year.' And he was just Digger. He came in confident and said, 'This is how life goes. This is what happens.'"

On April 15, 1991, Richard "Digger" Phelps resigned the only coaching job he had ever wanted. His exit statement was a perhaps-typical three pages long, and he spoke for more than an hour at his farewell news conference.

Conspicuous by their absence at the press conference were the three men for whom Phelps worked. Fr. Beauchamp was in Alaska for a Notre Dame fundraiser, although he issued a one-page statement praising Phelps for his dedication to Notre Dame and the graduation rate of his players. Dick Rosenthal was at NCAA meetings in Orlando.

In their defense, some believe Phelps timed his resignation to ensure that Rosenthal and Fr. Beauchamp couldn't be there in person. But the apparent lack of administration support for Phelps in his closing hours rubbed some people the wrong way.

Gary Brokaw: "The way it happened, yes, I wasn't happy. The things he stood for were developing players and the games we talked about. But he never allowed guys to go on and not do the best they could in the classroom. I felt those were the two things Notre Dame was looking for, and he did that in his 20 years.

"Yes, I thought he could have gone out a little bigger. But Digger had an ego satisfaction in his 20 years at Notre Dame that he doesn't need it. He's fine."

Skip Meyer: "In most schools, it comes down to wins and losses. I would like to think that Notre Dame looks at the whole picture—the kind of person he is, the kind of coach he is, the atmosphere of the program, the direction of the program, the things off the floor like community service. I think

Notre Dame took consideration of all those things. But I also think that sometimes it does come down to wins and losses."

LaPhonso Ellis: "When people have served you for so long, have given all of themselves to your program, and have not only pursued athletic excellence but also committed to making sure that the majority of the players graduate on time, those people should go out with class. And I didn't feel they handled that situation with the class it deserved."

The task of replacing Phelps proved daunting. A number of names came up, including Duke's Mike Krzyzewski, Georgia Tech's Bobby Cremins, and former Irish assistant Pete Gillen, who had become head coach at Xavier. In the end, all turned the opportunity down, some publicly.

Dick Rosenthal: "In some instances there was press speculation that maybe Coach X would be in line for the position. And when we weren't responding to that, it probably put a little pressure on the coach. He didn't want to say Notre Dame wasn't interested in me. In fairness, maybe some of them made a comment just because they were committed to the institutions they were with. It really didn't mean much. In those years too, our conversation levels weren't quite as competitive as they are today."

Lou Somogyi: "[The job] wasn't attractive. Coaches hated being an independent. The recruiting hadn't been very good the last couple of years. Football was king; you were always going to play second fiddle. It had no high appeal. So why leave this job to go to ND?"

Equally discomfited were the Irish players.

Keith Tower: "I remember walking back from the meeting with Phonz. He had just come off ineligibility and was considering going pro. If you are a new coach coming in and you've got guys coming off the season we just had, and then you've got a stable full of young guys, would you go with one-year guys or would you start building your young guys, get them experience and phase players like us out? We were concerned, kind of scared. What's this new guy's philosophy going to be?"

It would be a couple of weeks before Tower and his teammates would have the answer.

The
John MacLeod
Years

(1992–1999)

30

A Quiet Approach
(1992)

His hometown of New Albany, Ind., had four Catholic parishes for its 30,000 or so residents. He faithfully attended games between Notre Dame and the University of Kentucky in nearby Louisville. As a player at Bellarmine, in a game he called "schedule fodder" for the Irish, he saw the exploits of Gene Duffy and Tommy Hawkins up close.

With those influences, it's no surprise that John MacLeod grew up a big fan of Notre Dame. So when the call came from South Bend in 1991, he didn't let a little thing like a date with Michael Jordan stop him.

John MacLeod: "I was coaching the Knicks when my name came up as a candidate. Dick Rosenthal and I got together in Cleveland one night before a game. I met with Fr. Beauchamp and Fr. Malloy and Dick Rosenthal in Chicago the day before one of our playoff games against the Bulls. That was the beginning of it."

While some basketball pundits felt the selection of MacLeod was the result of the Irish running out of options, his positives were obvious to the men making the choice.

Dick Rosenthal: "John had been very successful. He was one of the win-ningest coaches in the NBA. I liked the kind of basketball he had always played, a little up-tempo. And John was a great competitor. He was willing to play anybody, anyplace, anywhere."

Fr. Edward Malloy: "He had strong pro credentials. He was a Catholic, and although he had not gone to Notre Dame, we felt he'd be a good institu-tional fit. He seemed to have a personality that would work well with col-lege students—he wasn't the yeller-screamer type you'd sometimes get in pro basketball."

For people used to the "yeller-screamer" coaching style of Digger Phelps, MacLeod's more laid-back attitude came as quite a change. For some, the change was welcome.

Carl Cozen: "It was a really big contrast to playing for Digger. Digger would motivate you by putting pressure on you. With John, it was more of a quiet approach, more instructional. That worked better for me and the way I played."

But as Keith Tower found out, MacLeod was not always quiet.

Keith Tower: "Every year, the NCAA comes in with a referee and they explain to you the new rule changes and that kind of stuff. And every year at the end of that meeting, Digger would stand up and say that if anybody on this team ever got in a fight on the court, they'd be off the team.

"Our junior year down at Butler, Daimon Sweet went to the basket. They had a big 6-foot 6-inch guy who played football and some basketball who just laid Daimon out. Just flat out took a flagrant foul. My nature is to be kind of an enforcer. I don't do well when somebody takes a shot at one of my guards. But I also knew I couldn't do anything about it. So I went over and I remember patting the guy on the rear end. But I whispered in his ear, 'The next time you leave your feet, I'm ending your career.' That way Digger wouldn't know.

"Well, John watched every game from the year before so he could get a feel for our talent. He called an emergency meeting with the four captains: Daimon, Elmer, LaPhonso, and me. He put in the tape of the Butler game from the year before and played where this guy just laid out Daimon and I walked over and patted him on the rear end. On the tape, it looks like this guy knocks my guard down and I go over and slap him on the butt for it.

"John absolutely came unglued. It's the only time I've seen him lose his composure. He challenged our manhood and said if something like that ever happened and one of us didn't take that guy out, we were off the team. It was a complete 180 from before. For me it was kind of freeing, because I felt like a total sissy at that meeting.

"And lo and behold, the first game of the season, we played Butler and somebody tried to punk one of our guys. LaPhonso grabbed him right in front of our bench, put a chokehold on him, and lifted him off the ground. It was definitely a different mind-set."

One of the first things MacLeod did was alter the training regimen to fit his style. Though the players came in forewarned, it still took them by surprise.

Keith Tower: "My family lived in Boston, so I got to know Dennis Johnson of the Celtics pretty well. Dennis had played for John in Phoenix, so I was picking his brain. And he said, 'Expect to run. You will never in your life be in as good a shape as you will be for him. If you don't go into camp in shape, you will die.'"

"Going back to campus for the summer, LaPhonso weighed about 280, Daimon Sweet had about 18 percent body fat. . . . I was telling these guys that from what I was hearing, this guy was a fanatic about conditioning. If you look at him, he's lean and toned, even at his age. So we all got a little bit scared."

LaPhonso Ellis: "I had been lifting weights very heavily the second semester of my junior year. People close to me were saying that if I was going to be an NBA ballplayer, I needed to be big and powerful like a Karl Malone. I was probably about 271 pounds when Coach MacLeod came in. He asked, 'Why are you so big?' I told him, and he said, 'No, no, no. They are looking for the more athletic power forwards.' With his encouragement, I began to run all summer long. And by the time we started the preseason, I was probably about 235, 230 maybe."

With this new regimen, the players trimmed down and improved their endurance—which was fortunate, because the schedule waiting for them that season would test that endurance.

John MacLeod: "I was at the podium answering questions after I had been introduced, and a hand slipped me a piece of paper. It was a Notre Dame schedule. I didn't have a chance to look at it closely. But we had nine straight games on the road and we were out of the building for 45 days. That was the toughest schedule I had ever gone through. And in the pros, you are playing tough teams every night.

"To play the teams we did says a great deal about the kids on that team because it was as difficult a collegiate schedule as I have ever seen in my life. They never backed up. They never wavered. They were one of the hardest-working groups I ever had."

The season opened with only a five-point win over Valparaiso to show for the first six games, so the Irish went into the holidays looking for answers. The break turned out to be just what they needed.

Keith Tower: "In one of our first games we went down to Indiana against Bobby Knight, a defensive specialist, and we had one offensive set. It took them about 30 seconds to deny our entry pass, and then we were shut down. We got just annihilated. Then we went to Boston College and got our doors blown off. We had two days off for Christmas, and then when we came back we had about a week where we had no games. So we just practiced.

"After that Christmas break, everything turned around. We had gotten beat early by teams that we were better than, but we didn't have our sets in. We were trying to adjust. During that Christmas break it was just like, boom, we got it. It just clicked. We had a new toughness level. You could just feel the air shift."

Billy Taylor: "Everybody was getting comfortable with their role and trying to figure out what was needed for us to win. I was going to provide defense. Elmer Bennett was going to provide ballhandling and scoring, so he was going to run the floor and score for us in the halfcourt. Phonz was our low-post presence. Keith Tower was a good defensive presence, rebounder, and shot-blocker.

"We started to get closer as a unit. As the season went on, we figured out each other's games, what we could bring to the table, and what Coach MacLeod wanted and expected from us."

With this higher level of confidence, the Irish began collecting some attention-getting wins. But they were still fighting the fatigue of the killer schedule.

Fran McCaffery: "USC was ranked, had just beaten Ohio State, and had a big crowd. We beat them pretty good. Our next game was against LaSalle and Lionel Simmons. We beat them in Philadelphia. And then we bussed to New York, where we beat North Carolina. So that's a pretty good run. But after we've just crisscrossed the country instead of coming home and playing somebody we knew we could beat, we went on the road at West Virginia and got beat.

"The scheduling made no sense. It didn't give that team a chance. We were on the bus to go to practice at West Virginia, and I have never seen a more exhausted team. I don't care who we played; we weren't going to win that game.

"We needed to come home and play somebody we knew we could beat. You've beaten three ranked teams in a row and you're going to be ranked. Instead, before we come home, we've already lost to West Virginia."

John MacLeod: "At the end of that nine-day trip we played Carolina in the Garden on a Saturday. Then Monday, we played West Virginia at West Virginia, and then went back to South Bend. The next Friday we got on a flight and took a bus to Charlottesville to play Virginia. Those kids were wiped out. As soon as they got on the bus to make the trip to Charlottesville, everybody was sound asleep. And I remember saying to myself, 'My gosh, they are worn out.' "

Still, the team continued to knock off ranked opponents. No. 10 Syracuse went down by three in the Carrier Dome. The Irish beat No. 2 UCLA by 13 in the Joyce Center, and St. John's followed a week later.

That strength of schedule—No. 1 according to the Sagarin ratings—kept a bid to the NCAA Tournament alive despite a 14-12 record as the Irish headed to Chicago to face No. 15 DePaul. But in the final five seconds of the game, their strong hand went bust . . . in part because of an emotional reaction by the normally taciturn MacLeod.

Fran McCaffery: "We were winning the whole game. Then Howard Nathan stole the ball from Elmer Bennett, went down, laid it up, and gave them a little boost of momentum. But we still had the ball in a tie game."

Brooks Boyer: "The play was designed to go to Elmer Bennett. Elmer was going to penetrate. If he got to the basket, great. If he could dump it on the right side to Daimon Sweet for a jump shot, great. If he could throw it to the left side to me standing on the wing for a jump shot, great. Elmer is right-handed, so odds were he was going to go right. I wasn't even going to be in the play.

"Daimon was taking the ball out. My guy came off of me and they doubled Elmer, so he threw it in to Keith Tower. Keith turned around and threw it to me. With five seconds left, I knew I had one thing to do: put my head down and go to the basket. Every coach since I was in the sixth grade has told me that.

"I went through two guys and came away with a few touches out of that, and then I went up in the air. I was low-bridged and knocked over. Stephen Howard was standing back there and got his fingertip on the ball that I had released. So up there, everything was clean. But I was laying on the floor because I had been cross-body-blocked."

Keith Tower: "He went clear to the basket and he got absolutely creamed. He was either going to get a lay-up or get fouled, and he clearly got fouled.

"John blew his top and got T'ed up. But you know what? He should have. I was ready to get T'ed up. It was ridiculous that we didn't get that call. That was a huge game for us. If we won that one, we were in the tournament. And we knew it. We really needed that game."

Billy Taylor: "We thought he got fouled, and there was no call. Coach MacLeod was typically very calm on the sideline, but he took his jacket off and threw it down. I guess that just kind of shows the importance of the game and importance of the moment.

"The referees observed that as being disrespectful, a slap in the face, so they gave him a technical foul. Coach didn't mean any disrespect by it. He wasn't trying to show the officials up. He was just frustrated."

John MacLeod: "I can tell you, I rarely complained. I rarely have ever said anything about officiating. And that was one of the worst officiating jobs I have ever seen in my life. Brooks made a great play—he put his head down and drove it to the basket. And he did get fouled.

"I did jump up and I did throw my coat down, so I guess you'd say that deserved a technical. I didn't swear at the official. But some of the calls that were made or weren't made were incredible. And those kids deserved a better fate than the way those guys officiated that game."

Stephen Howard's free throw off the technical gave the Blue Demons a 66-65 victory. That, for all intents and purposes, killed the Irish tournament bid, although a season-ending wipeout at the hands of Evansville didn't help matters.

Yet some members of the team still believe that a .500 record against a schedule that featured 11 top 25 teams should have been good enough.

Billy Taylor: "The fact that we were .500 was the big sticking point, obviously. But we had so many quality wins that I thought it made us a very interesting tournament team. That's kind of what the tournament is all about: what team gets on a roll and gets an upset. It's exciting to watch, and we were exciting to watch."

Fran McCaffery: "That schedule was absolutely ridiculous. We were out of our building 45 straight days. We took them all on.

"We lost some games we shouldn't have lost. The Detroit loss at home really hurt. But today, with the emphasis on RPI and encouraging people to play better schedules, we probably would have been in."

The NIT didn't hesitate to invite the Irish, who got to the championship game and a rematch with Virginia. But the championship game proved too much for the Irish, who fell to Virginia for the second time that season. The fabulous class of Ellis, Tower, Sweet, and Bennett departed for the professional and international ranks. And John MacLeod was about to find out how difficult the Notre Dame job could be.

31

Give Me Liberty . . .

I n the days of the Revolutionary War, patriots like Patrick Henry believed in independence so strongly they were willing to die for it. In the early 1990s, the Notre Dame basketball program seemed to hold the same ideal, although it's not entirely certain the goal was a beneficial one.

Notre Dame had a long history as an independent in college athletics. That independence got the Irish access to the NCAA Tournament in the days when only one team per conference could participate. The lack of ties to other schools enabled Notre Dame to market its program nationally and successfully as Johnny Dee and Digger Phelps did in the 1960s and 1970s. Freedom in scheduling created the rivalries like UCLA that captivated audiences in the arenas and on television.

In the salad days of Irish sovereignty, the program's wheelhouse was the Northeast. With a number of large urban areas—and corresponding strong Catholic populations—from which to draw talent and no major affiliation of schools to counterbalance Notre Dame's influence, Irish coaches were able to keep the machinery humming for years.

But in the early 1980s that began to change with an alignment of high-profile, mostly Catholic schools that became known as the Big East. Dave Gavitt, the first Big East commissioner, recognized the importance of television just as Phelps had, and the conference received immediate exposure and increased it every year by partnering with ESPN, the fledgling all-sports cable network that needed programming. Established coaches like Jim Boeheim at Syracuse, John Thompson at Georgetown, and Rollie Massimino at Villanova now had an effective weapon against the Irish publicity machine, and they started to use it.

Frank McLaughlin: "A lot of our success in recruiting was getting players like A.D. out of Washington, Toby Knight out of Long Island, Billy Paterno out of New Jersey. . . . We were getting those kids. Then they formed the Big East, and Notre Dame was an independent. I remember saying to Digger around then he was going to have a really tough time. It's one thing recruiting against the ACC, but now we had this Big East Conference."

Lou Somogyi: "The 1970s were the perfect era for Notre Dame as independent. Notre Dame almost had a monopoly on the television market for weekends. Now you have ESPN created in 1979. You have the Big East created in 1979. The pendulum started to swing toward those schools in that region of the country. You had John Thompson at Georgetown building up power sort of the way Digger Phelps had. You had Jim Boeheim doing the same. And suddenly they were saying, 'Hey, we can be our own attraction.'"

Notre Dame recognized the developing situation but was slow to react. While conference affiliation with teams such as Marquette and DePaul had been discussed as early as 1950, it wasn't until the 1985 season that the self-titled "Great Independents"—Notre Dame, Marquette, DePaul, and Dayton—started playing each other in a round-robin each season. At that time there were 17 schools that played Division I men's basketball as independents, and the conventional wisdom of the time said the Irish could (and probably would) be the last team standing because of their program quality.

Some writers were sounding the alarm that conference affiliation was necessary, but it went unheeded. The "Great Independents" group was never more than a scheduling agreement. The other three participants decided conference affiliation was in their best interests. The number of independent programs dropped from 17 to seven by the early 1990s, and the pressure on the Irish increased on a number of fronts.

Roger Valdiserri: "It was very difficult to get into the NCAA Tournament as an independent. The committee would pick five or six teams from a conference, and that left little room for independents. You had to have a very good record.

"It was also tough getting officials. We'd used the Big Ten, but we didn't feel comfortable playing Big Ten teams with Big Ten officials. So we went to the ACC because we felt the ACC had some really good officials. And that worked out pretty well, but. . . ."

Fran McCaffery: "It affected us in every way. In recruiting, we constantly had to defend our independent status. The ongoing theme of our opposition was our games were meaningless, we didn't play for anything. There was no conference tournament, there was no automatic bid, so every game we played was sort of like an exhibition game.

"So here we go out and sell that we are the only team in America that will play Duke and Carolina in the ACC, Boston College and Providence in the Big East, UCLA and USC and the Pac 10, Michigan in the Big Ten, DePaul and Marquette in Conference USA, Missouri in the Big Twelve. . . . Our schedule was the nation, and when we played on television it was national television.

"But television had changed in that era. We were fortunate because of our great football connections to have the NBC contract and get some NBC games. But the prospects were now watching ESPN, and we weren't on ESPN. We had our SportsChannel deal, and that was great. But the players were watching ESPN. We needed to get on Big Monday."

Slowly but surely the Notre Dame administration saw the need as well, and the wheels began turning to end the days of the Last Independent. The first option was the conference that already housed most of the other Irish sports programs.

Fr. Edward Malloy: "We were in the Midwest Collegiate Conference for most of our other sports, and it didn't have enough clout. So even if our teams did well, they didn't get an automatic bid into the NCAA. We felt to properly serve the range of sports we offered, we needed to be in a conference that would give those sports an advantage at the end of the season."

The Irish began to look to the ensemble that had started their trouble: the Big East. Dave Gavitt had always considered the Irish a natural fit and had talked informally to Dick Rosenthal about the possibility of Notre Dame joining in the late 1980s. His successor, Mike Tranghese, took the discussions a step further.

Mike Tranghese: "We took Miami in 1990, and then announced we were going to have a football league. We had a bunch of schools like Rutgers and West Virginia that were in our league just for football but not for everything else. They were pressuring us to come into the league.

"In 1995 when we made the decision to invite Rutgers and West Virginia as full members, it was difficult because it was going to expand our conference from 10 to 12 teams. Even though it would strengthen us, the basketball schools were concerned this was a football expansion and we needed to make a basketball statement. They posed the issue of Notre Dame coming in and joining us as our 13th team.

"When I spoke to the school presidents at that time, I asked they not view Notre Dame as someone we were bringing in to offset what we did with football because I thought both Rutgers and West Virginia would be good conference members in a lot of other sports. I made the claim at the time—and a couple of people told me I was wrong—if Notre Dame could be given a home and a little bit of time, they could become a national program again. I felt very strongly about that, even though there was some debate in our ranks. Our presidents then agreed to bring Notre Dame along as our 13th team, and that's where it all began."

Notre Dame administrators and coaches saw the synergies of such a relationship.

Fr. Bill Beauchamp: "It was founded as a basketball conference, so there wasn't any expectation that Notre Dame would bring in football. We weren't going to be the only team that would be in for basketball but not football. There were a number of private, Catholic schools. We had a lot of alumni in that part of the country. We had a number of conversations, but in the end, we felt there was a good fit."

Dick Rosenthal: "We looked at it and said the only detriment was the distance we'd have to travel. But the Big East, by virtue of their scheduling process, accommodated us in the number of classes missed. There wasn't the rigidity that we play every Tuesday night, because we couldn't do it. The mandate we had was not to miss more than three classes in a semester, and you can't do that if you've got to play every Tuesday night—too many Tuesday nights you are on the road."

It seemed like a win-win scenario. The Irish would get a home for their basketball team and a chance to rejuvenate their program. The Big East would bring in a nationally recognized university (and basketball program) that would increase its exposure.

But some Big East coaches didn't see it that way. Syracuse's Jim Boeheim wondered why the Big East had to "help that poor little college in South Bend," asking what the Irish had done for them. Boston College's Jim O'Brien feared the Irish would get well in a hurry at the Big East's expense. The coaches felt Tranghese not only had awakened a sleeping bear, he had also invited it in for dinner.

John MacLeod: "There was some complaining about it. But if you were in a conference and you needed another team, wouldn't you want one of the top schools in the country? I know one thing: Jim Boeheim never complained when we went to Syracuse to play and they had 32,000 people watching the game."

Fran McCaffery: "We understood it. It was a small number of teams, and five or six of those teams were guaranteed a bid to the NCAA Tournament. Now we were taking players away from them and we were going to compete with them and maybe take an NCAA bid away from them.

"But the bottom line was, when we would go to West Virginia, they would get bigger crowds. When we would go to Georgetown and Syracuse, they would get big crowds. That's what the Big East wanted, and that's what TV wants. So ultimately it was the right move for the Big East and the right move for Notre Dame."

Mike Tranghese: "I don't think Jim O'Brien's and Jim Boeheim's comments were necessarily directed at Notre Dame. They were directed at the fact we had expanded. Once you get past 10, you get into the world of no-wins in scheduling, because there's no easy solution in scheduling that many teams.

"I told both coaches they were right: what we did by going from 10 to 13 was not in the best interests of basketball if you looked at it from just that perspective. But if we hadn't done it, teams like Syracuse, Boston College,

Pittsburgh, and Miami might ultimately think about leaving the Big East in order to take care of their football interests."

Most of the players on the Irish roster at the time the decision was being made saw independence as a virtue. But they came to understand the need for the change and embraced it.

Carl Cozen: "One of the reasons I wanted to go to Notre Dame is that we'd be playing the best teams all the time. When the rumors about joining a conference started during my junior and senior years, none of the players I talked to wanted to do it. When your schedule had a lot of the best teams on it, you can finish 16-13 and still make the NCAA Tournament. Additionally, we'd have the advantage of having played top competition to get there."

Ryan Hoover: "I thought being an independent was a good thing because we got to play the best teams from each conference. Then I came to realize you needed to be in a conference. When you talk about the NCAA tournament . . . I realized that was going to be a more important thing."

Keith Kurowski: "I thought being affiliated with the Big East Conference would help the program get to that next level. Before we joined the Big East, the program as a whole was down. Many times we were overmatched. Our talent level didn't match the schedule. Not only did we not have speed, quickness, and athleticism, we were lacking skilled players. Joining the Big East attracted a lot of recruits, so it really helped."

In 1993, Notre Dame and the Big East announced the Irish would begin conference play in the 1996 season. But that would be three years down the road . . . three very long and painful years.

32

The Down Years
(1993–1994)

T he Irish certainly were not on Big Monday in the 1993 season, and given the preseason prospects, that was to be expected. The class of 1992 had graduated, taking 79 percent of team scoring and 65 percent of team rebounding with them. An NCAA reduction in scholarships from 15 to 13 left Notre Dame with only four scholarships to award in two years. The 1993 schedule featured 13 teams that would play in the NCAA Tournament, including three of the eventual Final Four: Indiana, Michigan, and Duke.

And on campus was one player who could possibly keep the Irish from being completely destroyed by the buzz saw that awaited them. Monty Williams, sidelined for two seasons with his heart ailment, had suffered being away from the court and took every opportunity to keep his skills sharp in preparation for a possible return.

Brooks Boyer: "Everyone knew he was the best player on campus. He just couldn't play with us. He was at the Rock every single day, and every once in a while he would come to practice. He rarely came to games. I don't think he could stand it."

"Any guy on the team, if you took the game away from us at that age, it would be devastating. But Monty just kept plugging away. He wasn't going to quit school and he wasn't going to quit on his dream, which was to play in the NBA. He was going to graduate and then he was going to go and try and play in the NBA. He'd sign any waiver.

"I'm sure he would have found other colleges that would have let him play. But he loved Notre Dame, he liked being there, and he knew he was going to be successful in whatever he did."

Carl Cozen: "The first two years, he wasn't supposed to be doing anything, but in the preseason he'd always play pickup games with us. He was really upset with the fact he wasn't allowed to play—not so much at the administration, the doctors or the school, but rather in general. Taking away something that was so important to him really shattered him."

But the two years had given doctors time to learn more about his problem and to determine how much danger Williams would face if he played.

Skip Meyer: "They were able to put a number on and categorize the problem. Yes, he still had the problem, but what percentage of these problems would likely crop up after doing all the tests? He was in a group where the percentages were very low.

"Did they have the science initially to tell us that? No. It was either you had it or you didn't have it. In those two years they developed the science to differentiate the degree of the problem. It made for more enlightened decisions. The new technology could predict whether he was in the high-risk category. Had he not been in that lowest category, he wouldn't have been allowed to play."

Williams was retested, and while he would still be at risk if he played, the risk was statistically very low—low enough that he could return to the team.

Brooks Boyer: "I was in summer school. I went in and Monty had his eyebrows shaved because they had so many things hooked up to him. I walked in and he was lying on his bed. He looked up and he said, 'I passed.'

"We had a star player, and we were pumped. He came and assumed the leadership role. He was our star, and it was great to have him back."

John MacLeod: "Once the medical staff said he could play, we just played him. We didn't limit the number of minutes. It's one thing to play three-on-three in the Pit. It's another thing to be playing Duke or Kentucky on national TV banging against some of the top talent in the country. So it took a while for Monty to get back to game shape."

Williams's return was pretty much the only silver lining in the 9-18 cloud that was the 1993 season. The schedule was just as brutal as advertised, and the talent was put in a tough position.

Lou Somogyi: "When you recruit players, your absolute worst case scenario is one out of three of them have to be 1,000 career point scorers. At the top programs, it's two out of three. And only one of Digger's last nine recruits was even a 500-point player: Billy Taylor scored 577 point and averaged 3.6 as a senior."

Brooks Boyer: "We didn't have any seniors because Monty was now in our year. We didn't have high expectations. We didn't expect to make the tournament. We weren't naïve. We just wanted to come and compete and get the respect of the teams, knowing our senior year we'd get some more horses in here."

As the losses mounted, so did the frustration of students, alumni, and fans. That frustration found a convenient target—the class of 1994, which had become the symbol of the decline of Irish basketball fortunes.

Carl Cozen: "When we came in, we heard a lot of things, like Digger knew he was going out so he didn't care who he recruited. And we'd be the first to admit we weren't the most talented class that had ever come to Notre Dame. But we never felt like we were given as much of a chance as we should have. The only times we ever played together were on Senior Day and one or two games in our freshman and sophomore years. So we never got a chance to play together and jell as a class."

Brooks Boyer: "We knew what we were brought in there to do—be good, smart ballplayers. We weren't there to run, jump, and dunk over people. We all had a specific role. None of us were going there to be superstars. But we all came in there to play, and we contributed to making Notre Dame basketball better."

Joe and Jon Ross, the twin centers, quickly became the butt of numerous campus jokes, including skits at the university's annual talent show, the Keenan Revue.

Jon Ross: "I let it go in one ear and out the other. I hung onto the important stuff and tried to listen to the coaches because that was the only thing that was going to get me playing time and make me better, not what people from the outside were saying."

Joe Ross: "We went through a lot. But it was a two-way street. These articles would come out in the *Observer* or whatever and have certain comments, and I'd get letters from students throughout the campus saying, 'Keep your chin up, you are doing great.'

"But when you got around the family—the basketball team family—people knew what you were doing. They appreciated what you were doing, they knew what your role was."

Brooks Boyer: "Joe and Jon took a beating. That's the unbelievable thing about those guys. Some of the stuff they went through, some of the things that were said about them, some of the Bookstore Basketball team names that were named after them, they took it all in stride. They come from a great family. They are great guys. They were good basketball players. And they proved it. In the final eight of the Bookstore Basketball Tournament our senior year, Joe's team was left, Jon's team was left, and my team was left."

Saddled with off-court baggage, the Irish prepared for 1994 bound and determined to make some improvement. The schedule was easing, with only four ranked teams and a reasonable number of home games. The senior leadership was strong, and the underclass talent included backcourt players Ryan Hoover and Keith Kurowski, who had recovered from the broken foot that sidelined him the previous year.

Fran McCaffery: "When we signed [Keith], we thought he was a major piece. We had to beat Kentucky and Villanova for him, and going into New

Jersey to get a guy away from Villanova was difficult. He was clearly one of the best players at the Nike camp, and at that time they only had 120 players, so if you were at the Nike camp and you were one of the best players, you were a pro."

The results did improve somewhat. The record was 12-17, but included tough losses like 74-72 to No. 2 Duke, and some big wins at the Joyce Center over No. 25 Missouri by two points, and a 13-point drubbing of No. 2 UCLA.

Billy Taylor: "It was a noon game on NBC. UCLA has always been a big game, and they had lost just one game before ours. We knew their quality of talent.
"We were excited—a big opponent, a nationally televised game. And you want to come out and have a good showing, perform well and make your university, your friends, family, and yourself proud. So we came out with great energy. We had a terrific crowd—it was packed, a great environment to play college basketball. We fed off of that emotion and energy and were able to play at a very high level."

Jon Ross: "You get through the first five minutes against ranked teams, especially at home, and you realize, 'Hey, we can play with these guys, let's get the job done.' It was a great win at home against an awfully good team, and it was great to have the crowd and the student body behind us."

But the problems persisted. Keith Kurowski was injured again, missing six weeks with torn cartilage in his knee. Lamarr Justice missed the first semester for academic reasons. The great wins were offset by head-scratching losses, such as a 70-58 defeat by an awful Loyola (Illinois) team at the Joyce Center. The team seemed to be missing focus and cohesion, and the students stayed away in droves—student season tickets plummeted from 4,500 in Digger Phelps's heyday to around 1,500 for the 1994 season.

Matt Gotsch: "It didn't seem like our students were very interested in the basketball program. Part of that falls on the team itself, and Notre Dame basketball had not seen a lot of success for a period of time. If you win, they come; if you don't, they don't show a lot of interest."

Billy Taylor: "When you go on losing and you are trying to figure out how to win, a lot of times it's a lack of confidence. Sometimes it just takes a couple of wins to start feeling good about yourself. Sometimes it takes making shots or making a big play. But it helps if a guy or two or three really starts feeling good and puts things together. There was a lack of confidence on how to win and get to a point where we could win a ballgame and feel good about ourselves."

Keith Kurowski: "I guess my years were a dark period in Notre Dame basketball. Those were the down years. And I will be the first to tell you we struggled during those years. When you are not successful, you are not going to have sellouts. I didn't think we had the talent to perform at a consistently high level when I played."

The Irish ended 1994 with the program at a crossroads. They were hopeful that the pending Big East membership would make a difference, but that was two seasons away and it would probably take a while for the program's momentum to shift. Notre Dame needed something to recapture the fans' interest in short order if it hoped to get its program back on the national map.

And from out of Monument, Colorado, someone came.

33

Arnzen Reincarnated
(1995)

Colorado isn't exactly a hotbed of high school basketball, so Pat Garrity wasn't ranked very highly by the recruiting services during his senior year. But something about him caught the eye of the Notre Dame coaching staff and they were determined to make him a part of the Irish program.

Fran McCaffery: "I was going through some recruiting lists, and his name kept coming up. I called Russ McKinstry, his high school coach, and I said, 'What can you tell me about him?' And I don't know if I've ever gotten a better recommendation from a high school coach.

"I flew out to see him, and it was one of the worst blizzards I've ever seen. I'm surprised they even played the game. They were telling people to leave during the game because of how bad the weather was. When the game ended, I was the only person left. I said, 'I'm not leaving. This kid is too good.'

"I went down and talked to Russ after the game. We really turned the heat up and encouraged him. He took an unofficial visit, which is difficult for a kid from Colorado. His father had to pay his expenses. His father appreciated that we were showing the interest. Coach MacLeod offered the scholarship. He came in for an official visit and he fell in love with the place."

John MacLeod: "I remember watching Pat Garrity in one of the AAU games, watching him move easily and make one jump shot after another. He had a knack for being in the right place at the right time, he always got himself open, and he helped his teammates out. That's one of the things I always looked at: Can a player help his teammates? Can he play in the system? And Pat did that."

College coaches give incoming players a training regimen to prepare for the rigors of Division I basketball. Garrity's adherence to it was an example of a work ethic that set him apart.

John MacLeod: "In the spring of his senior year we gave him a strength and conditioning program and asked him to start working out. When he came to campus in September he looked totally different. I said, 'How much work have you done?' And he said, 'Well, I've done a lot of work.' And right then, I knew we had a champ.

"Every year at the end of the year I'd give him something special to work on for the next season. And he would work all summer long on that thing we talked about. Then he would come back, and it was incredible what he'd done."

Ryan Hoover: "When we signed Pat, I remember the coaches saying he was a hard worker who was Mr. Basketball in Colorado. But who in Colorado would give him competition? When he was on his visit I hosted him and he wasn't even the big recruit that weekend.

"But Pat Garrity grew from being a really good high school player into one of the hardest working teammates I've ever had the opportunity to play with. He was so focused on what he wanted and what he wanted to become. And nobody got in his way."

Pete Miller: "The first time I played with him it was a football Saturday, and we would usually scrimmage on the court at the Joyce Center. They were only pickup games, which meant they were competitive, but not so much that guys were taking charges and that kind of thing. The first time we played, he was wearing everybody out. He was incredibly competitive, getting in people's faces. He was tireless, beating everybody down the floor. And this was as a freshman."

Lou Somogyi: "Every year he worked on an aspect of his game. From freshman to sophomore year it was rebounding. From sophomore to junior year it was defense. From junior to senior year it was three-point shooting. You want to talk about the poster boy for development? That was Pat Garrity."

Jack Lorri: "When I first saw him play, I told somebody, 'Oh my gosh, it's Arnzen reincarnated.' He was the only player I've ever seen at Notre Dame who was the most improved player three years in a row. He was the hardest working player I've ever seen in practice. Limited, disciplined with his feet. But he made himself a great player.

"And tough. Here's this good-looking super-A student with the world by the tail who was tough as nails. If somebody was giving him a hard time in practice, that guy would end up in the second row. That's why he's survived in the NBA—he's smarter than most, and always knew how to adjust his game accordingly."

An intelligent, talented forward with an unrelenting thirst to improve was a good tonic for an Irish program that had become stagnant. And Garrity wasted no time making his presence felt. In the season opener against Valparaiso he had 18 points and seven rebounds in 17 minutes of play. He supplemented 16 points apiece from Hoover and Kurowski with 14 of his own to help the Irish overcome a 13-point deficit and stun No. 9 Indiana in overtime. The Irish were 8-3 out of the gate—their best start since 1989—and confidence was high.

Billy Taylor: "To finally get off and feel good about ourselves was certainly a bonus. You wanted to keep building on that and try to keep the streak going as long as you can and feed off of that confidence."

Matt Gotsch: "We had a young team, Pat being a freshman and me being a sophomore, and we had a couple of other guys who were young like Marcus Young and Admore White. We were excited. We felt like this was our team now—our program, our opportunity to start producing and taking things and turning them around. That sophomore year was our chance to come out and show something and put Notre Dame back on the map."

But nothing came easy in the decade of discontent. Keith Kurowski, perhaps the most hard-luck player in Notre Dame history, was diagnosed with

Wolff-Parkinson-White Syndrome, a short circuit in his heart. The surgery to correct it was successful, but he ended up missing the rest of the season.

John MacLeod: "Not every player has that kind of explosiveness or can go for a big number in a short period of time like Kurowski. When Keith went down, the defense obviously focused on Pat Garrity. So it made it that much more difficult to compete."

Pete Miller: "Keith was like Pat in that when you saw him play when he was healthy, he was a step above everybody else. He really made a difference when he played because he was a fearless scorer. He also had a great personality—an extremely confident guy whose confidence rubbed off on his fellow players. Losing someone like that was a killer."

Pat Garrity: "Keith was a guy who could go for 25 or 30 any given night. He wasn't too great in shooting, but he was an explosive, veteran player, and we needed that at that time. We had young guys who were inexperienced. We needed a guy who was comfortable in the game. So when he went down, that took away one of those guys for us."

Without Kurowski's points and leadership, the Irish skidded, losing nine of their last 13 games, including a loss at Madison Square Garden to unranked Fordham. Scheduling difficulties in the pre-Big East season meant the Irish played their last game on February 28, so they were left in limbo for two weeks waiting for a postseason invitation . . . that never came.

John MacLeod: "You might be able to make a case for us. But we weren't strong enough to really be competitive in the NCAA. We weren't, at the time, quite ready for the NIT. We hadn't attracted enough attention. We didn't have a long winning streak. We didn't knock off a lot of opponents on their floor, which are some of the things you have to do."

Derek Manner: "We expected there'd be a decent chance for the NIT. The only thing everyone was upset with—and Coach definitely expressed his feelings about—was the embarrassment we took losing to Fordham at the Garden that year. That wasn't a team we should have lost to, particularly at the Garden with the NIT Commissioner and everyone else there. If we had won that game, 16-11 would have been enough to get us in."

The season was not without its highlights. For the second straight year, the Irish improved on the previous year's winning percentage. Their debut in the Big East would be the next year, and it was already having an effect on recruiting. And they had found a future star in dean's-list scholar Pat Garrity.

But John MacLeod was now 54-62 in four seasons in South Bend, and some players and writers wondered if the coach's laid-back approach was the right one for college basketball. An article in *Blue and Gold Illustrated* after the season suggested that perhaps a more forceful, vocal approach was needed, a claim MacLeod is quick to refute.

John MacLeod: "I'm about as laid back as Rambo. You don't have to scream and holler every minute and jump up and down all over the place to be competitive. I'm very competitive. But our players understood exactly what they were supposed to do. They knew when we were going to practice, it was going to be a demanding practice. And I don't think anybody could ever say I was laid back."

Derek Manner: "There were definitely people on the team who could have used getting yelled at a little more. But it's hard to say because every player has his own reaction. If he'd been hard on us, you'd probably get a different group of players complaining and they wouldn't perform as well as the other ones would."

Lou Somogyi: "He got that question a lot at press conferences, and he really took umbrage to it one time. He said, 'Look, we do our chewing out behind closed doors. I'm not there to do it in front of the crowd to let them know what a tough coach I am.' He was getting tired of that question that he was perceived as maybe too laid back.

"But that was the nature of his personality. He was kind of even-keeled, calm. John Wooden was the same way, but he won, so he was the 'quiet genius.' When you lose, you are perceived as not emotional. This school feeds off a shake-down-the-thunder guy. That's what Notre Dame wants. Maybe not the administration necessarily, but the fans love the Ara Parseghian–type emotion, that demonstrative spirit."

But any concerns about MacLeod's demeanor would have to take a backseat to more pressing matters like life in a conference, which the Irish would be experiencing firsthand the next year. The Big East was loaded . . . and Notre Dame was not.

34

Growing Pains
(1996–1997)

The All-Big East squads for the 1996 and 1997 seasons read like a list of NBA lottery picks: Kerry Kittles, Danya Abrams, John Wallace, Ray Allen, Allen Iverson, Tim Thomas, Richard Hamilton, and Austin Croshere. Conference coaches included Connecticut's Jim Calhoun, Georgetown's John Thompson, Syracuse's Jim Boeheim, and Boston College's Jim O'Brien; experienced, savvy veterans who were not about to give any slack to a newcomer. The teams oozed talent, with Connecticut, Villanova, Georgetown, and Syracuse making top 10 appearances. Of the 13 conference teams, seven received a postseason bid in at least one of the two seasons, with Syracuse losing in the NCAA Tournament Championship game in 1996 and Georgetown and Providence appearing in the Elite Eight in 1996 and 1997, respectively.

This was the atmosphere that awaited a Notre Dame program still trying to right itself. A reasonable person would not expect the Irish to contend immediately, and few outside of campus did—pollsters picked the Irish no higher than 10th in the conference preseason, and they were expected to battle fellow newcomers West Virginia and Rutgers to avoid the basement.

But that sentiment did not find its way into the Irish locker room. The team was realistic about its chances, but not ready to use its youth and inexperience as a crutch.

Matt Gotsch: "We talked a lot about how it took Miami over three years to win a road game in the Big East, and we told ourselves we weren't going to wait that long. We were going to compete at every opportunity, and we weren't going to back down from anybody."

Phil Hickey: "There was some excitement, but at the same time we were going into it with some caution. We only had one senior, so we were a very young team. And I don't think anyone knew really what to expect. There wasn't an off night in the Big East, especially that first year. We wanted to come in and season ourselves and see what happened."

The Irish welcomed their most heralded recruiting class in years, highlighted by two potential difference-makers: Doug Gottlieb, one of the best point guards in the class, and wing man Gary Bell, runner-up to Kevin Garnett for Mr. Basketball in the state of Illinois.

Pat Garrity: "My first impression of Doug was he had a swagger. He was cocky. And that's the kind of guy you want running your team. You see Chris Thomas with that swagger, and it's a real swagger. Doug's came from a little bit of insecurity, maybe, so he wasn't really the leader he could have been. But my first impression was it was going to be fun playing with him because this was a guy who loved to pass."

Antoni Wyche: "Gary had a lot of talent. The one thing that impressed me was his muscular physique—6 foot 4 inches, 225 pounds, and he was solid. For a high school player, that's ridiculous. Then I saw his ability. Even though he was only 6-foot-4, or whatever, he managed to score in the post on people 6 foot 8 inches or 6 foot 7 inches due to his strength. He could go to the perimeter.

"With the recruiting class we had—Doug at the 'one,' me at the 'two,' Gary playing either the 'three' or 'four,' and Phil Hickey at the 'five'—around Pat, along with Admore White, Ryan Hoover, and Keith Kurowski . . . I thought we had a pretty good team."

But problems developed almost from the start. Bell, accustomed to being the focus of his team in high school, was having a hard time adjusting to the college game and keeping himself healthy.

Pete Miller: "Gary was definitely used to being the man in high school. He was tremendously talented physically, but didn't understand the team concept very well. The coaches got on him because he tended to shoot the ball every time he got it.

"Gary would've had a great career, but he had a lot of injuries. Every time he'd start to make improvements, he'd break a foot or something. We were practicing in the Pit one day his freshman year and he was really playing well, but he hurt his knee. Usually when someone would get hurt in practice, practice would move to the other end of the floor while Skip Meyer would come out to get the guy quietly. When Gary got hurt, practice just stopped. Usually Coach MacLeod was a pretty even-keeled guy and you couldn't read his emotions too well. But when that happened, you could tell he was thinking, 'Here we go again.'"

Fran McCaffery: "That was really a sad situation. We got probably more publicity for signing Gary Bell than anybody we ever signed because he was from Chicago and we had to beat all the Big Ten schools to get him.

"It became a distraction because he'd play and play well, and then he'd get hurt again. We couldn't plan on having him in the lineup. The plan originally was he would be the 'three' and Garrity the 'four.' You would be hardpressed to find two better forwards in the country. It's really a shame—it was one injury after another with Gary."

Gottlieb, meanwhile, had to deal with the pressures of running the team as a freshman point guard . . . and, according to some players, with the added pressure brought on by his father, Bob Gottlieb, a coach himself who didn't agree with how MacLeod and his staff were utilizing his son.

Keith Kurowski: "His dad was a very intense individual. He was often traveling with the team and sitting behind the bench. And at times it appeared he was trying to coach his son during the game. So his presence presented some conflicts of interest, because I'm not so sure he always would coach his son from an objective standpoint with the betterment of the team in mind.

Looking back at it now, it turned out to have some negative impact on how Doug played and on the chemistry of the team."

Phil Hickey: "His dad really, really pushed him hard. And there wasn't anything wrong with that. He wanted basketball to be his career, so his dad was pushing him for that. He was thinking of being in the NBA, which was his goal and the goal of most college players.

"I know there were some differences between him and his dad with the coaching staff. That was reflected in the chemistry occasionally. Doug got along really well with his teammates, but he needed the space a little bit from his dad. There was a lot of pressure when his dad was around."

Fran McCaffery: "Very definitely. And to his credit, he apologized for it and backed off, because it became very confrontational, and there was a confrontation. And to his credit, he backed off and let the kid play."

With turmoil on and off the court, the Irish embarked on their maiden Big East voyage. In the grand scheme of things, it was a forgettable one—another 9-18 record, with four Big East wins against 14 losses and the Irish learning very quickly what they would need to compete in the league.

John MacLeod: "I remember Dick Vitale saying we joined at the wrong time. Well, what are you going to do, wait until everybody's down and then say OK, now we are going to join? We joined at the right time, because we took some licks. Pat Garrity was the recipient of some of the most physical basketball play I've ever seen at the collegiate level. We knew we needed to be stronger. We knew we needed to be quicker and deeper. So we set out to get bigger, stronger, quicker kids."

Fran McCaffery: "You have to go through it to understand what the Big East is. I don't know if people truly understand what it's like every night to play somebody who is really good and really physical in a hostile environment on the road. It's really difficult to win on the road in that league. I know we beat St. John's in the Garden. But all of our other wins that year were at home, and we only won four games. So it's the whole idea of every night having a big, big game."

But there was reason for optimism. After getting their first Big East win at home in a rematch against Rutgers, the Irish picked up their first conference road win in short order, stunning St. John's by three at Madison Square Garden. The Irish felt they were on the move with four conference wins in their inaugural season. They had survived relatively intact and wiser for the experience, setting the stage for what was sure to be improvement in year two.

No sooner had the season ended, however, than the optimism was tested. Doug Gottlieb informed the coaching staff in late June he would be transferring, a decision that didn't necessarily surprise his teammates.

Ryan Hoover: "I heard it about the same time everybody else did. I talked to Doug, and he just said he was transferring. He didn't say anything about the fact they were telling him he had to go. He kind of covered it all up. He just said he was leaving school. It was not too long after everything came out about the credit cards."

Gottlieb had been accused of stealing one of his dorm-mates' credit cards and using it at some local stores. The stores provided security tapes that showed Gottlieb making the purchases. Gottlieb made restitution to his classmate, but his Notre Dame career was over.

Fran McCaffery: "There was a lot of discussion. He had some problems that were fairly well documented, and we were trying to help him through those issues and not bury him—sort of let him leave with his dignity, but at the same time knowing he couldn't be a part of the team anymore based on what happened. We had assurances from his family he would take care of his problem, which he did.

"I'm happy for Doug that things worked out well for him. He just had a problem. A lot of people have problems. It was immaturity, and he overcame it. His family supported him. His father and I are good friends to this day. But we had some issues at that point that needed to be addressed, and we addressed them."

The turbulence wasn't over. Keith Kurowski, back for a fifth year because he had missed his first season with a broken foot, began to experience back pain as the 1997 season began.

Skip Meyer: "He came back from summer break with a sore back. Usually we're not very concerned about those things, but because it was him, we wanted to check it out more closely. We came to find out he had a disc problem. There was nothing we could do—it was a nonsurgical case. We rested him and put him on an exercise program. But he determined he had had enough. His back was just not going to allow him to play."

Kurowski's departure meant Pete Miller, a walk-on who had been forced to leave the team because a scholarship was not available for him, could return to the squad. Given the strong friendship between the two young men, the ending was probably as good as either could hope for given the circumstances.

Keith Kurowski: "If I had to pick one person who my injury could have benefited in terms of my scholarship, Pete Miller's name was right at the top of the list. It could not have happened to a better individual. Pete Miller is someone you would want your daughter to date. He was that type of squeaky-clean individual. So I was extremely happy he was able to come join the team as a result of my injury."

The Irish made definite improvements in their second conference year, with Pat Garrity coming into his own. He led all scorers with 36 points in a one-point loss to No. 8 Indiana. At one point in the first half of a game against Syracuse, he had personally outscored the Orangemen 16 to 15. In the second game against them, he barely missed the first triple-double in the history of Irish basketball with 22 points, 13 rebounds, and 9 assists.

Pete Miller: "Pat definitely became a star that year. In the conference, you could hear other coaches yelling at their players 'There's Garrity' and 'Watch out for Garrity.' People would be heckling Garrity when we played on the road. He was not just an above-average player in the conference but also a great player nationally. We didn't play anyone in the conference that year better than Pat, which meant something to us. We may not have been as talented as those guys, but we had the best player on the court."

Garrity's performance didn't go unnoticed by conference-mates. He was voted Big East Player of the Year, only the third in Big East history who didn't play on a first- or second-place team, and first-team all-conference, while MacLeod's peers voted him Big East Coach of the Year.

Pete Miller: "We were very happy for him when he got the award. Everybody respected him so much, and he had caught so much flak and not had a lot of success. I was excited for him. It meant a lot to him. It was the first tangible sign of people affirming him as a coach at ND."

An NIT bid was extended, and the Irish knocked off Oral Roberts and TCU before falling by one to a Michigan team that would go on to win the championship at Madison Square Garden.

Notre Dame had endured its conference growing pains. The question became: could they take the next step and finally return to the NCAA Tournament?

35

Exodus
(1998–1999)

John MacLeod ended the 1997 season on a high note. He had won eight conference games in his second season in the Big East, double the previous season's total, and was named Big East Coach of the Year. The team had come within one point of a trip to New York City and the NIT semifinals. Big East Player of the Year Pat Garrity would be back for his senior year and was a preseason All-American.

But all was not well in the House of MacLeod. His original five-year contract had been fulfilled, and as was customary at Notre Dame at that time, the agreement became a year-to-year arrangement—a definite detriment when they hit the recruiting trail.

Fran McCaffery: "They would not allow us to recruit on an even playing field. We felt that him being Coach of the Year would propel the administration to give him a contract extension and put the rumors to bed and allow us to continue to get the best players in the country. Instead, they gave him one other one-year contract and told him they were going to evaluate him on his recruiting."

Mike Wadsworth, who had replaced Dick Rosenthal as athletic director in 1995, had attempted to quantify what the administration was looking for in terms of success. The team understood the effect.

Phil Hickey: "It was tough when recruits would come in because they would say, 'Is Coach MacLeod going to be here next year?' We would say, 'We can only hope, you know, but we enjoy him.' Coach MacLeod is an honest person. He's not going to say, 'Well, I'll be here for five years,' when it's a year-to-year contract. So it was hardest on incoming recruits because I know I had the same concerns going to other schools."

As big a concern as the players coming in, however, was an increase in the number of players transferring out. Immediately following the 1997 season, David Lalazarian followed fellow Californian Doug Gottlieb out the door, transferring to Pepperdine to be closer to home. Then in August, the oft-injured Gary Bell became the sixth player to transfer during MacLeod's tenure, leaving for North Carolina State.

Antoni Wyche: "It was a downhill slide for him. Having back surgery before coming to school, not performing his freshman year the way he wanted to, and then suffering injury after injury really took a toll on his confidence and his whole perspective and his outlook on things. Everyone handles adversity differently, and this was the first time he was ever really faced with it.

"It wasn't really that the coaches were upset with his actions on the court. It was the decisions he was making outside of basketball that ultimately doomed him—being ineligible, getting into trouble on campus, stuff like that."

The reasons varied, but there was a steady stream of talent leaving Notre Dame, and the university administration noticed.

Fr. Bill Beauchamp: "You look at the top 100 players in the country coming out of high school, there's a big percentage that you have to lop off and can't even consider because of our academic standards. Having said that, there are a lot of high-caliber, talented athletes out there who can be successful and admitted at Notre Dame. We expected to be successful in that regard.

"Was the number of outbound transfers a concern to the administration? It always is. We want our students to graduate and we want them to graduate from Notre Dame. If they leave Notre Dame and graduate somewhere else, fine, they've graduated. But at the same time, if a student comes to Notre Dame and is unhappy here, we'd be concerned. Was it not a good fit to begin with, or did something happen?"

With Pat Garrity becoming more of a target in 1998, the Irish needed a second offensive option to keep opposing defenses honest. And as the season progressed, they found one in Keith Friel, a 6-foot 3-inch sophomore guard. Friel's last-second jumper gave the Irish an early-season upset win over No. 20 West Virginia, and he set what is still the Irish record for three-pointers in a game with eight against No. 15 Syracuse. Starting against St. John's at Madison Square Garden, Friel scored 16 points in a 73-65 win that bumped Notre Dame's record up to 11-7. But that would be his final contribution that season.

Skip Meyer: "In the last 20 seconds of the St. John's game, he came to the bench and he couldn't walk. He got hit in the worst place possible. Keith, unfortunately, was a slow healer and he never recovered that season. He missed a ton of time at the wrong time."

Derek Manner: "That made a huge difference. Friel was off and on, but he had a killer shot. He really helped spread the court and got Pat some relief and it was really a good combination. When he went down, that impacted our ability to attack."

With Garrity left on his own, the Irish staggered to a 2-7 finish and were knocked out of the Big East Tournament by Providence in front of about 5,000 people at Madison Square Garden. Worse, the Irish learned after the season that Friel would add his name to the growing list of transfers.

Derek Manner: "You get a feeling about guys—how hot they are about the school in general, how they get along with the coach, how they're enjoying school and the academics. You get a feel for their happiness. Friel never bought into the system as much as other people did."

The outlook seemed grim. Garrity, a second-team All-American and the school's No. 3 career scorer, was gone to the NBA, and Friel, who had been counted on to pick up some of the offensive slack had left for the University of Virginia.

But all was not lost for 1999. After years of criticism of his recruiting, MacLeod and his staff were bringing in a top-20 freshman class: David Graves, Harold Swanagan, and Troy Murphy.

Troy Murphy: "I went to high school with [NBC broadcaster and Notre Dame alumnus] Don Criqui's son. He was a couple of years older than me, and he was a friend of John MacLeod. So Don Criqui kind of put the bug in my ear about Notre Dame basketball and got me interested in it."

John MacLeod: "Don Criqui called during Troy's sophomore year and said, 'John, you've got to look at this Murphy kid. He's real young and he's not real strong now. But somewhere down the road, it looks like he's going to be a good player.' So we started the recruiting process. And boy, was Don Criqui right. He turned out to be one heck of a player."

Fran McCaffery: "I probably spoke to [David's father] Steve Graves 500 times before we offered David a scholarship. We got a call from his high school coach when he was a freshman. His father called and said they might make an unofficial visit. Then we developed a friendship, and it was evident to all of us that if we offered, he would come.

"I loved Swanagan because I had seen him play at the same tournament I had seen David in during the summer. David's high school coach said, 'You guys ought to turn the heat up because he's getting some heavy recruitment. But I think David's relationship with Harold will help you.' So we turned the heat up on Harold and got David involved."

The coaches and players believed this was the difference-making recruiting class they'd been waiting for. But there didn't seem to be much of a difference in the early part of the 1999 season. After getting blown out by No. 1 Duke in the first round of the Great Alaska Shootout, the team bottomed out with an 88-82 overtime loss to the host school, Division II Alaska-Anchorage.

Fran McCaffery: "We played a team that was perimeter-oriented with terrific shooters, and they came out with incredible energy. From the opening tip they were just draining threes. We were working hard; we were not flat.

But they were hitting jump shot after jump shot after jump shot, and they got ahead. Troy really put us on his back and got us into overtime.

"I can still see the play. The kid came off of a double-team and banged a three with Wyche right in his face, one of the most incredible shots I've ever seen. That broke our back. We were up one, and that gave them the lead back by two."

Inconsistency continued as the season progressed. Four days after the loss in Alaska, the Irish took No. 16 Indiana into overtime before falling by four. The elation from a 23-point win over Pittsburgh was snuffed out by a 31-point loss to Villanova two nights later. The transfer train continued, with Hans Rasmussen, Leviticus Williamson, and little-used Peter Okwalinga leaving during or after the season, reportedly raising the temperature on John MacLeod's hot seat.

David Graves: "We really didn't think about it. The only thing we heard was 'John MacLeod is my guy,' and we believed it. We had both feet in with Coach MacLeod. He spent extra time after practice, especially with me, watching films and breaking down the game and helping me understand it's not just what you do, it's what you do to help your teammates and what your teammates do to help you. That really opened our minds up."

Troy Murphy: "The funny thing is I was given a vote of confidence late in the season—Coach MacLeod was going to be back. I remember talking to one of the assistant coaches and he said we would hear some stuff about Coach MacLeod being let go or asked to resign and it was simply not true. He was going to be back the next year."

The Irish finished 14-16 and were eliminated in the first round of the Big East Tournament by Seton Hall, a team they had swept during the regular season. But the staff went into the off-season hopeful, because another top-50 recruit, Matt Carroll, would be joining Murphy, Graves, and Swanagan the next season.

Little did they know they wouldn't be there to see it.

Fran McCaffery: "John and I were supposed to fly to see Romeo Augustine, who had committed to us but was sort of wavering. We were going there to lock him up. It was snowing, so the pilots called and said we weren't going to fly. We were in our offices working and John's door was closed for a long time. Then he came out and called us into the meeting room and told us he had resigned."

Was it in fact a resignation? All involved describe it that way, but when the details emerge it becomes less clear.

Mike Wadsworth: "John wanted to stay at Notre Dame. John was hopeful that his recruitment of Troy Murphy and the fact that Matt Carroll was coming in—and to be fair to John, those were major breakthroughs—was an indication that the corner was being turned after eight years. But at the end of that season, there was no chance we could say we were making progress.

"It was a very difficult decision for all of us, because John MacLeod was a tremendous asset to the university as a person. John is the sort of person you would want to have representing the university, the kind of person who if you were a parent you would want to have coaching your son. But there were these other realities we had to deal with, and those were the factors that led to John's resignation."

Fr. Bill Beauchamp: "He had been there eight years. In his first year he had a number of successes, but we didn't go anywhere from there. Our teams didn't get any better, it seemed. Obviously he needed some time because he didn't inherit a bunch of talent. But we didn't seem to be in the ballpark for enough good players."

Whether forced or otherwise, many felt MacLeod should have been given one more season to see what he could do with the young talent coming into the program.

Jack Lorri: "John did not attend his press conference announcing his resignation, and neither did I because it insulted my intelligence to tell me he'd resigned. He didn't resign. I really liked the man a lot, so I didn't want to participate in that charade. I felt very bad because I thought he might have a chance to turn it around. But that's a part of sports."

Troy Murphy: "I don't think it was very fair how he was dismissed so quickly. I really think we were turning the corner. We had a great recruiting class with Dave, Harold, and me, and then we had Matt Carroll and Mike

Monserez coming in the next year. We were one year away from turning the corner."

David Graves: "Business is business, and people try to sugarcoat things a little too much. There probably could be an argument. But Notre Dame had to do what it had to do, and if there was going to be a change that was probably the time for it because you had young guys generating a lot of excitement and who were going to be good. You need new excitement."

Regardless of their opinion about his departure, all agree that John MacLeod made a critical contribution to Irish basketball.

Lou Somogyi: "He really set the table. I will never, ever mention Notre Dame's revival without mentioning John MacLeod because he sort of had to be Moses. Moses never got to see the Promised Land. His job was to get across the river, and he did his job. But to get to the next level, they needed somebody else."

Skip Meyer: "You develop relationships, and you hate it when bad things happen to good people. You won't find a nicer, more gentlemanly person than John MacLeod.

"The players respected John as a coach and as a person. The night we won the Big East [Western Division] championship, the whole team called John at his home and thanked him for bringing a championship to Notre Dame. Every player who he had recruited talked to him and thanked him. John was very proud of their accomplishments."

The
Matt Doherty
Year

(2000)

36

Emotional Rescue
(2000)

S ometime during the late 1970s, the story goes, a talented Irish Catholic
high school basketball player from Hicksville, New York, received a
recruiting letter from Notre Dame. The letter exhorted Michael
Doherty to consider a basketball future with the Fighting Irish.

One problem: the young man's name was Matthew.

Clerical error notwithstanding, Matt Doherty thought long and hard
about the Irish before casting his lot with North Carolina. That process
would be repeated 20 years later with similar results, but not before
Doherty had revitalized a moribund Irish program with his enthusiasm
and emotion.

Although he won a national championship with the Tar Heels,
Doherty still considered himself a Notre Dame fan. Throughout his
coaching career, as a three-year assistant at Davidson and then through
seven seasons with Roy Williams at Kansas, Doherty kept his Irish eyes on
South Bend, wondering if he might have a future there. And when John
MacLeod's resignation was announced, he saw his chance to slip in under
the radar.

Matt Doherty: "The best thing about the process was no one thought I was involved. So I wasn't getting calls from the media and I wasn't getting calls from other assistant coaches wanting to be on my staff if I got the job.

"I was at the Final Four in Tampa and I was walking the street. A guy came up to me and said, 'Notre Dame ought to consider you for the job. You would be a great fit there.' And I just smiled and waved and said, 'Yes, I know.' I was meeting with Fr. Malloy the next day for my second interview."

As an assistant, Doherty was well known for his recruiting fervor. He employed the same tactics in his pursuit of the Notre Dame job.

Matt Doherty: "I would find out what they were looking for, what their interests were. I knew Bubba liked to play golf, so I'd send him golf balls with my name on them. I was recruiting them like I was recruiting a great high school player."

Doherty's pedigree appealed to Notre Dame administrators who viewed him as a sociological fit for the job.

Fr. Edward Malloy: "Matt came from a high-quality program. He was young. He didn't have a lot of experience, which was a negative, but he seemed to have a lot of energy, good ideas and had a pretty good sense of what it took to succeed."

Fr. Bill Beauchamp: "He was very heavily involved in recruiting at Kansas. He knew the recruiting scene. For us, that was critical. He had a lot of enthusiasm. You're not going to get an overnight fix, but we felt Matt could turn around the program quickly."

Most of the attention during the search had centered on Utah's Rick Majerus, with Xavier's Skip Prosser, Delaware's Mike Brey and Sienna's Paul Hewitt also being mentioned, so Doherty's candidacy took Notre Dame observers by surprise.

Lou Somogyi: "I was really stunned. We [Blue & Gold] put his name in as an afterthought. We thought they would be looking for a head coach with experience, and Skip Prosser was the safe choice. So when they chose Matt Doherty, I didn't know what to think."

On March 30, 1999, at his introductory press conference, Doherty was overcome with emotion and wept. This emotional fervor would come to characterize his tenure with the Irish . . . sometimes for good and sometimes for ill.

Doherty jumped into his new position with both feet, and his first order of business was recruiting. The Irish had Matt Carroll and Mike Monserez as freshmen for the 2000 season, but Doherty augmented the class with two Croatian players, Ivan Kartelo and Jere Macura. He also knew of a young man at Oklahoma named Ryan Humphrey who Doherty had recruited when he was at Kansas and who had just announced his intention to transfer. Although Notre Dame wasn't known for accepting many athletic transfers, Doherty viewed Humphrey as a difference-maker and decided to roll the dice.

Ryan Humphrey: "My relationship with Coach Doherty made Notre Dame attractive. That was the big picture. If I didn't make it to the league, I wanted to get a quality degree. I had two things in mind: a chance of being seen a lot on TV and getting a great degree. Notre Dame did those things for me."

Humphrey's decision to join the Irish was a wake-up call to the program's long-suffering fans that things were going to be different. All around the Irish nation, fans who had wandered away from the program during the lean years of the 1990s began to perk up, wondering who this energetic go-getter was and what he was going to do next.

If the players were asking themselves the same question, it was answered quickly.

Lou Somogyi: "In basketball, when you take a charge, everybody rushes over to pick up their teammate—that's like a thank-you for doing it. The first practice I went to, they had a scrimmage. After a player would take a charge, everyone would just stand around. Doherty was screaming, 'Pick up your teammates!'

"The third or fourth practice I went to, somebody took a charge, and it was instinctive. Everyone was rushing to pick up their teammate. And I said, 'Wow, this guy has definitely got motivational skills. I don't know how he is strategically, but he's got the fire. He's got that burning passion.' "

That passion always seemed to be burning, which meant the players would bask in its warmth in the good times and burn in its intensity in the bad. One of their first exposures to the latter came after a loss to Marathon Oil in an exhibition game. Stung by the South Bend Tribune's description of the effort as "lackadaisical," Doherty decided to call a special practice.

Matt Doherty: "We had a scheduled day off that day, but we had already given them a day off that week. So NCAA-wise, we could practice. I told the staff to tell the managers to get the team there. No balls. We were just going to run. I'd be darned if anybody was going to call my team lackadaisical."

David Graves: "That was the worst day of my life. We ran and we had to make times. We were running and running and running to the point where nobody was making their times, but we had to keep running. We had people vomiting. Saliva would get so thick you couldn't get it out of your mouth. I thought it was a little extreme at the time. But that's the way Coach Doherty does it. When he wants to make a point, he makes a point."

Troy Murphy: "I remember garbage cans in the four corners of the court. Jere and Ivan were cursing in Croatian. It was an unbelievable physical and mental strain. It was the hardest practice I ever had. At the time it didn't make any sense, but it brought us closer—got us to band together and want to show the coaching staff we were better than they thought we were."

Opening the season at fourth-ranked Ohio State in the preseason NIT, the players were anxious to send that message to the coaches. The Buckeyes had been to the Final Four the previous season, and ESPN would be televising Doherty's Notre Dame debut.

Troy Murphy: "We were on the bus, and everyone was still pretty worked up about the whole wind-sprint incident. There wasn't going to be anything harder than doing that. We were in pretty rare form, pretty keyed up."

Matt Carroll: "It was my first college game, and there were over 20,000 people there. I was nervous. But after a while, I was thinking, 'These are the guys that are supposed to be one of the top five teams in the nation, and we're hanging right with them . . . ahead of them, actually.'"

They stayed ahead of them through most of the game, but the lead see-sawed back and forth in the closing minutes. As the clock ran down, David Graves came off a Harold Swanagan screen and buried a jumper from the wing with less than a second to go, giving the Irish an attention-grabbing 59-57 victory.

Troy Murphy: "It was one of the top feelings I've had playing basketball when Dave hit that shot. No one really believed we could win a game like that—go into someone else's place and beat a team like Ohio State that was ranked very high in the preseason. It was a great win for us, and gave us a lot of confidence as a young team."

Emotions were riding high. Doherty's enthusiasm was infectious, and the team, the fans, and even the media were drawn into it. But while that enthusiasm magnified the highs, it also seemed to deepen the lows, and the Irish embarked on a season-long roller-coaster ride.

After winning their first three games, the Irish dropped five of six. They went to No. 2 Connecticut for their Big East opener and upset the Huskies 75-70 behind a spectacular performance by Murphy, but followed it up with a 76-51 clunker at lowly Rutgers. A second victory against Connecticut was offset by a devastating loss to Providence, where previously unknown Donta Wade shot the lights out from beyond the three-point line as the Irish would not come out of their zone defense to contest him.

Off the court, things were growing contentious as well. Doherty had decided to replace two-year starter Martin Ingelsby at point guard with senior Jimmy Dillon. He cited Dillon's personality and toughness, but the decision did not sit well with Ingelsby and some of his friends on the team. Against Indiana, Doherty subbed in the four freshmen to send a message to his starters that he thought they were playing soft. After losses to Pittsburgh and Villanova, he pleaded with the team to tell him if there was something wrong with his approach.

The question began to surface: Was Doherty's emotional nature a good or bad thing? Were the Irish getting inspired or too tightly wound to function properly?

Troy Murphy: "His fiery approach was good. We were young, and there were a lot of knuckleheads on the team. We needed a kick in the butt sometimes, and he was right there to do it."

Martin Ingelsby: "In the beginning it was definitely a good thing for our team, because he brought a lot of intensity and a lot of passion to the practice court and to the game. He was passionate about turning the program around. But after a while it just got old. The yelling and screaming wore on the players a lot."

Ryan Humphrey: "Before he got there, Notre Dame was kind of known as a pushover. People said the only thing to do with Notre Dame is be physical with them and they will back down. But Coach Doherty brought that attitude and that aggression, and it showed. He had those guys believing in themselves. And confidence is a dangerous thing."

David Graves: "After a while it was like, all right, something needs to change. We need not to be so emotionally involved with this, or somebody needs to change their way of handling things. Basketball is a huge part of all of our lives, no doubt about it. But it shouldn't be this big. You always want to win, and you always do the best in everything. But when it's making you miserable, something needs to change.

"It got a little frustrating after a while. We didn't talk to him about it. People were scared to say anything to him. We just went about our business, and if he was having a day like that, then I guess it was just him having a day like that."

The players weren't the only ones riding the roller coaster; the student body was right there with them. Doherty had met with student leaders in the months before the season, making the point that a strong home-court advantage would help the team succeed. The students took the lesson to heart, forming "Matt's Outrageous Bunch," or the M.O.B., a fanatical cheering squad for the Joyce Center.

The new enthusiasm made a difference, but that difference was not always positive. Taunts at Connecticut player Khalid El-Amin before the game at the Joyce Center forced the athletic department to issue a public statement regarding sportsmanship. In the closing seconds against Syracuse, a student reacted to a referee's call by throwing a water bottle onto the court. It was not the first such incident of the game, so the officials called a technical foul on the crowd and the resulting free throws cost the Irish any chance they had at victory. Some Irish officials believed Doherty had created a monster that he was now unable to control.

Matt Doherty: "How ironic that at the beginning of the year we were just hoping somebody would show up, and the end of the season we were having some crowd-control issues."

Troy Murphy: "I really didn't know what had happened. I thought Jere had kicked a bottle or something and they were trying to give him a technical for it. It was pretty weird to find out someone had thrown a bottle."

David Graves: "It was kind of a bittersweet moment. You hate the fact that somebody outside the game had affected its outcome. However, we were excited they were passionate enough that they felt they needed to do that. So it was kind of frustrating, but yet these are the people who are backing us.

"I've always been taught to let the [players] decide the outcome of the game. So it was pretty frustrating."

The frustration wouldn't end with the Syracuse game. The Irish finished the season 18-14, with wins over Ohio State, Seton Hall, St. John's, and Connecticut. But the emotional tide was not enough to sway the tournament selection committee, which looked instead at defeats against Vanderbilt, Miami of Ohio and Providence, and decided Notre Dame's NCAA drought would not end that season.

Martin Ingelsby: "I was disappointed because we felt we deserved to be there. I know we had double-digit losses and maybe the selection committee thought we lost too many games against teams we should have beat. But we thought we had a very good year and had brought Notre Dame basketball back to where it should have been."

Matt Carroll: "People were saying, 'You can do it, you're right on the bubble, you're one of those teams.' You hear you're in and you hear you're not. It's so many different things along the way. We felt we were in—at least I did, and I think most of the players did. You've got ESPN, CBS, and all those cameras around and you're thinking, 'Why are these people here if we're not in?' "

Matt Doherty: "My game plan was if we were not invited, I was going to get them in the locker room and tell them we were going to be excited about going to the NIT. We were going to show the NCAA they should have invited us and not sulk or cry or say no, we don't want to go. I'd seen teams do that, and then they'd perform without emotion in the NIT."

As they had many times before, the Irish took advantage of their NIT bid and went all the way to the championship game. But they didn't have enough to win the championship, and Wake Forest ended Notre Dame's season 71-61.

The immediate concern in the postseason was Troy Murphy, who had been named Notre Dame's first consensus All-American since Adrian Dantley 24 years before. His value in the NBA was high. Would he forego his last two years of eligibility and enter the draft?

Matt Doherty: "I tried to educate him and his family on the process. Having been at Kansas and at North Carolina, I knew how Coach Smith and Coach Williams handled it. I tried to gather information about where he'd be drafted and then give him and his family the information and let them make the decision."

Troy Murphy: "I was having a great time in college playing basketball. The NBA was more of a business or a job. I was there with my friends like Matt Carroll, Jimmy Dillon, Todd Palmer, David Graves, all those guys. It was fun, and I wanted to continue to do it. I thought we could accomplish great things my junior year—we had Ryan Humphrey coming in along with some good recruits. So I was excited and looking forward to my junior year."

Fans who had anticipated Murphy's departure rejoiced in his decision to stay. But their fears had not been unfounded. There would be a departure before the 2001 season began, and it would come from an unexpected source.

On June 30, North Carolina coach Bill Guthridge resigned unexpectedly. Attention quickly turned to Kansas coach Roy Williams, who was invited to return to his alma mater. With ties to both institutions, Matt Doherty quickly became a hot topic of conversation.

Matt Doherty: "My mind was racing a lot of different ways—what's going to happen, how do I prepare for it. I remember calling Coach Smith saying, 'Coach, what if Kansas were to call me. How should I handle this?' I wanted to make a quick decision if Kansas were to call. Coach Smith said, 'Well, things aren't done here with Coach Williams yet, and you are still on the list.' And I said 'Oh, that's a no-brainer. That's not going to happen. Coach Williams is going to take the job.' "

But it wasn't a no-brainer. Williams, after some public soul-searching, declined the offer, leaving the Tar Heels with a very public job opening. As other candidates like Larry Brown and George Karl fell by the wayside, Doherty began to emerge as the favorite.

Skip Meyer: "When Roy Williams turned it down, that made Matt a more viable candidate. I got a call from Larry Gallo, the associate athletic director at Carolina who coached here—we're very close friends—to ask me what I thought about Matt. That's when I knew they were getting serious."

Doherty flew to North Carolina to interview for the job and was left with a decision to make. After reflection and a much-publicized early-morning phone call from Michael Jordan, he decided to return to his alma mater. He told Kevin White of his plans, asking for an opportunity to talk to the team.

Some players, however, had hoped the talking would have been done before then.

David Graves: "He had always said he wanted us to find out the day before it happened. Well, I found out three hours before he was talking to us. That kind of contradiction between what he would say and what actually happened was pretty upsetting to everybody. I found out at 10 or 11 AM, and we didn't even have a meeting scheduled. That was disheartening to a lot of us, and that was where a lot of our ill feelings came from with the way he left. It was an opportunity he had to take, and we all understood that. But we felt used."

His final meeting with the players was a typically emotional time for Doherty. Opinions differ as to whether that meeting provided the closure he sought.

Martin Ingelsby: "I wasn't there when he told the guys he'd taken the job. He called me. I was at home, and he called me on his way to the airport to say he had taken the North Carolina job. The phone call lasted like 30 seconds. And that's the last time I talked to him."

Hans Rasmussen: "There wasn't a lot of emotion on the team's side. We were all kind of dumbfounded. But he was very upset. He teared up. Everybody gave him a hug and said their goodbyes, and he went out and left. I remember walking out and he was talking to Troy right before he got in his car and left. And I went up to him and said I was really looking forward to playing for him, and I was sorry I couldn't. That was the last time I talked to him."

David Graves: "It was a shallow meeting. You felt he was uncomfortable with the decision he made. You could tell it was a tough decision for him. He almost apologized. We felt sorry for him. Carolina is a great opportunity. But again, we felt it was a little bit shallow. It was so emotional for him that that was probably the way it had to be."

Doherty certainly brought enthusiasm and attention to the Notre Dame program. He brought in talented players like Ryan Humphrey, got the students interested in the program again and pointed the Irish toward a brighter future.

But he had also left after only one year. The returning players would be dealing with their third coach in as many seasons. The question was who would it be this time?

The
Mike Brey
Years

(2001–)

37

A Happy Medium
(2001)

K evin White had been on the job as athletic director at Notre Dame for about four months when he was suddenly faced with finding a new basketball coach. Fortunately, he had recent experience on which he could draw.

Kevin White: "Not too many years earlier we had conducted a national search for a head basketball coach at Arizona State. So we had been, to some degree, in the market. We had a sense of who was mobile, what the financial aspects were, and coach's reputations in terms of who were the up-and-comers.

"Although we found ourselves in the search mode unexpectedly, we really thought we were pretty well positioned to move quickly. We contacted everybody in the game that we really respected—people who were directly involved in the game as well as ancillary people like conference commissioners and TV people—wherein we tried to secure a profile of possible successors. So we were well on task before Matt chose to take the position at North Carolina."

One of the names on White's short list was Mike Brey, the young coach at the University of Delaware who had been a finalist for the job the year before. So confident was Brey in the possibilities at Notre Dame at the time that he put the University of Georgia on hold to see how things would develop in South Bend. By the time he was told he was no longer a candidate at Notre Dame, the Bulldogs had already hired Jim Harrick. Brey and his family were happy to return to Delaware, where they had put down roots and felt comfortable, and he began to think he might make his career there.

But in the upheaval that accompanied the North Carolina search, both Brey and some friends like ESPN analyst Jay Bilas believed he would get another opportunity.

Jay Bilas: "When the job came open [when John MacLeod left], I remember telling Mike, 'That job would be perfect for you, and that's a job you should really go after.' And when he became a candidate, I was excited about the possibility of him getting it. Matt was a terrific choice, but I thought Mike was *the* guy.

"Then the North Carolina thing happened and it looked like Doherty might go to Kansas. The first thing I thought of was that this would be the perfect time for Mike to go to Notre Dame. He's been ready for that job for so long. He'd be modest about it and say he needed this or that in his coaching career first, but he was ready a long time ago for that opportunity."

Brey recognized the opportunity as well, telling his wife, Tish, on the front porch of their vacation home in Rehobeth, Delaware, to "get ready for South Bend" as he read about Williams's decision to remain at Kansas.

While White also interviewed former Seton Hall coach P. J. Carliesemo and Oregon's Ernie Kent for the position, he was impressed right away with Brey's suitability. So impressed that within 72 hours of Matt Doherty's departure Mike Brey was being introduced as the new head coach of the Fighting Irish.

Kevin White: "We really felt he would be a wonderful fit at Notre Dame because of a combination of things. First, his background at DeMatha High School as a player and a coach with Morgan Wootten, truly one of the most successful guys who ever coached at that level; second, his eight years at Duke where they went to six Final Fours and won the NCAA Championship twice, while coaching for arguably one of the very best college coaches in NCAA history; and finally, his successful run at Delaware where he won 99 games in five years. You put that whole pedigree together and it's a pretty impressive track record—certainly a distinctive profile we thought would fit really well within the Notre Dame family."

Brey's affability made a big impression on the media folks covering the team.

Lou Somogyi: "If you can't get along with this guy, you better seek professional help. He's the most approachable, easiest to converse with coach. It was easy to get along with him."

Jack Lorri: "The guy who was a radio broadcaster in Delaware, Don Volts, called me and said, 'You won't believe this guy. You will think, 'No, he can't be that nice, there is something wrong here.' But without being syrupy and without playing favorites, he treats everybody terrific.'"

Brey needed little time to familiarize himself with Notre Dame. A product of the Washington, D.C., basketball community, he was familiar with the Irish program from his youth, having gone to basketball camps where Adrian Dantley was a counselor. But he did need time to get to know the players who would be dealing with their third coach in as many seasons.

Mike Brey: "I met with the team that afternoon. It was such a dysfunctional situation, what happened to them. The only thing I said to them was, 'I watched you last year when you didn't get the bid. You walked out of this locker room disappointed in front of the ESPN cameras. Whether you deserved it or not is a moot point now. I know what you want to do: you want to get back. As a program, we haven't been back in a long time. Where I've been, I can help you with that.' That was about the strongest comment I made."

Troy Murphy: "He was more like John MacLeod than he was Matt Doherty. Because he came in the middle of the summer, his coaching style that first year was a lot different than it is now. The team was, I guess, wounded mentally a little bit by the departure of Coach Doherty. Coach Brey did a really admirable job that year just holding us together."

David Graves: "Coach Brey was a happy medium between Coach MacLeod and Coach Doherty with respect to emotions. Coach MacLeod was a very stoic guy. In the NBA, you win some and you lose some, and you can't dwell on it. Coach Doherty probably dwelled on it a little too long, and he was really involved emotionally. Coach Brey was involved, but he understood that you need to be a leader and you need to be calm out there. He had that fiery personality, but he knew when to back it off and be the calming influence on a group."

Matt Carroll: "What you see is what you get with him. He's not two different people. He's going to tell you how it is and that's how it's going to be."

Brey's most important introduction was yet to come. He wanted to make sure that senior point guard Martin Ingelsby, whom he had recruited at Delaware, could get his confidence back after being demoted the previous year.

Martin Ingelsby: "I was down the Jersey shore at my brother's house. His phone kept ringing at like six in the morning. It was my mom calling to tell me Coach Brey got the job. I guess he had called my house at 5:30 that morning because he was catching a flight out to Notre Dame to accept the job or have his press conference and he was flying back the next night. He wanted to come to my house and take me out to dinner and just talk basketball."

Mike Brey: "I was in the car to the plane at Newcastle airport to come out here. He had already left summer school, so I wasn't going to meet him. I got him on the phone and I said, 'Martin, I've never been a guy to overanalyze things, but you're my guard next year. You're my guy.' That was important for him to know right off."

Ingelsby came away from their dinner knowing that a lot would depend on him that season. And even when his confidence was tested, Brey's faith didn't waver.

Mike Brey: "[Indiana's Tom] Coverdale had a hell of a game on him here. After what he went through his junior year, he probably thought that I was going to make some drastic changes. When he came in I said, 'Tough one last night. He was rolling. He was playing pretty well. We have to get you going over ball screens better, and we've got to give you some help. But I'll tell you one thing: you're my guy. You're playing 37 minutes on Saturday, so be ready.' Of course we lost that game, too, against Miami. But I didn't want him going back thinking about not being the guy and wondering what Coach is doing. 'You're the guy,' I told him. 'So how can we get better?' "

Another new dynamic was transfer Ryan Humphrey, who would be seeing his first action in a Notre Dame uniform. Few doubted the effect Humphrey would have on the Irish.

Martin Ingelsby: "He was like a man playing with boys. Every day he brought it. I know he saved a lot of my turnovers just by his athleticism."

David Graves: "On the south end of the arena, we had the best rim in America. It was loose, it was soft, and it kind of hung down a little bit. We always played on it during the second half, and we'd always make big shots.

"The Bulls and Pacers came in for an exhibition game and they broke the springs on the rim because it was so loose. When they put the new rim up, it was too tight. Ryan went up to dunk it once and kind of slipped off the rim. The rim was so tight that it shattered the backboard. It was pretty impressive. I'd never seen that before."

But there was a snag. Humphrey had transferred to Notre Dame with the understanding that he would be given the opportunity to develop his perimeter game. With Doherty gone and Brey in place, the agenda had changed.

Mike Brey: "We went to lunch at North Dining Hall in September once we were in the routine of school. I sat down and said, 'Now Ryan, I know why you came here. I'm going to get you facing the bucket. But I don't think we can go heavy doses of you out on the three-point line. I'll get you facing in the high post. I'm thinking that high-low with you and Murph will be very hard to guard. You'll work on your face-up stuff. All I'm asking is that you meet me halfway. I'll work with you. You have to trust me.' "

Ryan Humphrey: "He gave me more freedom to use my quickness on the perimeter and drive past people to shoot jump shots. And he said, 'Just go out there and play.' With Coach Brey, you never had the sense that if you made a mistake, you were going to immediately come out. He let his players play."

With the tandem of Murphy and Humphrey, the Irish came into the season with higher expectations than they'd had in years. A 4-0 start, a win in Indianapolis against No. 13 Cincinnati, and Notre Dame's first top-10 ranking in 15 years added fuel to the fire of enthusiasm. The players believed in themselves—maybe too much.

Mike Brey: "I knew we had good players and we potentially had a good team. I did think they thought they were better than they were, but I certainly was in no place to tell them that one week into the job, one month into the job, or even three months into the job. That was the tricky dynamic of coaching this group. Not until we got beat by Indiana and Miami in that one week did they say, 'OK, maybe we have to be a little more open-minded to what we need to do better.' "

The losses to Indiana and Miami of Ohio knocked the Irish off their top-10 perch, and through the holidays the team struggled. But Brey remained confident in them.

Mike Brey: "Those six guys—Murphy, Ingelsby, Humphrey, Carroll, Graves, and Swanagan—given that I was new, needed to know they were going to play the bulk of the minutes. So we never even changed jerseys around the first three weeks of practice. Six men wore gold shirts. Nobody else got in a gold shirt—not Torrian Jones, not Ivan Kartelo. Those six guys needed to know I wasn't going to mess with their minutes. They needed to be the guys, and we needed the stability."

Still, the team searched for a spark to rally around. They found it in Lexington, Ky., after the Kentucky Wildcats had handed the Irish their third loss in four games. Kentucky native Harold Swanagan made his feelings known in the postgame locker room.

Hans Rasmussen: "I was sitting near the doorway and Harold came in. There was a cooler of Gatorade sitting on the table. He walked in, he took one hand and swiped the cooler off the table like it was a rag doll, and ice spilled everywhere.

"Harold just went off. He told everybody we were playing like a bunch of women and if we wanted to make the NCAA tournament, we'd better step it up. He was sick and tired of getting embarrassed, especially on his home floor, being from Kentucky. He lit into everybody. He lit into the walk-ons, he lit into the starting five, he lit into the guys who sat on the bench and didn't really play that much. He wasn't taking any prisoners.

"It was really eye-opening. The last time I had seen that was a face-to-face confrontation with Pat Garrity. It was kind of cool for me, because I had never seen him try and take a lead position. But he definitely was in that locker room, because he was telling everybody that they needed to suck it up or go home."

Swanagan was in the starting lineup three days later against Pittsburgh in the Joyce Center. The 16-point win was the first of eight in a row for the Irish, halting their downward spiral and propelling them to the Big East Western Division title, their first title of any kind in the conference. Unlike the previous seasons, the team jelled down the stretch instead of folding.

Torrian Jones: "We got more down to business and back to doing the things that win games. What Swanagan always brought to the table was that hard-nosed attitude—the tough-guy attitude we needed on the floor. Just that one guy to spark everybody else and make everybody feel like, 'Well this guy is giving all he has. No reason why I shouldn't be doing it.' We were feeling too good about ourselves. We had our noses up in the air, thinking we were better than other people and forgetting the things that got us to that point."

Matt Carroll: "That was a turning point in our season. Swannie is the type of guy who, if he's talking, you're going to listen. If you don't listen, you don't want to get in his way. He was one of our captains, and he was right. We had to turn it around—we couldn't lose games like that. And we did."

When Selection Sunday dawned, the Irish were confident as they gathered to watch the announcement of NCAA Tournament bids. Not 30 seconds into the telecast, the players learned that an 11-year monkey would finally be off their backs.

Martin Ingelsby: "It was one of the greatest moments of my life. You grow up and you think about playing Division I basketball, and then you think about playing in the NCAA tournament. To see Notre Dame's name flash up there for the first time in 11 years, you're like, 'Wow, we really did it.' We accomplished something that we had set out to do at the beginning of the year."

Torrian Jones: "It felt great, especially for the guys like Swanagan and Graves who were here when the team was down and was the joke of the Big East. For them to see how far they had brought the program, and being part of bringing the program back up and making it to the tournament."

The Irish were off to Kansas City to face Xavier. Although they were evenly seeded, the Musketeers were favored because of a three-game slide with which Notre Dame had finished the season. Behind a balanced scoring effort, the Irish earned their first NCAA tournament win since 1989 and would play Mississippi on the day after St. Patrick's Day for the right to go to the Sweet 16.

Troy Murphy: "We were playing in our green uniforms. The hotel we were staying at had a fountain shooting green water. I figured there was no way we could lose that game. Come on, Notre Dame on St. Patrick's Day weekend? We were going to be all right."

But it wasn't all right. The Irish lost in the final seconds 59-56. Their season was over . . . as was Troy Murphy's Irish career.

Martin Ingelsby: "We understood that this was the last go-around for Murph. He had a great opportunity to play in the NBA as one of the top-15 picks in the draft.

"Going into the season, we wanted the NCAA tournament. We wanted to win the Big East championship. We had goals to go to the Final Four. And we accomplished a lot of those going to the tournament. So we all knew that it was Murph's time to move on."

Troy Murphy: "Going into the season, I wanted to look at all the options. Coach Doherty leaving kind of showed me how basketball is a business and I had to take care of *my* business. I felt it was a good time for me to go to the NBA, and it was a challenge that I wanted to see if I could handle."

The Irish had survived the upheaval that preceded the season, and for the first time since 1998 they would be going into the next season with the same coach with whom they'd finished the previous one. And though they'd have to replace Murphy, they would be adding an electrifying player, the type Irish fans hadn't seen in a while.

38

Gaining Confidence
(2002)

Chris Thomas, a point guard from Indianapolis who had been a McDonald's All-American and Indiana's Mr. Basketball, arrived on the Notre Dame campus in the summer of 2001. He was Notre Dame's most high-profile recruit since LaPhonso Ellis and was being compared with former Duke All-American Bobby Hurley. What would prompt such a decorated player to take a flyer on the Irish program?

Chris Thomas: "I never really thought about Notre Dame being a basketball school and the place where I would end up, even when Coach Doherty stepped on the campus. I just figured they were an in-state school and I'd see what they had to say. When I took my visit up here with my parents, it was a sense of family and community and a great sense of pride. They went out of their way to make everybody feel comfortable."

The coaching staff realized how important it was for Thomas to make a good first impression on his new teammates.

Mike Brey: "I felt it was important for Chris to come up here and play with the guys a little bit and get a feel for them. So he came up for a week of camp to hang out and play with our guys.

"I asked him to come back to my office. I said, 'You're going to play pick-up for three or four days with these guys. I think it would be very important for you, being our point guard next year with seniors and veterans, that you give the ball up to a fault. Turn shots down to get people involved. It's really important because this is the first time you'll play with these guys, and they're going to go back to the dorm tonight and say 'I like him' or 'I'm worried about him.' How you get off to start is extremely important.' He's a very sharp kid, and he understood it. That week went well."

David Graves: "He earned our respect from the start. He wasn't an arrogant or cocky kid when he came in. We knew we needed a guy like him to really spread us out. With Matty and I on the perimeter and the inside presence of Harold and Ryan, it would free Chris up to do the things he does best—penetrate and create. And he did a great job with it."

Irish fans didn't have to wait long to see Thomas's impact. In his first game, against New Hampshire, Thomas recorded the first triple-double in school history with double-figure totals in points, assists, and steals.

Ryan Humphrey: "I had to sit out that game [for a suspension due to a minor NCAA rules violation]. I knew he had played a good game, so I checked his stats. I told him to get two more assists and that would put him over, because I would have been upset if that was me and didn't get it."

Chris Thomas: "I figured my assists and steals were getting up there. And throughout the game it was so much fun to play, I didn't even think about it until two minutes left when Hump said, 'Chris, one more steal, one more assist, and you've got a triple double.' The next play down, I stole the ball and I passed it to somebody and he scored. The next time I got another steal and another assist.

"With Hump playing, it probably wouldn't have happened, because I wouldn't have had to do much. But it was a good experience for me. That kind of set the tone for the whole season."

The tone had indeed been set. Thomas scored 32 points and had 11 assists against Rutgers. He was named Big East rookie of the week six times over the course of the season. And in a four-overtime game at Georgetown, Thomas scored 22 points, dished out 12 assists, grabbed eight rebounds, and got three steals in a conference-record 60 minutes of action.

Jordan Cornette: "That was just an amazing game. It's something I'm proud to have been a part of. It was two teams fighting for it all. They had beaten us earlier in the year, and that was probably one of our worst losses of the season. So we knew we had to come and get this one. It was a big game for us, and we weren't going to lose, no matter what the cost."

Mike Brey: "I was trying to put Tom Timmermans back in the game when he had already fouled out. In the third overtime I said, 'Tom, get in there,' and [associate head coach] Sean Kearney said, 'He fouled out.'

"At the end of one of the overtimes I turned to Sean and said, 'How many is this? What number?' He said, 'This is the third one.' Hump was coming off the floor and we were laughing, going, 'Can you believe this?' "

Chris Thomas: "It was very scary in the overtimes. We had controlled the whole game, but it seemed like every time Georgetown would come back and make a five-point run and they would have the last shot to win the game and barely miss it.

"At the end of the game, my feet were white and my toes were blue. I couldn't feel my legs. I couldn't run. But at the same time, when I stepped into the locker room, everybody's emotions took over. They had beaten us up physically and mentally when we played them at home. That could have been our biggest win of the season."

The 116-111 win helped propel the Irish to a second straight season of double-digit conference wins. They managed a 20-point win against St. John's in the conference tournament—their second win in the tournament ever—before falling by five to No. 19 Connecticut. And once again, the NCAA Tournament came calling, seeding the Irish ninth and sending them to South Carolina.

But there would be a subplot to this tournament trip. Awaiting the Irish in the second round after their 82-63 win over Charlotte were the top-ranked Blue Devils of Duke University and Brey's former boss, Mike Krzyzewski.

Mike Brey: "I had played him before when I was at Delaware, so I never was distracted with it being Mike and it being Duke. If it was my second or third year of coaching, maybe I might have been. But I had been around for a while and played in some big games. I was really into our team. I looked at it as an unbelievable opportunity for our program.

"I thought we had it set up where we had a great chance to beat them. All our guys grew up watching those Duke teams dominate, and I didn't want a mental block there. The night before the game, I told them I was always amazed that by the time teams figured out that Duke was normal, they were down 17."

Energized by the fact that they were playing the only nationally televised game of the tournament that day, the Irish grabbed the lead at the opening tip and held it for most of the way.

David Graves: "That was another one of those games where everybody was playing at a high level and great players were making plays. We were hitting big shots; they were hitting great shots. I felt confident going in because I knew we matched up as well as anyone in the country could against them. We really neutralized their offensive power with the type of personnel we had.

"The biggest turning point of the game was when we were up five with about three minutes to go. Chris was on the line shooting one-and-one. He missed it, and they came down and hit a three. Say he would have hit those two. We would have been up seven. Now we were only up two. A five-point swing is a big swing, especially against a team like Duke. I thought at that time it was probably going to be a monumental task to beat these guys, because I knew they had another run in them. We needed that cushion to absorb that run, and we didn't get it."

Without the cushion, the Irish couldn't absorb that game-ending run that gave the Blue Devils an 84-77 win. But even in defeat, the team felt a corner had been turned.

Mike Brey: "Not that you ever want to talk about moral victories, but after not being in the NCAA tournament for a decade and then going one time and going back another year, we did need a few. I don't know if you could get more mileage out of a loss than that loss, because everyone watched that game. When I went around that summer, people would say things like, 'That was a heck of a game. I was watching it here. We were cheering for you.' It legitimized us because we hung with a heck of a program and had a chance to beat them."

Four years before, Graves and Swanagan had begun their Irish careers with a 20-point pounding by Duke in a small gym in Alaska. Now they had given the Blue Devils everything they could handle in front of a national television audience.

David Graves: "The one thing I was most proud of, and I was quoted a couple of times saying it, was that 'Irish' meant something now. When people talked about Notre Dame, it was because Notre Dame was a great team and a great program. That's what I was more excited about than anything. I was excited about Coach Brey and his staff and what they could accomplish in the future because of what we had accomplished. It's a team game. We played our part."

Jordan Cornette: "You had guys like Dave and Harold who built this program from almost nothing and brought it to the point where they could play a Duke close. That game was something I know our program is building on. We had the confidence knowing we should have beaten Duke, and if we had a chance the next year, we would beat a team like Duke consistently."

39

Sixteen after Sixteen
(2003)

Slowly but surely, Notre Dame was shaking off the malaise of the 1990s. Interest was strong on and off campus. Ticket sales were increasing each season, and ten games in the 2003 season were sold out, the highest total since 1986. Mike Brey's profile away from campus was expanding: he served as guest singer for the seventh-inning stretch at Wrigley Field.

But there were still steps to be taken, particularly in the NCAA Tournament. The goal for 2003 was to take the next step: Notre Dame's first Sweet 16 in 16 seasons.

To reach that goal, they would need help. Ryan Humphrey had taken his toughness and athletic ability to the NBA, and David Graves's perimeter proficiency and Harold Swanagan's leadership had to be replaced. The preseason questions centered around whether two newcomers could help fill the voids: Dan Miller, a senior transfer from the University of Maryland, and freshman forward Torin Francis, Notre Dame's second McDonald's All-American recruit in as many seasons.

Miller's situation was unique. Notre Dame hadn't been known to take in many transfers, let alone one-year players. But his brother had played for Brey at Delaware, so the coach had a history with the family.

Mike Brey: "People would talk about how we only had him for a year, but we really had him for two. When he practiced against Graves and Carroll the previous year, he made them better. He played with a little bit of anger in him. There's a toughness in him that helped Matt Carroll and Chris Thomas, who are nice kids, be a little crueler. He's kind of a cruel competitor, and that helped our demeanor.

"He also kept us old. Instead of turning to a 19-year-old, we turned to a 23-year-old in that lineup. He'd been in big games. And as we got into the NCAA tournament, I thought it was only fitting that when we broke into territory we hadn't seen in 16 years that he was the guy who said, 'Follow me, I'm going to set the tone.' "

Francis, on the other hand, would have to be nurtured the way Thomas had been the previous season . . . with a bit of a twist.

Mike Brey: "We weren't going to mess around with his minutes. He needed to be in there right away. Like Chris Thomas, he was going to be playing with some veterans, but it was a veteran perimeter. It was kind of inverted. All he had to do was get his hands ready.

"My big thing to our team was that our leading rebounder of the big guys was going to start, and it was going to be hard to take him out of the game. Through our first five practices, he was, by and large, our leading rebounder. He established himself in there.

"It was a matter of bringing him along. He had some tough games early, but we weren't going to waver. He was the guy. We were going to develop him and stay with him, and he was going to have to be physically able, like Chris Thomas as a freshman, to play 30+ minutes a game. And he got himself in shape to do that."

To facilitate the development of Francis and his fellow freshmen Chris Quinn and Rick Cornett, Brey included them in the team's summer program. Thanks to new NCAA rules, the freshmen could get a head start on their classes and have some academic credits under their belt when September rolled around. But the biggest benefits would be intangible—the chemistry of a very close team.

Matt Carroll: "What we did best was show them we were going to be good this year. It didn't matter what people were going to say, we were going to work hard in the weight room, and we were going to play a lot. We wanted to build chemistry and develop their confidence so when they came in to start the school year they knew what to expect."

Mike Brey: "It was a little bit of a training camp retreat atmosphere for six weeks. You can only do that if you feel you have good captains, because they're setting the tone for your team during those six weeks. I'm not involved; I can't coach them. But I was confident in Matt Carroll and Dan Miller running our team."

The results of that team-building would be seen quickly. In early December in the span of seven days, the Irish defeated three top-10 opponents—No. 5 Marquette, No. 9 and defending national champion Maryland, and No. 2 Texas—two of them away from the Joyce Center.

Matt Carroll: "That's probably the most memorable week I've had since I'd been here at Notre Dame, and maybe in all of college basketball. How many teams play three top-10 teams in a week, let alone beat them? That gave us so much confidence going into the rest of the year, knowing we could play and beat anybody in the country."

Mike Brey: "It was huge. I didn't know how historic it was overall in our history. I knew it was pretty big in recent memory in college basketball.

"It gave our team a lot of confidence. Looking back, it was another mark of credibility nationally as a top-20 program that could be in the mix on a national basis. It was a reestablishment of being back on the map and credible again."

Their big December week catapulted the Irish from the ranks of the unranked into the top 10, and they stayed in the rankings for most of the rest of the season. In February, they would add Pittsburgh to their list top-10 victims. They would once again reach double-digit wins in conference, the only team to do so for three straight years. They also became the only Big East team to receive an NCAA Tournament bid for those same three years.

But all was not rosy as the Irish entered postseason play. They had lost four of their last five games to end the season, including a three-point upset by St. John's in the first round of the Big East tournament. Then, in their opening game of the tournament against 12th-seeded Wisconsin-Milwaukee in Indianapolis, they needed 27 points from Chris Thomas and a missed layup by UWM's Dylan Page to survive 70-69. If they were going to realize their Sweet 16 dream, they would have to pull it together against the No. 4 seed, Illinois.

Mike Brey: "Winning the Milwaukee game the way we did gave us some more juice in that setting. We were a very confident team going into the Illinois game. Watching us in the locker room, it was almost like, 'Get through the scouting report stuff, because we're ready to go.' We were very mature about our preparations from the end of the Milwaukee game through the day in between."

Their early-season confidence returned. Dan Miller, suffering from occasional shooting slumps during the season, scored a career-high 23 points and hit five of his seven three-point shots. Torin Francis followed a 23-point, 14-rebound performance against Wisconsin-Milwaukee with another 14 rebounds against the Illini. The Irish overcame Matt Carroll's ankle injury, broke out to a 13-point lead at halftime, and withstood the inevitable Illinois runs in the second half to win 68-60.

Matt Carroll: "That was one of those games where everyone was playing great. Shots were falling, and everyone was having a fun time. I was like, 'This is it. We're going to get to the next weekend and the Sweet 16. We worked hard to do it, and it's finally here.' I had played in two NCAAs where we'd lost, and I figured I'd rather win a game and not be 100 percent and move on."

For the first time in 16 years, the Irish had survived the first weekend of the NCAA Tournament and were in the Sweet 16.

Mike Brey: "The buzz around our program and the attention was huge. Considering where we were in the 1990s, we needed that next step. Our guys handled it very maturely. They were a confident team. By no means did I want to create an atmosphere of 'Arizona, Kansas, Duke, look at that company.' I wanted us to feel like we belonged in that company, even if we had not been the consistent programs those teams had been."

Awaiting them in Anaheim were the Arizona Wildcats. The Irish hoped to make them their sixth top-10 victim of the season, and it was close for the first 10 minutes. But then the Wildcats went on a 22-3 run that turned the game into a rout.

Mike Brey: "I thought we were going to have to score like we had against Illinois and put some numbers up, and we did for about 10 minutes. Then they went on a roll.

"I never wanted us tight. That was easy to say but hard to do coming out of the Big East, because you're thinking, 'We've got problems, how are we going to get this going again?' We still wanted to be loose and to go for it because we had nothing to lose. Once we got through the Milwaukee thing, we were in that territory."

Matt Carroll: "The teams that were there were great teams, established programs. I don't know if we're there yet, but we're going to be there. We can play with them. Arizona obviously had our number that day. They're a very good team, and probably a little deeper than we were. But we enjoyed it, and we played for next year."

The hoped-for steps had been taken. Torin Francis had again been the bright spot against Arizona, making 10 of 11 shots and scoring 25 points. Chris Thomas had decided to forego the NBA draft to return for his junior year. And the Irish nation hoped that 2004 would bring another step forward.

40

Past and Future

With a firm grasp on the program's present thanks to three consecutive NCAA trips and a plan for the future with young stars like Torin Francis and Arizona transfer Dennis Latimore, Brey and his staff took some time to focus on the past.

Mike Brey: "I sensed during my first five months on the job there was a big separation from our former guys. We weren't very good in the 1990s, so people weren't really attracted to coming back. With three coaches in three years, there wasn't a lot of reaching back. There weren't a lot of organized things to get those guys back.

"My first two years, I called a lot of them. If I was in New Jersey, I called Tripucka. If I was in California, I called Branning. I went to a D.C. summer league game, and I couldn't have been prouder. I walked in with Bob Whitmore, Collis Jones, and Adrian Dantley, and they all had their Notre Dame rings on. Talk about impressive."

Determined to reconnect the Irish program with its storied history, the coaching staff redoubled its efforts to make the alumni comfortable around the program. They sent e-mail updates about the program and players to the alums. Reunions were held before the 2002 and 2004 seasons, with former players enjoying a football weekend along with each other's company. The 1974 team that had ended UCLA's winning streak returned in January of 2004 to celebrate the 30th anniversary of their feat, the first time the group had reunited on campus since they had graduated.

Jim Gibbons: "He knew that could be a lifeline with this program, so he's bound and determined he's going to bring those alumni back. He communicates with us. He sent out a folder with all the names and the e-mails and the phone numbers and the addresses. He's got the system going again and doing a good job of communicating with the former players so he can get them back on board and involved in the program."

John McCarthy: "The last few years I've become close to it, mostly because of the wonderful group of coaches who keep in close contact with us. I get an e-mail probably every day from Notre Dame on different things going on with the team. It's wonderful."

Brey even got involved in some of the little things noticed and appreciated by the former players, even those who never suited up for him.

Joe Fredrick: "I took my wife and children up to a game and we stopped in the basketball office just to say hi. I'd never met these guys, but they took the kids down in the locker room and introduced them to the players. They let us watch practice, and they brought the kids on the floor after practice to meet the players."

Carl Cozen: "I called him to introduce myself and said we'd like to come down for a game. When we got there, even though he had some recruits there and I had never met him or his assistants before, he came right up to us and knew exactly who I was and what I had done not only at ND but also in high school. I was thinking, 'Geez, were you guys up all night memorizing who the alumni were?' But it really impressed us and meant a lot."

Bruce Flowers: "At Notre Dame's basketball camp at night, once the kids are in bed, there really isn't anything to do. It's 10:30 PM, but we counselors have to stay around the dorms to make sure they're not jumping out the window or anything. So I started this game called Wizard's Golf, where you hit a tennis ball all around the North Quad, hitting various monuments along the way. We renamed some of those monuments, such as 'And-One Moses' in front of the Library, 'Three-Point Jesus' in front of the admin building.

"Mike's first year, we tried to get him and the coaching staff to come out and play. Mike didn't come out, but some of his assistants did. The next night, at the coaches' dinner, Mike shows up with this four-foot-tall trophy, and tells me, 'Bruce, here's the new Wizard's Golf trophy for the winner of your tournament. You give me the names of the winners and we'll display this proudly in our basketball offices.' First time I meet this guy and he does something like that."

An anchor to the past will help stabilize any program when things get rough, and rough certainly was a good descriptor for the 2004 season—a roller coaster ride that featured a little of the past and future before it was over.

For the first time in three years, the Irish wouldn't be dependent on freshmen to contribute immediately. Chris Thomas was back with a renewed intention to get his teammates involved and show the NBA scouts he was worthy of a high draft pick. Torin Francis had ended 2003 with tremendous performances in the NCAA Tournament and looked to build on his effort for a good sophomore year showing.

But there were still some unknowns. Defensive specialists Torrian Jones and Jordan Cornette would be asked to contribute on the offensive end more. Someone would have to provide the in-your-face leadership Dan Miller had brought to the 2003 Irish. And sophomore Chris Quinn would have to take up the scoring slack from the departed Matt Carroll, with some help from freshman Colin Falls, and learn to play alongside Chris Thomas rather than in place of him.

Chris Quinn: "All through my freshman year, when we'd separate the teams, both teams would need a point guard so we'd split up. So this summer and in the preseason, even when we were playing pickup games, Chris and I wanted to make sure we had a lot of time on the court together, and once we had some experience playing together, it just went from there.

"As a freshman, I didn't have too much pressure on me. If I came in and hit a couple of threes, that was great, and if not, I could move the ball on offense. This year, it was totally different. The team needed me to step up and be a part of the offense."

Unlike Brey's previous teams, this was an Irish squad that was going to have to craft its identity on the fly. Even if everything else went as expected, there were probably going to be bumps in the road while that identity was established. But almost from the get-go, it was apparent things weren't going to go as expected, as the injury bug that had for the most part stayed away from the Irish the previous three seasons returned with a vengeance. Freshman Omari Isreal missed the entire season rehabbing a knee that had been surgically repaired in the offseason, and only Quinn and Falls escaped the season unscathed as the bruises—and missed playing time—mounted for their teammates.

Skip Meyer: "This was probably the worst year we've had for injuries in my 25 years here. Chris Thomas had a significant knee problem and played the whole year hurt. Jordan and Rick were both out for a while, which meant we had a numbers problem with our big men. It was constant all year, and it really tied Mike's hands because he had no options. It was one of those years—sometimes you're lucky and sometimes it catches up to you, and this was one of those years where it caught up to us."

Mike Brey: "Injuries are part of your team each year and you try to antici-pate them, but we probably had a little more this year than the average num-ber and it messed up our ability to get into a rhythm or a rotation for the season. I thought it was important for us to get into a rhythm because we had some guys in roles they'd never been in before and we were asking them to do more—pretty much everybody but Chris [Thomas] and Torin. I think it distracted us and probably hurt our practice rhythm some."

Chris Thomas: "It was tough because you never knew who would be prac-ticing. If you don't take the time to practice the plays with your teammates, it's hard to get that camaraderie and understand how they play the game."

Jordan Cornette: "It was one of those times when things just weren't going my way. I was pretty confident I was going to be a starter this year and I nailed that down, and then I got hurt. But it showed how much resolve this team had, because every time we got knocked down, we'd get back up and make the most of it. I just got myself healthy and moved on."

Rick Cornett: "It was difficult to get the chemistry together, but I think we all came together. Everyone was feeding off of one another and trying to use each other as a catalyst to push ourselves to be more hungry and aggressive on the court."

The adjustments and injuries took their toll early. The team struggled in its exhibition games, requiring overtime to dispatch an Illinois All-Star team that featured former Irish star LaPhonso Ellis. The players squandered a big lead at home before defeating Northern Illinois and were embarrassed on national television in Milwaukee against Marquette.

Then, with only seven players available in their next home game against a Central Michigan team that would win only five games against Division I opponents all season, the wheels came off. Joe Carr beat the buzzer and the Irish with a three-pointer from the wing for the 69-68 win.

Torrian Jones: "Any time you know you could help your teammates win a game and you see them struggling a little bit, it's hard to sit there [injured] and let things happen. I was the leader of this team, and more than anything else I think my leadership was the most important thing I brought to games. I saw things in that game we needed that I could have brought to it."

Chris Thomas: "They seized the opportunity. We took things for granted and put ourselves in a position to lose. We were up seven points in the last minute, and we fouled twice and I let the guy get an open shot. We didn't approach the game situation the way we should have."

Mike Brey: "We had the game won, and the frustrating thing was we just didn't handle the game situation well. We missed free throws, we fouled a three-point shooter, we gave up a three-point shot at the end—little things that we had been pretty consistent with when finishing up games, but we didn't do there. As Joe Carr was driving the length of the court at the end, we almost deserved to get beat. We hadn't shown enough attention to detail, and they'd earned it."

Things didn't get better quickly. Four days after the CMU debacle, an undermanned Indiana team upset the Irish by three. Rick Cornett moved into the starting lineup and scored a career-high 10 points to help the Irish win at DePaul and snap the three-game skid, but went down with a foot injury and missed the next three games.

Mike Brey: *"Who knows what we would have seen if he hadn't hurt his foot after the DePaul game, because I think we were ready to see [his improvement] then. But then he turned the ankle and sprained the foot in a scrimmage on a fluke play—I think he was stepping around a block-out and he wasn't even up in the air. By the time he was back, Tom was playing pretty well and he had to reinvent himself."*

The Irish went into the new year looking for some luck and seemed to get some. They opened Big East play 2-0 including their first-ever conference win over Villanova, and played No. 13 Pittsburgh down to the wire on the road before falling by three.

But it didn't last. Lackluster performances against Syracuse and Kentucky on national television snuffed out the positive momentum. Winnable games at Boston College and Rutgers were lost. And in the rematch against Pitt at the Joyce Center, the Irish blew a 13-point advantage and lost not only the game but also Torin Francis to a season-ending back injury.

Torin Francis: *"It had been a recurring problem, but it had never been too bad. I'd just keep it stretched out and it wouldn't slow me down. But in the layup line at the Pittsburgh game, I went up for a layup and when I came down, I felt a sharp pain. I got it stretched and I thought I'd be all right, but during the game, I couldn't run without pain. It tightened up and I starting having back spasms.*

"A couple of days later, we played UConn, I was out there for only a few minutes and I wasn't effective at all—I still couldn't run. That's when I knew it was something serious."

Mike Brey: *"As a staff, we had pushed a lot of buttons going into the Pitt game because we knew that weekend was a big one. We do have a confidence against Pittsburgh because we'd been pretty good against them [lately], so I knew the kids would be confident because we'd played them well in Pittsburgh. I thought we were really psychologically ready, and we came out 15-2. With Chris, it was like the Law of Averages was kicking in— he had not shot the ball particularly well, but he hit his first couple of shots.*

"But then we couldn't finish. They were too old and too mature and they beat us up in the second half. That was demoralizing because we had the thing under control and we were putting it to them, but we couldn't finish it.

"We didn't know the day before the game Torin would only give us nine minutes. We knew he was in discomfort. In the first half, I turned to him and said, 'Are you ready?' and he couldn't answer me. He didn't want to say no.

"When I looked at the weekend, I felt if we could get a split that would be pretty good. But I also felt if we didn't get Pittsburgh, I wasn't sure if we could turn around and get Connecticut from a psychological standpoint."

To call Notre Dame's situation grim would be an understatement. They sat at 10-9 overall, 4-5 in the league. Francis' 14 points and nine rebounds per game wouldn't be very useful to them on the bench, and his absence would increase the pressure on an already thin front line. Thomas continued to struggle through his knee problems. Their next four games featured two against No. 5 Connecticut sandwiched around Top 25 Seton Hall at home and a road game against Syracuse team that had blown their doors off in the Joyce Center weeks before. The stage was set for a meltdown, and since seven of the eight remaining regular-season games would be televised to nationwide audiences, it seemed a whole lot of people would be there to watch it happen.

But a funny thing happened on the way to the meltdown.

Mike Brey: "We only practiced for 30 minutes on Sunday because the Pitt game had been really physical. We started talking about the scouting report for Connecticut. I had up on the board the keys for the game, and it said we needed transition defense, to control the tempo on offense and to execute our 'number six' play. Well, we don't have a 'number six' play. As the assistants are going through Connecticut's personnel, you could see Chris Quinn and Chris Thomas and Jordan Cornette muttering, 'What's our number six play?'

"Then I got up to review the keys. I said, 'Defensively, we need transition D—you gotta get back. Offensively, we're going to control the tempo because we don't need to be going up and down on them, and we're going to run our number six play a lot.' They started to ask what the number six play was, and I said, 'Six passes. That's all I want. When I hold up six fingers, I want us to make six passes, and that'll remind us to slow down in the half-court and swing the ball around a couple of times.'

The number six play did the trick. The pieces of the puzzle suddenly clicked, as the Irish went 7-3 the rest of the way. Thomas snapped out of his shooting slump, scoring a season-high 31 points in the win over Connecticut,

26 against Seton Hall, and 25 against Syracuse in another big win at the Carrier Dome. Quinn was sharing the point guard duties, finding Thomas for open looks while draining treys himself. Tom Timmermans was finally in game shape, throwing his weight around in the low post.

Jordan Cornette: "The underground phrase in the locker room became 'play with nothing to lose.' We were playing carelessly out there—carelessly in a good way, without worrying about messing up or making mistakes. We played fearlessly and got it done."

Chris Quinn: "Tom and Torrian did a great job helping keep our heads even. We went through a lot this year, and after the Pitt loss it probably would have been easy to throw in the towel. But we knew what this team was capable of doing, and with our talent, we were capable of beating anybody."

Torrian Jones: "Everybody stayed together. Some teams faced with that kind of adversity would cash in and start blaming each other and not put forth the effort to end the season up the right way. The closeness of our group really helped us stay together. We knew we wanted to do what it took to make a run at the tournament, and that's exactly what we did."

In the final season push, two players who had not had to contribute before took advantage of their time to shine. Freshman Colin Falls became a dependable offensive threat off the bench, with his last-minute three-point shot giving the Irish a win over West Virginia in the first round of the Big East Tournament.

Colin Falls: "At the time, I didn't realize how big a shot it was because it was just a shot from the corner with 12 seconds left. But it was cool afterwards to realize I'd done that in Madison Square Garden in the Big East Tournament."

Mike Brey: "If you think back to December, he was the one taking the big shot for us in the Indiana game, and he was the guy to take that shot. He had to take it, and we were confident in him in that situation. Against West Virginia, we subbed him in to have another shooter on the floor, and Chris Quinn didn't hesitate getting him the ball in the corner. He's getting more and more confident, and I'm very pleased with what he gave us."

And Rick Cornett, now recovered and ready, more than picked up the slack in Francis' absence, pulling down critical rebounds and besting his scoring mark set against DePaul with 15 points against Connecticut in the Big East Tournament.

Mike Brey: "I wanted to play as long as possible in the postseason because of Rick Cornett. He had to get 18 to 22 minutes per game, and to his credit, he embraced it and ran with it.

"As Kevin White said at our banquet, we reinvented ourselves again because we were back to a low-post presence. When Torin went out, there weren't many low-post feeds—maybe some to Tom every now and again, but our low-post buckets were drives by our perimeter players based on our big guys being out on the floor and opening things up. We came back around after the second Connecticut game, and I said, 'We have a low-post presence again. Rick's the guy, and we're going to go back to some of the sets we ran for Torin and we're going to run them for Rick.' We had two or three sets where we'd bring him high into the low post and throw it in to him. And he really responded."

Torin Francis: "Rick really stepped up once he got the chance to play. That was a real confidence-builder for him, and he was pretty much able to have his way down low. He was confident being that low-post presence with me out."

Torrian Jones: "You can't even put into words how big Tom's and Rick's play was. For a guy like Torin to go out and those guys having to come in and fill his shoes was a very tough thing, especially considering the roles they had been playing all season like Rick not getting a lot of minutes. They handled it like men. They stepped in right away and gave us instant progress and instant success."

Rick Cornett: "It's weird because I was happy and not happy at the same time. We lost one of our leading scorers and rebounders, but I was excited because I got the opportunity to step in there and fill his shoes. Looking ahead, we're going to have a great season next year and he's going to be a part of it, but I want to make sure I'm a big part of it as well because I think I deserve it."

But would the late-season surge be enough? Like 2000, the Irish sat on the NCAA Tournament bubble, but this time had a strong finish in a highly ranked conference to make their case for a bid. Thanks to the unbalanced schedule the Big East had played that season, they had played six games against the top three teams in the conference, Connecticut, Pittsburgh, and Syracuse. Some pundits felt the team had earned its fourth consecutive trip to the NCAAs.

But conventional wisdom doesn't always pan out. In 2003, a strong week in December had offset stumbles down the stretch. But in 2004, a bad week in December had offset a fantastic final month, and the Irish were NIT-bound.

Mike Brey: "[Central Michigan] was very hard to recover from. The only way we could have recovered from that in the eyes of the NCAA Tournament committee would have been to get another win against Pittsburgh, Kentucky, or Connecticut. That's the only way that game would have been dusted off the board. We weren't able to do that, and it hurt us Selection Sunday when it came down to crunch time."

Chris Thomas: "I felt we built ourselves a good resume, but the NCAA committee chooses teams based on what they do the whole year and not just the last 10 games. So I don't think we got screwed. I think we were blessed to be where we were at the end of the season."

The NIT, however, brought the Irish back to the past as much as it prepared them for the future. Their opening round 71-59 win over Purdue was the old rival's first-ever trip to the Joyce Center and the first matchup between the schools anywhere since 1966. In the second round, the Irish returned to their old stomping grounds of Fort Wayne for the first time since 1967 to play another old foe that had been missing from the schedule for a while, St. Louis. Given a chance to play where his father had starred, Chris Thomas scored a new career-high 39 points in a 77-66 Irish win.

Chris Thomas: "Playing the way I did in Fort Wayne was really meaningful for me. My family and friends were there. It was tournament atmosphere, and I did what I had to do to help the team win. That was a night where they needed me to score. It was a career night and I was blessed my shots were going in. I had the opportunity, and I seized it."

The Irish now had a chance to succeed where they'd failed in the past. Awaiting them in New York City was their old postseason nemesis, Michigan.

If they got past the Wolverines, they could try to finally bring home the banner that had eluded them in their previous four trips to the NIT Finals. All they needed to get there was one more victory.

But it wasn't to be. Notre Dame's hot shooting deserted them against the Ducks of Oregon. Thomas was harassed into 7-25 from the floor and had to earn every one of his 18 points in the 66-61 loss. The Irish had fallen short of the 20-victory mark for the first time since 1999, but perhaps had learned a couple of other lessons along the way.

Mike Brey: "I talked to our guys Sunday night after we knew we were in the NIT—we were pretty prepared for that, even though there was some wishful thinking and some things did happen where we got close—and reminded them this was our lot this season and we were honored to be in it. After 10 years of not being in the NCAA Tournament and being the whipping boy of the Big East, who are we to turn our noses up at the NIT?

"But I also told them this was a good lesson to not take the NCAA Tournament for granted and assume it's their birthright. Tom and Torrian played in three of them and they didn't get in. It's a great lesson for the guys coming back that you have to be focused and you have to be hungry every day because everything you do once things start officially is analyzed at the end of the season, and we hadn't done enough."

Torin Francis: "We had a lot of ups and downs because it seemed there was always someone sitting out with some kind of injury, and that contributed to the rough start we had. But it was a good learning experience for the team to come out and face this kind of adversity. It made the team closer, and since we're only losing two guys, next year we'll be coming back ready. As long as we're healthy, we'll have even higher expectations."

Jordan Cornette: "We'd never been in that position before—watching Selection Sunday and wondering if you're going to get in there. The other years, we were wondering about our seed, who we were going to play and where we were going to be. It was definitely a reality check. We sat there and realized we were going to the NIT. Obviously we wanted to advance in the NIT as long as possible, but right then I realized I never wanted to feel that way again. I've got one more year left, and I refuse to feel that way sitting on that couch realizing we belonged in there but didn't prove we belonged in there. There'll be nothing to doubt next year."

Afterword
Mike Brey

R ight after I was hired, a lot of people said to me, "You must have been one of those people who watched Notre Dame football every Saturday." And I always replied, "Absolutely not." Notre Dame's basketball presence in D.C. was very strong, so my connection to this university was always through the basketball program and its pipeline of Washington, D.C., guys. Growing up in the Washington, D.C., area, these were the best players out of my neighborhood, so I followed their careers. I aspired to be like them, I worshipped them.

The only time I'd ever been on the campus before I was hired was when I was an assistant at Duke University and I came here for basketball games. I didn't really get a chance to know the school then because we'd usually just drive in the back tunnel of the Joyce Center, play the game, and then leave. So there was still an air of mystery about the place for me.

I'll never forget being at our place in Rehoboth getting ready to go on the road recruiting for Delaware. I picked up the paper on July 7 and read that Roy Williams had turned down North Carolina and was going to stay at Kansas. As unbelievable as I thought that was, the dominoes were all falling down in my head, and I said to my wife, "Depending on how this unfolds, we may have to start thinking about South Bend again." That was on the 7th, and on the 14th, one week later, we were on the plane to South Bend for my introduction press conference. That's how quick things can move.

One thing that made Notre Dame attractive to me was its commitment to education. I'm a product of educators. My father is a lifetime high school teacher and athletic director; my mother also a teacher and coach. Those were the first influences on me—our dinner table conversations revolved around what I'd done in school that day. At Notre Dame, a high level of both academic and athletic success is expected from our student-athletes. What makes this place unique is the integrity and balance found here. I believe strongly in the mission of the university and the fact that we can provide our players not only with opportunities on the court, but opportunities off it as well.

I'm very happy with the progress we've made. In my first team meeting, there was one guy in the locker room who knew about the NCAA Tournament: Ryan Humphrey, and he'd done it in an Oklahoma jersey. Now we've got guys talking about how we've got to get to that Regional Final or to that Final Four. And it's not pipe dream talk. They've done it. They've lived it. I've talked so much about playing well at the right time and pacing a team during the season that our kids are thinking, "The NCAA Tournament's our time. We always play well there." They feel that now, and I like that. We're at our best at that time. And now I have help from our experienced upperclassmen to deliver that message.

We have a rich tradition, and we've had some special guys come through this program. Our reunions have been such a hit, and it has been a great pleasure to get to know the basketball alumni who have made it back to campus or come to see us on the road. Those guys are our best ambassadors. If Austin Carr says in Cleveland, "Mike Brey would be a good guy to play for," and Adrian Dantley is saying things about Notre Dame basketball in D.C. and in Denver, that helps us. I want them to be proud of us and know we're really proud of them.

We have had special players here in the past, we've got special ones here now, and we will have special ones here in the future. We are all truly honored to be a part of the upcoming 2004–2005 season, the 100th season of Fighting Irish basketball. We hope we can 'wake up the echoes' on the hardwood.

Mike Brey
Head Coach, Men's Basketball
University of Notre Dame

Epilogue

This poem was composed by Chris Stevens, class of 1974, for the 2003 Notre Dame basketball players' reunion.

Hoop Players at Notre Dame

Now there is a heavenly destination for those who love to play
The game called "hoops" that we grew up playing almost every day
And as young boys, some dream of playing at Chapel Hill or
    Pauley Pavilion
But the chances of playing for Our Lady in South Bend are maybe
    one in a million

Some of us started as prodigies achieving a great deal of high
    school fame
And some played hoops as a second sport and perhaps achieving
    much less acclaim
And some of us had chances to play at just about any school you
    could name
But there is something magical that drew us to our beloved Notre Dame

Now if you took a recruiting trip to some of the ACC or Big Ten
    schools
You got put up in fancy hotels that had in-room bars and kidney-
    shaped pools
But if you got recruited to visit the Dome on a football weekend
    or more
You usually ended up sleeping on some freshman player's cot or
    even the floor

But all who made the exciting decision to sign on the dotted line
    and play
For the Irish and get a Notre Dame education that would pay
    dividends every day
Can now look back with enormous pride no matter how much or
    little we played
We were that one in a million who realized our dream that as little
    boys we had made

Whether we played for Johnny Dee or Digger or MacLeod or the
    dapper Mike Brey
We are part of a legacy that has achieved hoop heaven in oh so
    many ways
The memories of Tom Hawkins, Jack Stephens, Bob Arnzen, and
    vets like Kevin O'Shea
And all-stars like Bob Whitmore and Austin, and Adrian and all of
    the DC Subway

And there were great teams like '78 when the Irish got to the Final
    Four
With Tripucka, Orlando, Hanzlik, and Jackson and host of other
    stars and more
And that great team in the '60s that routed top-ranked Houston
    and their star the Big E
And that team that knocked UCLA from the top, ending their
    88-game winning streak

Not every player fills the stat sheet and receives all the notoriety
and fame

And the prep teams and walk-ons were just as important a part of
our dear Notre Dame

Guys like Mike Franger, Tom Hansen, Tim Healy, Tom Varga, and
so many more

Are as much a part of hoop team history and members of Notre
Dame folklore

And some of us played on some teams that toiled through some
more difficult years

Like losing to national TV by 65 . . . six wins in a season can bring
you to tears

But it wasn't the record of teams we remember when we return
to the Golden Dome

It is the camaraderie of being a part of a family where we always
will feel at home

And to men like Father Riehle and the ageless Ed O'Rourke and to
those who aren't here

And to Coach Brey and his staff to Father Malloy, all of us want to
make it clear

Thanks for what you do to invite us back and make us feel we are
still a part of the game

And to continue to enjoy the dreams of little boys who were hoop
players at Notre Dame